A Routledge Literary Sourcebook

William Shakespeare's
Othello

First performed around 1601, *Othello* remains one of William Shakespeare's most controversial yet popular plays. This volume offers those new to the play all the information they need for an informed and wide-ranging study.

Andrew Hadfield first examines the historical and literary contexts of the play, through a concise, accessible overview, a chronology and reprinted documents from the period. He covers, among other issues, *Othello*'s Venetian setting and contemporary representations of Moors. The second section of the book traces various interpretations of the play, from the earliest responses through to modern critical texts as well as stage and film interpretations. In this section, all reprinted materials are accompanied by explanatory headnotes. The sourcebook then examines key passages of the play in detail. Each passage is reprinted in full, along with headnotes and annotations offering crucial guidance to Shakespeare's language and the critical issues which surround the text. Throughout the volume, cross-references link together the contextual materials, critical responses and key passages, enabling those new to the play to make their own original yet informed readings of the text.

Offering not only a wealth of documents but also the guidance required to make the most of what they offer, this Routledge Literary Sourcebook is essential reading for any student of *Othello*.

Andrew Hadfield is Professor of English at the University of Wales, Aberystwyth, and Visiting Professor of English at Columbia University.

Routledge Literary Sourcebooks

Series Editor: Duncan Wu, St Catherine's College, Oxford University

Also available are Routledge Literary Sourcebooks on:
Mary Wollstonecraft's *A Vindication of the Rights of Woman* edited by Adriana
  Craciun
E. M. Forster's *A Passage to India* edited by Peter Childs
Mary Shelley's *Frankenstein* edited by Timothy Morton

Forthcoming titles are:
The Poems of John Keats edited by John Strachan
William Shakespeare's *The Merchant of Venice* edited by Susan Cerasano
William Shakespeare's *King Lear* edited by Grace Ioppolo
The Poems of W. B. Yeats edited by Michael O'Neill
Herman Melville's *Moby-Dick* edited by Michael J. Davey
Harriet Beecher Stowe's *Uncle Tom's Cabin* edited by Debra J. Rosenthal

A Routledge Literary Sourcebook on

William Shakespeare's
Othello

Edited by Andrew Hadfield

Routledge
Taylor & Francis Group

LONDON AND NEW YORK

First published 2003 by Routledge
11 New Fetter Lane, London EC4P 4EE

Simultaneously published in the USA and Canada
by Routledge
29 West 35th Street, New York, NY 10001

Routledge is an imprint of the Taylor & Francis Group

Typeset in Sabon and Gill Sans by RefineCatch Limited, Bungay, Suffolk
Printed and bound in Great Britain by
TJ International Ltd, Padstow, Cornwall

British Library Cataloguing in Publication Data
A catalogue record for this book is available from the British Library

Library of Congress Cataloging in Publication Data
A Routledge literary sourcebook on William Shakespeare's Othello/edited by Andrew Hadfield.
    p. cm.—(Routledge literary sourcebooks)
  Includes bibliographical references and index.
  ISBN 0–415–22733–X—ISBN 0–415–22734–8 (pbk.)
  1. Shakespeare, William, 1564–1616. Othello.   2. Othello (Fictitious character)
3. Jealousy in literature.   4. Muslims in literature.   5. Tragedy.   I. Hadfield, Andrew.   II. Series.

PR2829.R68 2002
822.3'3—dc21   2002026939

ISBN 0–415–22733–X (hbk)
ISBN 0–415–22734–8 (pbk)

For Richard Shields

Contents

4: Further Reading

Illustrations

Series Editor's Preface

The Routledge Literary Sourcebook series has been designed to provide students with the materials required to begin serious study of individual literary works, all in a single volume. This includes an overview of the critical history of the work, including extracts from important critical debates of recent decades, and a selection of key passages from the text itself. Volume editors provide introductory commentaries and annotation for the reader's guidance. These handy books provide almost everything most students will need for the contextual and critical overview of literature expected in schools and universities today.

This aim is reflected in the structure of each Sourcebook. Section 1, 'Contexts', provides biographical data in the form of an author chronology and contemporary documents relating to the author and their work. In Section 2, 'Interpretations', the editor assembles extracts from the most influential and important criticism throughout the history of the work. In some cases this includes materials relating to performances or adaptations. The third section, 'Key Passages', gathers together the essential episodes from the literary text connected by editorial commentary and annotation so as to relate them to ideas raised earlier in the volume. The final section offers suggestions for further reading, including recommended editions and critical volumes.

Annotation is a key feature of this series. Both the original notes from the reprinted texts and new annotations by the editor appear at the bottom of the relevant page. The reprinted notes are prefaced by the author's name in square brackets, e.g. '[Robinson's note.]'.

Routledge Literary Sourcebooks offer the ideal introduction to single literary works, combining primary and secondary materials, chosen by experts, in accessible form.

Duncan Wu

Acknowledgements

I would like to thank the following for permission to reprint copyright material:

BLACKWELL PUBLISHING for Terry Eagleton, *William Shakespeare* (Oxford: Blackwell, 1986), pp. 64–70.

CAMBRIDGE UNIVERSITY PRESS for Stanley Wells, 'Shakespeare Production in England in 1989', *Shakespeare Survey 43* (1991), pp. 191–4; Virginia Mason Vaughan, *Othello: A Contextual History* (Cambridge: Cambridge University Press, 1994), pp. 94–6, 181–2, 187–90, 197–8; Patricia Tatspaugh, 'The Tragedies of Love on Film' in Russell Jackson, ed., *The Cambridge Companion to Shakespeare on Film* (Cambridge: Cambridge University Press, 2000), pp. 144–6.

HARVARD UNIVERSITY PRESS for William Empson, 'Honest in *Othello*' in *The Structure of Complex Words* (Cambridge, Mass.: Harvard University Press), pp. 218, 224–5, reprinted by permission of the publisher, copyright © 1951, 1985 by the Estate of Sir William Empson; for Elmar Edgar Stoll, *Shakespeare and Other Masters* (Cambridge, Mass.: Harvard University Press), reprinted by permission of the publisher, copyright © 1940 by the President and Fellows of Harvard College.

LIVERPOOL UNIVERSITY PRESS for G. K. Hunter, '*Othello* and Colour Prejudice', from *Dramatic Identities and Cultural Tradition: Studies in Shakespeare and his Contemporaries*, published 1978 by Liverpool University Press, pp. 31–2, 45–6, 53.

OXFORD UNIVERSITY PRESS for Andrew Hadfield, *Literature, Travel and Colonial Writing in the English Renaissance 1545–1625*, pp. 232–6, © Andrew Hadfield 1998, reprinted by permission of Oxford University Press.

PALGRAVE for A. C. Bradley, *Shakespearean Tragedy: Lectures on Hamlet, Othello, King Lear, Macbeth*, 1918 [1904], Macmillan, pp. 176–82.

THE RANDOM HOUSE GROUP for extracts from *The Structure of Complex Words*, by William Empson, published by Hogarth Press. Used by permission of Lady Empson and The Random House Group Limited. (1951, pp. 218, 224–5.)

Extract from *The Common Pursuit* by F. R. Leavis, published by Hogarth Press (pp. 138, 150–2). Used by permission of The Random House Group Limited.

ROUTLEDGE for Lisa Jardine, *Reading Shakespeare Historically* (London: Routledge, 1996, pp. 25–31, 33–4, 165–70; G. Wilson Knight, *The Wheel of Fire* (London: Routledge, 1993 [1930]), pp. 97–100; Karen Newman, ' "And wash the Ethiop white": Femininity and the Monstrous in *Othello*' in Jean Howard and Marion F. O'Connor, eds, *Shakespeare Reproduced: The Text in History and Ideology* (London: Routledge, 1987), pp. 151–3, 157–9, 161–2.

THOMSON LEARNING for William Shakespeare, *Othello*, Arden 3, ed. E. A. J. Honigmann (London: Thomson Learning, 1996)

UNIVERSITY OF DELAWARE PRESS for David McPherson, 'Othello and the Myth of Venice' in *Shakespeare, Jonson and the Myth of Venice* (Newark, Del.: University of Delaware Press, 1990), pp. 81–4, 86–90; Marvin Rosenberg, *The Masks of Othello* (Newark, Del.: University of Delaware Press, 1993 [1961]), pp. 5–7, 209–10.

Every effort has been made to trace and contact copyright holders. The publishers would be pleased to hear from any copyright holders not acknowledged here, so that this acknowledgements page may be amended at the earliest opportunity.

My thanks to Michael Neill for reading an earlier version of the text and generously sharing his formidable knowledge of the play with me, and to David Scott Karstan and Joy Hayton for answering some queries. It has been a pleasure to work with Liz Thompson, Rosie Waters, Liz O'Donnell and Duncan Wu. My special thanks, as always, to Alison, Lucy, Patrick and Maud.

Introduction

It is hard to imagine that any of Shakespeare's plays has a more obvious contemporary relevance than *Othello*. The plot of the play is directly centred on questions of gender, sexuality, race and status, all key issues for us today. There have been a significant number of film and TV versions of the play, in addition to stage productions, throughout the twentieth century. In fact, there have been six major films of *Othello*: 1922, 1952, 1956, 1962, 1965 and 1995. Of all Shakespeare's plays only *Hamlet* with nine can boast more screen productions. There has also been a huge amount of critical analysis of the play. Early in the twentieth century *King Lear*, *Macbeth*, *Hamlet* and *Othello* were named as Shakespeare's 'principal tragedies' by the literary critic A. C. Bradley, who was keen to define the essence of Shakespeare's genius. He regarded these four plays as the pinnacle of the career of the world's greatest ever writer, a view still held by many readers and commentators. As a result *Othello* is commonly set at school and university level in the UK, the USA, Europe and Australia.

It is a sign of the cultural importance of *Othello* that the lead role has come to define how black actors should appear on stage and how theatre and film directors often want them to act. Black male actors have often been represented as superficially dignified and in control, while beneath the surface lies a bestial savagery ready to be released – exactly how Othello changes when he learns of Desdemona's supposed infidelity. It has become a commonplace of theatre criticism that the crowning glory of any black actor's career should be a successful performance of Othello. This is a neat reversal of the assumption that, in the interests of historical accuracy because there were no black actors in Elizabethan England, the role had to be played by a white actor blacked up. However, *Othello* clearly troubled and stimulated audiences in different ways in different places. *Othello* was rarely performed in South Africa before the overthrow of apartheid, because it raised the explosive issue of race and so made the authorities nervous of the consequences. In India, colonised by England, the play was frequently staged because it was seen by a native theatre public to be a play that challenged English rule through the positive representation of a tragic figure of colour. Such reactions reveal that the character Othello has provoked widely divergent reactions, sometimes angering and upsetting readers and audiences, sometimes being hailed as a challenge to Western superiority and prejudice. Shakespeare has been seen as a man of his times, articulating the received ideas of his fellow countrymen in dismissing people of colour as savages. He has also been seen as a staunch critic of these received ideas, ennobling Othello and granting him the status of a tragic hero alongside more conventional figures such as Hamlet, Macbeth and Coriolanus. Critics are equally divided on these issues (see the essays in the Modern Criticism section by Leavis, Hunter, Newman and Hadfield, **pp. 62–3, 66–70, 74–8, 92–3,** and the extracts from Rymer in the Early Critical Reception section, **pp. 44–7**). It is likely that the issues of race and colour will dominate the ways in which productions of *Othello* are staged and the ways in which readers will respond to the play for the foreseeable future.

Othello deals with one of the central scandals of Western thought and culture, the marriage of a black man and a white woman, and the fear of miscegenation – the production of children of mixed race who do not know where they belong.[1] Theories of race in the early modern period (*c*.1500–*c*.1800) generally stressed the importance of purity and the need to preserve a 'race' or nation from contamination with the seed and blood of other peoples, especially if they were thought to be of an inferior stock or breed. English writers often assumed, explicitly or implicitly, that God had made them in his own image – i.e. white – so black people must be either inferior or an aberration of some form.[2] It is not surprising that *Othello* has proved to be such a controversial play, which has led to not only lively and sometimes acrimonious critical exchanges but also radically different evaluations of its meaning and significance. While some critics have argued that Othello himself is one of the most foolish and least credible of Shakespeare's tragic heroes (see the comments by Rymer, **pp. 44–7**, and Leavis, **pp. 62–3**), others have seen him as a figure of heroic stature damned by a racist society in which he stood no chance of living a normal life (see especially the analyses by Hunter and Newman, **pp. 66–70, 74–8**, and Vaughan's account of Paul Robeson's Othello, **pp. 100–4**). While some critics have felt that Shakespeare was a racist and accepted a pervasive Elizabethan and Jacobean xenophobia, others have seen the play as sharply critical of a blind hostility to foreigners (see Hadfield, **pp. 92–3**). Equally important is the question of Othello's treatment of Desdemona: are Othello and his wife star-crossed lovers who are undermined by a hostile society, or does Othello accept the perception of Venetian women presented to him with as little resistance as Iago and Roderigo show towards stereotypes of black Africans (see Eagleton, **pp. 70–4**, and Jardine, **pp. 84–91**)?[3]

The aim of this Sourcebook is to give readers the material to explore these challenging and exciting questions themselves. The book contains material that will help to illuminate the play in its historical context as well as in its subsequent

---

1   On 'miscegenation', see Hazel V. Carby, ' "On the Threshold of Woman's Era": Lynching, Empire, and Sexuality in Black Feminist Theory', in Henry Louis Gates, Jr., ed., *'Race', Writing and Difference* (Chicago, Ill: University of Chicago Press, 1986), pp. 301–16.

2   See Kim F. Hall, *Things of Darkness: Economies of Race and Gender in Early Modern England* (Ithaca, NY: Cornell University Press, 1995).

3   For a nuanced reinterpretation of the Othello story, see Caryl Philips, *The Nature of Blood* (London: Faber, 1997).

history on stage, as a book and on screen. There is, of course, no easy answer to any of the questions I have posed, and it is likely that readers will continue their arguments without ever resolving all of their differences. I hope that anyone who reads this Sourcebook will feel that they are in a better position to argue whatever case they wish to make.

The book consists of three main sections. There is an introduction to each section, and a headnote prefaces each extract. I have also tried to provide a series of cross-references to help the reader find his or her way about the book and make connections between the play and the various types of material included in the Sourcebook. While guiding and helping the reader, the text is also designed to help readers to think independently, make their own connections and develop their own ideas. The first section provides a series of contexts which will enable the reader to understand the intellectual and social milieux in which Shakespeare wrote *Othello*. A chronology gives an outline of the important events in Shakespeare's own life and the key events that are relevant to *Othello*. There is a collection of contemporary documents: plays, historical accounts, travel writing and literary sources, which should help a reader to understand what Shakespeare might have read when writing the play, or the opinions and beliefs he would have been familiar with, even if he did not hold them himself.

The second section, 'Interpretations', gathers together a number of readings of the play which provide a sense of the nature of the debates the play has generated. There are some extracts from early criticism of the play from the end of the seventeenth century to the start of the twentieth century, followed by a substantial range of modern criticism dealing with questions of race and identity, gender issues, tragic form, style, language and historical context. There are also a series of comments on productions on stage and screen from the first recorded performance (1604) to the late 1980s.

The third section, 'Key Passages', consists of a series of annotated extracts from the play, providing headnotes and footnotes that I hope readers will find helpful. These gloss difficult and unfamiliar words, interpret individual sentences, provide details of probable source material and analogues, point out similar episodes and events in other plays and provide historical and literary information, as well as cross-references to material elsewhere in the sourcebook. These notes are not intended to be definitive but to help readers find their way through a complex and rewarding work.

There is also an annotated guide to further reading, providing information on editions and critical works. Throughout there are a number of illustrations that readers might find interesting and helpful.

The book is best read – as are most books – from cover to cover. However, I hope it might also be used as a handy guide for those keen to use it as a reference work. If it stimulates readers to explore one of Shakespeare's most intriguing, complex and brilliant works more thoroughly, then I will feel that I have succeeded in my task.

1

Contexts

Contextual Overview

Shakespeare clearly drew on a variety of sources when composing *Othello*. The play is a consciously intellectual work that makes use of a wide range of different types of writing. Shakespeare must have been aware of contemporary plays which represented Moors and Turks such as Robert Greene's *Selimus, Emperor of the Turks* (1594), part of which is reproduced here (**pp. 28–30**). Greene's play narrates the life of the Ottoman emperor Selim I, who reigned from 1512 to 1520, poisoning his father, Bajezet, and murdering his elder brothers, Acomat and Corcut, so that he could become sole ruler of the empire. Selimus, as the extract included here demonstrates, is a tyrant who behaves with despicable cruelty to support his own ambitions before meeting a justifiably nasty end. A similar play to Selimus is Christopher Marlowe's more celebrated story of the heroic conquests of the Scythian shepherd, *Tamburlaine* (*c*.1587). This work was so popular that a second part appears to have followed immediately after the first, indicating that there was a significant demand for plays telling spectacular tales of exotic cruelty.

Shakespeare's *Titus Andronicus* (*c*.1594) contains an evil Moor from North Africa, Aaron, who, like Selimus and Tamburlaine, was ambitious, brave and violent. I have included an extract here which shows the similarity between Selimus and Aaron (**pp. 30–1**). *Othello*, I would suggest, works by denying the audience's expectation that they will witness a gory play dominated by barbarous tyrants. Othello is represented as a noble but flawed character who resembles other Shakespearian tragic heroes rather than Greene's or Marlowe's compelling tyrants. Shakespeare transforms the direct source of *Othello*, 'The Moor of Venice' – one of a collection of Italian novellas, *Gli Hecatommithi*, compiled by Giraldi Cinthio (1566) (see **pp. 19–21**) – from a vicious morality tale into a tragedy that acknowledges the issues of race, place and gender. As the extract included here demonstrates, Shakespeare made numerous changes to the material. The most important one is his portrayal of Othello, who bears little resemblance to the unpleasant and violent character in Cinthio.

Shakespeare also made other significant changes to Cinthio's narrative. In 'The Moor of Venice' Iago does actually have a motive for his plot, a fierce lust for Desdemona. In removing this aspect of the story, Shakespeare transforms Iago into the 'motiveless malignity' that Coleridge saw in his famous comments on the play (see below, **pp. 48–50**). Iago's sinister promise in the last scene of the play to remain silent despite the tortures that will be applied to him is only possible because of the way in which Shakespeare developed Iago's character throughout the play. Cinthio's narrative includes a foolish corporal. Cinthio has the ensign (his equivalent of Iago) stab the corporal in the leg as an attempt to murder him after the Moor has become convinced of his adultery with his wife (hence the captain's wooden leg in the passage cited below, **pp. 19–21**). Shakespeare transforms this character into two, Cassio and Roderigo, allowing him to develop a more varied and interesting dramatic world than that contained in 'The Moor of Venice'. Shakespeare also develops the women characters significantly, making Desdemona a complex heroine (see Jardine's essay below, **pp. 84–91**). It is also worth noting that in Cinthio's story the ensign's wife (Shakespeare's Emilia) is aware of her husband's guilt from the outset. Shakespeare makes her a more complex and divided character, a woman trapped in an unhappy marriage who wants to do the right thing, not a mere cipher.

If Othello's character is compared with that of the Moor in Cinthio's story, one can see just how radically Shakespeare has transformed the protagonist. Cinthio's Moor is a brutal and seedy murderer, Othello a great and respected general who becomes a grand tragic figure. Othello is certainly less morally corrupt or terrifying than many of the other characters in the play. It is also significant that the Turkish threat to Venetian-controlled Cyprus fails to materialise when their fleet is dispersed in a storm. The real threat to Venetian interests comes from within, and Othello is undoubtedly right to warn his men not to do the work of the Turks for them (2.3.166–7). It is important that we appreciate what plays existed before Othello so that we can see that Shakespeare deliberately produces a work that challenges the stereotypes of cruel Moors and Turks who had appeared on the English stage.

Shakespeare also read other sources and did not just rely on drama for his ideas.[1] He showed an interest in the institutions of state and government in Venice and certainly knew Lewis Lewkenor's translation of Gaspar Contarini's *The Commonwealth and Government of Venice* (1599). Contarini, along with other English visitors to Venice in the sixteenth and seventeenth centuries, saw Venice as a fascinating and important European city. Venice was renowned for its fabulous wealth and its longevity as a stable political entity. Contarini was especially impressed at the ways in which Venice preserved the liberties of its citizens, granting them constitutional rights, allowing them to vote for leaders and making every effort to integrate foreigners resident in the city into the fabric of its political and social life. Contarini also praised the government of the city with its large elected assembly, council of ten (who made the most important decisions) and Duke (or Doge), a leader whose period in office was strictly limited. This rotation of offices was especially important as it was thought to help prevent corruption in

---

1   An invaluable recent guide to Shakespeare's reading is Stuart Gillespie, ed., *Shakespeare's Books: A Dictionary of Shakespeare Sources* (London: Athlone, 2001).

high places because offices did not become sinecures distributed as favours by the monarch, but serious and responsible positions. It was an honour – but also a burden – for a citizen to serve the city. Venice encouraged its citizens to participate in government but also showed that decisions could be made quickly and efficiently. In the third scene of Shakespeare's play we see the Council in session successfully making two difficult judgements: how to deal with the Turkish threat and how to sort out the accusations made by Brabantio against Othello and Desdemona (see below, **pp. 121–33**). It is unlikely that Shakespeare ever visited Venice, although he may have known some people who did, and he probably made use of sources such as Lewkenor for his view of the city (see the essays by McPherson and Hadfield below, **pp. 78–84** and **pp. 92–3**).

Many English writers also observed a less welcome aspect of Venice and the liberty it fostered. Venice was notorious for its prostitutes and courtesans, and many saw it as a city that had a dangerous excess of sexual licence. Venetian women were famed for their easy virtue and loose morals. I have included here the well-known description in the traveller Thomas Coryat's account of his epic journey through Europe and North Africa of his encounter with the beautiful courtesans of Venice (see below, **pp. 25–8**, and Figure 1, **p. 27**). Coryat is simultaneously attracted and repelled by the lady he encounters in Venice, seduced by her beauty and glamour but aware that he is experiencing something strange in a strange land. Shakespeare makes use of this particular myth of the desirability of Venetian women, who appear to male eyes like the beautiful but deadly sirens of classical myth, luring men to their doom, in his representation of Iago's plot against Othello (see below, **pp. 138–47**). Iago manages to undermine Othello's faith in his wife's virtue by suggesting that Venice is a permissive society in which adultery is tolerated, even encouraged – something the North African general, used to the harsh ways of camp life, has no experience of or means of understanding. Iago's plot is especially potent because the audience would have shared Othello's ignorance of and fascination with the ways of the women of Venice.

Shakespeare also seems to have made use of histories of Africa and the Ottoman Empire. The main source for the history of Africa used by English Renaissance readers was Leo Africanus (John Leo), *The History and Description of Africa*, translated into English in 1600 by John Pory, and I have included an extract from this work below (see **pp. 21–4**). John Leo was an African Muslim who converted to Christianity, and it is possible that he was a model for Othello.[2] Leo represents the Moors of North Africa as noble and honourable, but also superstitious, gullible and capable of savage violence, which is exactly how Shakespeare represents Othello (see the essays by Hunter and Newman below, **pp. 66–70** and **pp. 74–8**). Leo distinguishes between the indigenous North Africans who inhabit the deserts (rather like the peoples Othello claims he encountered on his travels, see below, **p. 128**), the Arabians and the Moors.

---

2   See Andrew Hadfield, *Literature, Travel and Colonialism in the English Renaissance, 1540–1625* (Oxford: Clarendon Press, 1998), pp. 238–9.

Othello, as the cast list of the play makes clear, belongs to the last group. Leo describes Othello's people as 'tawnie Moors' and makes it clear that they do not have a skin that is as dark as that of other African peoples. He also makes it clear that the Moors have an Islamic faith and are more like the Turks in this respect than their fellow Africans. Was Shakespeare aware of these distinctions between peoples? Is he exposing the crude racism of those, like his queen, Elizabeth I, who seemed unable to distinguish between the different peoples with whom she had to deal and simply dismissed them as black aliens? (See below, **p. 11**.) Is this how we should read the first act? Would a contemporary audience have been able to see that Roderigo and Iago were misrepresenting a sophisticated and noble Moor in terms of a generalised black stereotype which clearly did not apply? Or was Shakespeare actually unable to tell the difference between peoples himself because he was a bigot like Elizabeth? Such questions are difficult to answer with any certainty, especially given the difficult and controversial stage history of the play (see 'The Work in Performance' below). Perhaps our understanding of the play would be altered if it were the case that Othello was represented on the Jacobean stage as similar to the Turks he was employed to fight rather than to what we think of as Africans.

Shakespeare relies on the audience knowing the fear that the Turks of the mighty Ottoman Empire inspired in Christians. Venice was one of Europe's furthest outposts, an entrepôt which was situated on the Mediterranean frontier of the continent. The city absorbed numerous foreigners like Othello, which was one of the chief reasons for its success. (It had also absorbed a large Jewish population, which Shakespeare represented in his earlier play, *The Merchant of Venice* (1596–7).) However, it also had to defend Europe from being overrun by its enemies, hence the crucial strategic importance of Cyprus and the edgy fear experienced by all the characters until the Turkish fleet is fortunately destroyed in a storm (see below, **pp. 123–5, 130–1**). *Othello* is a play which takes place in the outpost of a city on the margins of Europe, which gives some idea of the importance of the geographical locations and peoples represented by Shakespeare. It is also worth bearing in mind that English people often saw themselves as an isolated people in a perilous state in the sixteenth century, after Henry VIII divorced Catherine of Aragon and married Anne Boleyn (1533) – an event which inaugurated the Protestant Reformation in England and left the country isolated from the Catholic states which made up most of mainland Europe.

One of the key motifs in the play is that of 'turning Turk' and doing the work of Europe's enemies for them, as Othello feels he has done in his suicide speech, before the 'good' Venetian Othello takes his revenge (see below, **pp. 168–9**). Although they do not actually feature in the play the Turks stand as a ghostly presence haunting Venice and threatening the wealth and liberties that the city has worked hard to produce over such a long period. A source Shakespeare may have used is Richard Knolles, *The History of the Turks* (1601), which is a comprehensive account of Turkish society, history and culture. I have included here an extract from Fynes Moryson's lively and bigoted travel narrative, not published until 1617 but based on his experiences in the 1590s (see **pp. 24–5**). Moryson visited

Turkey in 1596. He sees the Ottoman Empire as a ruthless military machine, run with cruel efficiency, and so concentrates on this aspect of Turkish society which he regards as its dominant element. The Turks are represented as brutal and brave, worthy and dangerous foes who are blindly loyal to their leaders. They are fearsome warriors who are the products of a competitive and tyrannous state. They are shown to be superstitious pagans keen to destroy the proper values of Christianity.

I have also included three representations of Turks on the Renaissance stage to give a sense of their importance for a Renaissance audience in England. If Othello was represented as a Muslim Moor who would have seemed to a contemporary audience to be similar if not identical to the Turks as I have suggested, then the importance of the Turkish aspect of the play becomes more evident. In Christopher Marlowe's *The Jew of Malta* (c.1590) (see **p. 28**), Ithamore is shown to be a cruel and malicious trickster eager to cause trouble with his equally immoral master, Barabas the Jew. The contrast to the noble Othello is clear, but we get a sense of the force of the fear of 'turning Turk' in *Othello*, as well as the fear of what will happen if the Turks do actually overrun Europe. In Robert Greene's *Selimus, Emperor of the Turks*, the principal character is proud, ambitious and ruthless in his pursuit of power and personal gain, in line with Fynes Moryson's depiction of the Turks.[3]

It is also likely, especially given the topical nature of drama, that Shakespeare had some knowledge of current affairs and events. Elsewhere he shows that he was keen to include topical references in his plays. *King Lear*, for example, makes clear allusions to King James's desire to unite the kingdoms of Britain, which he was attempting to achieve at the time that the play was first performed (c.1605). *Macbeth* (c.1606) makes similar allusions to James's interests, especially his obsession with witchcraft and his ancient lineage. Othello may also make allusions to contemporary political events and pronouncements. In 1596 Elizabeth ordered Edward Baines to have ten 'blackamoors' sent out of the realm, 'of which kind of people there are already here too many'. A week later she announced that 89 English prisoners were being released from Spain and Portugal in return for an equivalent number of 'blackamoors'. English subjects were told to behave like good Christians, get rid of black servants and 'be served by their own countrymen rather than with those kind of people'. In 1601, just before *Othello* was first performed, Elizabeth issued an edict banishing 'the great number of niggers and blackamoors which (as she is informed) are crept into this realm . . . who are fostered and relieved here to the great annoyance of her own liege people, that want the relief which those people consume'.[4]

3   On the Ottoman Empire and its relationship to Britain in the Renaissance, see Nabil Matar, *Islam in Britain, 1558–1685* (Cambridge: Cambridge University Press, 1998); Nabil Matar, *Turks, Moors & Englishmen in the Age of Discovery* (New York: Columbia University Press, 1999). See also Daniel Vitkus, ed., *Three Turk Plays from Early Modern England* (New York: Columbia University Press, 2000).

4   Cited in Julia Briggs, *This Stage-Play World: Texts and Contexts, 1580–1625* (Oxford: Oxford University Press, rev. edn, 1997), pp. 95–6. More generally see Eldred Jones, *Othello's Countrymen: Africans in English Renaissance Drama* (Oxford: Oxford University Press, 1965); Kim F. Hall, *Things of Darkness: Economies of Race and Gender in Early Modern England* (Ithaca, NY: Cornell University Press, 1995).

Elizabeth's statements raise the question of whether we should see *Othello* as a play which is of its time in accepting such attitudes (which raises the further question of whether we should still encourage productions of the play), or whether Shakespeare deliberately criticises such attitudes, provocatively producing a noble tragic hero and representing a society – Venice – that has a more inclusive ideal of citizenship.

The first scene of the play is certainly replete with racist attitudes. Roderigo refers to Othello as the 'thicklips'; Iago tries as hard as he can to force Brabantio to imagine his daughter actually having sex with Othello, an image he conjures up three times: 'Even now, very now, an old black ram/Is tupping your white ewe' (1.1.87–8); 'you'll have your daughter cover'd with a Barbary horse' (1.1.110); 'I am one, sir, come to tell you, your daughter, and the Moor, are now making the beast with two backs' (1.1.114–15). Brabantio's response to these lewd charges is fascinating: 'This accident is not unlike my dream' (1.1.140). He has already been tormented by nightmares of his daughter with the Moor, a fear of what we now call miscegenation, the interbreeding of different races and the subsequent production of children of mixed breed. For Brabantio, it is obviously perfectly acceptable to have a noble warrior such as Othello round for dinner and a bit of a chat, but he's not the sort of man one can permit to marry one's daughter.

However, as the second scene makes clear, these attitudes are not those generally held throughout the Venetian republic. We see the Venetian councillors dealing most effectively with the threat of the Turks to the city's outpost, Cyprus. In the absence of their first choice for commander, Othello is appointed to deal with the situation. Brabantio bursts in with the wedding party and the unwelcome guests, Iago and Roderigo. Brabantio demands that 'the bloody book of law' with its 'bitter letter' be used against Othello who, he claims, must have bewitched his daughter into marrying him because, were she in her right mind, she would not have married a black man. In fact, what we witness is the exact opposite. While Brabantio asserts that Desdemona would never 'fall in love with what she fear'd to look on' the council ask to hear how Othello and Desdemona came to be married and accept their version of events that they met at her father's house and fell in love when she listened to his stories of his exciting life in Africa. In stark contrast to Brabantio's allegations, the council listen to both sides attentively, being notably polite to both Brabantio and Othello, before deciding that there is nothing untoward about the marriage. The Duke gently rebukes Brabantio, claiming that 'Your son-in-law is far more fair than black'. Shakespeare shows that, for Venice to function successfully, the Venetians had to accept that they could not enforce the racial purity demanded by island dwellers such as Elizabeth I, suggesting that the play sets out to criticise existing attitudes to race.

The question of racial identity becomes even more complex as the scene develops. Othello's speech to the council, demonstrating how he accidentally wooed Desdemona through telling her tales of his past life as a traveller in Africa, forces the audience to confront his problematic identity:

Wherein I spake of most disastrous chances,
Of moving accidents by flood and field;
Of hair-breadth scapes i' th' imminent deadly breach;
Of being taken by the insolent foe;
And sold to slavery, and my redemption thence,
And with it all my travel's history;
Wherein of antres vast, and deserts idle,
Rough quarries, rocks and hills, whose heads touch heaven,
It was my hint to speak, such was the process:
And of the Cannibals, that each other eat;
The Anthropophagi, and men whose heads
Do grow beneath their shoulders: this to hear
Would Desdemona seriously incline . . .
. . . and with a greedy ear
Devour up my discourse.

(1.3.135–51)

Othello has, in effect, defined himself as an Elizabethan traveller, telling Desdemona how he escaped from the clutches of a whole series of primitive peoples who live in remote places and violate fundamental taboos by eating people. While Brabantio, Roderigo and Iago see Othello in ways similar to these stereotyped 'primitive' peoples, Othello tries to turn himself into a sophisticated citizen of Venice, to Europeanise himself. It is one of the key ironies of the tragedy that Iago is able to transform the noble Moor, who tries so hard to fit in, into a savage who plans to chop his wife up into little pieces. But then again, perhaps Iago's spiteful evil works on the problem of 'colour-blindness' that the liberal Venetians adhere to. The Duke, after all, describes Othello as 'more fair than black', indicating that colour distinctions have not been accommodated so much as ignored. Desdemona says that she 'saw Othello's visage in his mind', indicating that she ignores the colour of his face and sees the man beneath. Given that we have heard how far Othello tries to go to counteract a view that casts him as a savage, and so transform himself into a European, one might argue that the tragedy hinges very much on the issue of how effective ignoring racial differences really could be.

Shakespeare's representation of Othello and the question of whether he deliberately imagines Othello in racist terms – or, indeed, whether we should use such terms to analyse Renaissance texts – are key questions considered below in some of the essays from the Modern Criticism section (see **pp. 66–70, 74–8**). *Othello* should also be read as a fascinating and experimental mixture of the exotic and domestic tragedy, a fact which further suggests its complex nature and the debt it owes to a variety of types of writing available to Shakespeare. While the play makes use of exotic settings and peoples, it also belongs to a recognisable tragic form which takes place in the home of the victim. Such plays invariably involved the husband murdering his wife, or vice versa. They were notable for, among other things, the seemingly unbearable claustrophobic tension they generated, something that critics of *Othello* have noted has been a feature of numerous productions of the play (see the essay by Wells, **pp. 107–10**). The first example of this type of play is the anonymous *Arden of Faversham* (1585–92), based on an incident recorded in Holinshed's *Chronicles* and sometimes attributed to Shakespeare, in which the unfaithful Alice Arden has her husband killed.[5] Another example of this generic type is Thomas Heywood's *A Woman Killed with Kindness* (1603).[6] In this play no murder takes place but Anne Frankford pines away and dies after her husband discovers her in bed with her lover and she is banished from the heart of the family. Interested readers might find it useful to compare and contrast Anne's death with those of Desdemona and Othello.

5   *Arden of Faversham*, ed. Martin White (London: Black, 1982).
6   Thomas Heywood, *A Woman Killed With Kindness*, ed. R. W. Van Fossen (Manchester: Manchester University Press, 1961).

Chronology

Bullet points are used to denote events in Shakespeare's life, and asterisks to denote historical and literary events.

1562–8

* Sir John Hawkins slave-trading from Africa to West Indies

1564

● William Shakespeare born (probably on 23 April) in Stratford-upon-Avon, eldest son of Mary (née Arden) and John Shakespeare, a local businessman

1571

* Battle of Lepanto (7 Oct.); Combined fleet of Venetian, Maltese, Genoese and Spanish defeat fleet of Ottoman Empire; 12,000 Christian galley slaves are freed and 25,000 Turks killed; Ottoman Empire quickly recovers

1573

* Venetians conclude peace treaty with Turks, surrendering control of Cyprus; Turks dominate Mediterranean

c.1575–c.1580

● Shakespeare probably attends Stratford Grammar School

1576

* James Burbage builds The Theatre, London's first purpose-built theatre, in Shoreditch

1581

* Establishment of Levant Company to regulate trade with North Africa and Ottoman Empire; Laws against practising Catholicism

1582

● Shakespeare marries Anne Hathaway

1583
- Birth of Susanna, daughter of William and Anne Shakespeare

1585
- Birth of twins, Hamnet and Judith; Shakespeare leaves Stratford (?)
* Start of war with Spain

1587
* Mary Queen of Scots beheaded; Philip Henslowe builds the Rose Theatre on Bankside

1588
- Shakespeare perhaps now working in London theatres
* Defeat of Spanish Armada

1589
- First play, *Henry VI, Part 1*

1592
- *Richard III, The Comedy of Errors*
* Christopher Marlowe, *Dr Faustus, Edward II*; Successful English attacks on Spanish treasure fleet; plague in London

1593
* Church attendance (Church of England) made compulsory; plague continues; Marlowe murdered

1594
- *The Taming of the Shrew, Titus Andronicus*; Lord Chamberlain's Men founded – Shakespeare part of this acting company
* Two plots against Elizabeth's life

1595
- *A Midsummer Night's Dream, Romeo and Juliet, Richard II*
* The Swan Theatre built

1596
- *The Merchant of Venice, Henry IV, Part 1*; Hamnet dies
* Earl of Essex destroys Spanish fleet; food shortages and riots; Elizabeth orders expulsion of 'blackamoors'

1597
* Failure of second Spanish Armada when it is scattered by storms

1598
- *Henry IV, Part 2; Much Ado about Nothing*

1599

- Lord Chamberlain's Men begin occupying Globe Theatre; *Henry V*, *Julius Caesar, As You Like It*
* Publication of Sir Lewis Lewkenor's translation of Gaspar Contarini's *The Commonwealth and Government of Venice*; Transport of black slaves from Africa to the Americas is now estimated at 900,000 in total

1600

* Moroccan ambassador and entourage visit London. Publication of Leo Africanus (John Leo), *The History and Description of Africa*, trans. John Pory; Foundation of East India Company (had monopoly on trade with East Indies and was major force in trade and exploration)

1600–1

- Probable first performances of *Hamlet* and *Twelfth Night*

1601

- Death of John Shakespeare, William's father
* Earl of Essex's rebellion and execution; Elizabeth orders further expulsion of 'blackamoors'

1601–2

- Probable first performances of *Othello* and *Troilus and Cressida*

1603

- Shakespeare's last recorded stage performance, in Ben Jonson's *Sejanus*; Lord Chamberlain's Men officially adopted as the King's Men
* Death of Elizabeth (24 March) and accession of James I; Publication of Richard Knolles, *Generall Historie of the Turks*

1604

- *Othello* performed at Whitehall (1 Nov.); *Measure for Measure*
* Treaty of London establishes peace between Britain and Spain; Catholic priests banished

1605

- *King Lear*; Shakespeare purchases land in Stratford
* The Gunpowder Plot

1606

- *Macbeth, Antony and Cleopatra*
* Ben Jonson, *Volpone*

1607

- Susanna Shakespeare marries Dr John Hall; *Coriolanus*

1608

* Mary Shakespeare dies; The King's Men lease the indoor Blackfriars Theatre

1610

* *The Winter's Tale*

1611

* *The Tempest*; Shakespeare probably living mainly in Stratford
* King James authorises translation of the Bible

1612–13

* *Othello* performed for wedding of Princess Elizabeth, daughter of James I; William Shakespeare and John Fletcher, *The Two Noble Kinsmen*

1613

* Globe Theatre burns down

1616

* Judith Shakespeare marries Thomas Quiney; William Shakespeare dies on 23 April in Stratford

1623

* Publication of first folio

1636

* *Othello* performed at Hampton Court

1688

* Aphra Behn, *Oroonoko*

1693

* Thomas Rymer, *A Short View of Tragedy*, first sustained critical account of the play

1709

* Illustration for Nicholas Rowe's edition of Shakespeare – this may reflect contemporary performances

Contemporary Documents

Giraldi Cinthio, *Gli Hecatommithi* (1566 edn), 'The Third Decade',
Story 7. Reprinted in Geoffrey Bullough, ed., *Narrative and Dramatic Sources
of Shakespeare*, Vol. VII (London: Routledge & Kegan Paul, 1973), pp. 250–2

Many English dramatists made use of collections of Italian novellas as sources
for their work. More often than not they used a story as a useful starting point,
making a significant number of changes to the plot, developing the characters,
transforming a prose narrative into a stage play. Shakespeare made use of a
number of such tales throughout his career, mainly for comedies such as *The
Comedy of Errors, The Merchant of Venice* and *Much Ado about Nothing*. In writing
Othello, he used the bare bones of Cinthio's rather nasty story to create a major
tragedy. As the extract here shows, Shakespeare's play clearly resembles Cinthio's story but there are a series of important changes. In Shakespeare's play, it
is Othello who murders Desdemona rather than the Ensign, and the murder is
less spectacular and violent; in Cinthio's story the Moor suddenly realises the
guilt of Iago, whereas in the play this process is complex and protracted; when
the Moor knows of the Ensign's guilt a deadly feud develops, whereas the tragic
denouement in the play takes place quickly; the Corporal's lost leg is an important factor in Cinthio's plot, whereas Roderigo is only wounded in *Othello*; in
Cinthio the Moor is killed by Desdemona's relatives, while in Shakespeare
Othello commits suicide (see below, **pp. 168–9**); and the Ensign dies when
he repeats his slanders in his own country, while in the play Iago is led off to be
tortured by the Venetian authorities (see below, **pp. 167, 170**).

The unfortunate Disdemona got out of bed, and as soon as she was near the
closet, the Ensign came out and, being strong and muscular, he gave her a frightful
blow in the small of her back, which made the Lady fall down at once, scarcely
able to draw her breath. With the little voice she had she called on the Moor to
help her. But he, jumping out of bed, said to her, 'You wicked woman, you are
having the reward of your infidelity. This is how women are treated who, pretend-
ing to love their husbands, put horns on their heads.'

The wretched Lady, hearing this and feeling herself near to death (for the Ensign had given her another blow), called on Divine Justice to witness to her fidelity, since earthly justice failed; and as she called on God to help her, a third blow struck her, and she lay still, slain by the impious Ensign. Then, placing her in the bed, and breaking her skull, he and the Moor made the ceiling fall as they had previously planned, and the Moor began to call for help, that the house was falling. Hearing his cries the neighbours ran in and found the bed, and the Lady dead under the rafters—which made everyone grieve, for they knew what a good life she had led.

Next day Disdemona was buried, amid the universal mourning of the people. But God, the just observer of men's hearts, did not intend such vile wickedness to go without proper punishment. He ordained that the Moor, who had loved the Lady more than his life, on finding himself deprived of her should feel such longing that he went about like one beside himself, searching for her in every part of the house. Realizing now that the Ensign was the cause of his losing his Lady and all joy in life, he held the villain in such abhorrence that he could not bear even to see him; and if he had not been afraid of the inviolable justice of the Venetian lords, he would have slain him openly. Not being able to do this with safety, he took away his rank and would not have him in his company, whereupon such a bitter hatred sprang up between them that no greater or more deadly feud could be imagined.

The Ensign, that worst of all scoundrels, therefore set all his mind to injuring the Moor, and seeking out the Corporal, who had now recovered and went about with a wooden leg instead of the one that had been cut off, he said to him, 'It is time you got your revenge for the leg you lost. If you will come to Venice with me, I shall tell you who the miscreant was, for here I dare not tell you, for many reasons; and I am willing to bear witness for you in court.'

The Corporal who felt himself deeply wronged but did not know the real truth, thanked the Ensign and came with him to Venice. When they arrived there the Ensign told him that it was the Moor who had cut off his leg because of a suspicion he had formed that he was Disdemona's lover, and that for the same reason he had murdered her, and afterwards made it known that the fallen ceiling had killed her. Hearing this, the Corporal accused the Moor to the Signoria,[1] both of cutting off his leg and of causing the Lady's death, and called as witness the Ensign, who said that both accusations were true, for the Moor had approached him and tried to induce him to commit both crimes; and that, having then killed his wife through the bestial jealousy that he had conceived in his mind, he had told him how he had killed her.

When the Signoria learned of the cruelty inflicted by the Barbarian upon a citizen of Venice, they ordered the Moor to be apprehended in Cyprus and to be brought to Venice, where with many tortures they tried to discover the truth. But enduring with great steadfastness of mind every torment, he denied everything so firmly that nothing could be extorted from him. Although by his constancy he escaped

---

1   The ruling council of Venice.

death, he was, however, after many days in prison, condemned to perpetual exile, in which he was finally slain by Disdemona's relatives, as he richly deserved.

The Ensign returned to his own country; and not giving up his accustomed behaviour, he accused one of his companions, saying that the latter had sought to have him murder one of his enemies, who was a nobleman. The accused man was arrested and put to the torture, and when he denied that what his accuser said was true, the Ensign too was tortured, to compare their stories; and he was tortured so fiercely that his inner organs were ruptured. Afterwards he was let out of prison and taken home, where he died miserably. Thus did God avenge the innocence of Disdemona. And all these events were told after his death by the Ensign's wife, who knew the facts, as I have told them to you [. . .]

It appeared marvellous to everybody that such malignity could have been discovered in a human heart; and the fate of the unhappy Lady was lamented, with some blame for her father, who had given her a name of unlucky [unfortunate] augury. And the party decided that since a name is the first gift of a father to his child, he ought to bestow one that is grand and fortunate, as if he wished to foretell success and greatness. No less was the Moor blamed, who had believed too foolishly. But all praised God because the criminals had had suitable punishment.

Leo Africanus (John Leo), *The History and Description of Africa*
(1600), trans. John Pory. Reprinted in Andrew Hadfield, ed., *Amazons, Savages and Machiavels: Travel and Colonial Writing in English, 1550–1630: An Anthology* (Oxford: Oxford University Press, 2001), pp. 148–51

> John Leo (c.1495/6–1552) was a scholarly North African Arab, probably from Morocco. He travelled widely before being captured by Venetian pirates in the Mediterranean. He then converted to Christianity and worked for Pope Leo X until his death. He completed his long history of Africa in 1526 and it became the most frequently used work on the continent in Europe in the sixteenth century. John Pory (1579?–1635), also a traveller, translated it into English in 1600. Shakespeare probably used Pory's translation when writing *Othello*, and John Leo himself may even have been a minor source for the character of Othello (he had been a traveller, lived in Italy and converted to Christianity). Leo provides a balanced picture of the various peoples of Africa. While some are seen as savage and primitive, Leo also recognises the sophisticated culture of peoples such as the Arabs. Leo is very clear about the differences between the races and it is likely that Shakespeare knew exactly how he wished to represent Othello (see below, **pp. 66–70**).

THE COMMENDABLE ACTIONS AND VERTUES OF THE AFRICANS

Those Arabians which inhabit in Barbarie or upon the coast of the Mediterranean sea, are greatly addicted unto the studie of good artes and sciences: and those things which concern their law and religion are esteemed by them in the first place. Moreover they have beene heretofore most studious of the Mathematiques, of Philosophie, and of Astrologie: but these artes (as it is aforesaid) were fower hundred yeeres agoe, utterly destroyed and taken away by the chiefe professours of their lawe. The inhabitants of cities doe most religiously observe and reverence those things which appertaine unto their religion: yea they honour those doctours and priests, of whom they learne their law, as if they were petie-gods. Their Churches they frequent verie diligently, to the ende they may repeat certaine prescript and formal prayers; most superstitiously perswading themselves that the same day wherein they make their praiers, it is not lawfull for them to wash certain of their members, when as at other times they will wash their whole bodies. [. . .] Moreover those which inhabite Barbarie are of great cunning & dexteritie for building & for mathematicall inventions, which a man may easily conjecture by their artificiall workes. Most honest people they are, and destitute of all fraud and guile; not onely imbracing all simplicitie and truth, but also practising the same throughout the whole course of their lives: albeit certaine Latine authors, which have written of the same regions, are farre otherwise of opinion. Likewise they are most strong and valiant people, especially those which dwell upon the mountaines. They keepe their covenant most faithfully, insomuch that they had rather die than breake promise. No nation in the world is so subject into jealousie; for they will rather leese their lives, then put up any disgrace in the behalfe of their women. So desirous they are of riches and honour, that therein no other people can goe beyonde them. They travell in a manner over the whole world to exercise traffique. For they are continually to bee seene in Aegypt, in Aethiopia, in Arabia, Persia, India, and Turkie: and whithersoever they goe, they are most honorably esteemed of: for none of them will possesse any arte, unlesse hee hath attained unto great exactness and perfection therein. They have alwaies beene much delighted with all kinde of civilitie and modest behaviour: and it is accounted heinous among them for any man to utter in companie, any bawdie or unseemely worde. They have alwaies in minde this sentence of a grave author; Give place to thy superiour. If any youth in presence of his father, his uncle, or any other of his kinred, doth sing or talke ought of love matters, he is deemed to bee woorthie of grievous punishment. Whatsoever lad or youth there lighteth by chaunce into any company which discourseth of love, no sooner heareth nor understandeth what their talke tendeth unto, but immediately he withdraweth himselfe from among them. These are the things which we thought most woorthie of relation as concerning the civilitie, humanitie, and upright dealing of the Barbarians: let us now proceede unto the residue. Those Arabians which dwell in tents, that is to say, which bring up cattell, are of a more liberall and civil disposition: to wit, they are in their kinde as devout, valiant, patient, courteous, hospitall, and as honest in life and conversation as any other people. They be most faithfull observers of their word and promise; insomuch that the people, which before we said to dwell in the mountaines, are greatly stirred up with emulation of their vertues. Howbeit the said mountainers, both for learning, for vertue, and for religion, are thought much inferiour to the Numidians, albeit they have little or no knowledge at all in naturall philosophie. They are reported likewise to be most skilfull warriours, to be valiant, and exceeding lovers and practisers of all humanitie. Also, the Moores and Arabians inhabiting Libya are somewhat civill of behaviour, being plaine dealers, voice of dissimulation, favourable to strangers, and lovers of simplicite. Those which we before named white, or tawney Moores, are stedfast in friendship: as likewise they indifferently and favourably esteeme of other nations: and wholy indevour themselves in this one thing, namely, that they may leade a most pleasant and jocund life. Moreover they maintaine most learned professours of liberall artes, and such men are most devout in their religion. Neither is there any people in all Africa that lead a more happie and honorable life.

WHAT VICES THE FORESAID AFRICANS ARE SUBJECT UNTO

Never was there any people or nation so perfectly endued with vertue, but that they had their contrarie faults and blemishes: now therefore let us consider, whether the vices of the Africans do surpasse their vertues & good parts. Those which we named the inhabitants of the cities of Barbarie are somewhat needie and covetous, being also very proud and high-minded, and wooderfully addicted unto wrath; insomuch that (according to the proverbe) they will deeply engrave in marble any injurie be it never so small, & will in no wise blot it out of their remembrance. So rusticall they are & void of good manners, that scarcely can any stranger obtaine their familiaritie and friendship. Their wits are but meane, and they are so credulous, that they will beleeve matters impossible, which are told them. So ignorant are they of naturall philosophie, that they imagine all the effects and operations of nature to be extraordinarie and divine. They observe no certaine order of living nor of lawes. Abounding exceedingly with choler, they speake alwaies with an angrie and lowd voice. Neither shall you walke in the day-time in any of their streetes, but you shall see commonly two or three of them together by the eares. By nature they are a vile and base people, being no better accounted of by their governours then if they were dogs. They have neither judges nor lawyers, by whose wisdome and counsell they ought to be directed. They are utterly unskilfull in trades of merchandize, being destitute of bankers and money-changers: wherefore a merchant can doe nothing among them in his absence, but is himselfe constrained to goe in person, whithersoever his wares are carried. No people under heaven are more addicted unto couetise then this nation: neither is there (I thinke) to bee found among them one of an hundred, who for courtesie, humanitie, or devotions sake will vouchsafe any entertainment upon a stranger. Mindfull they have alwaies beene of injuries, but most forgetfull of benefices. Their mindes are perpetually possessed with vexation and strife, so that they will seldome or never shew themselves tractable to any man; the cause whereof is supposed to be; for that they are so greedily addicted unto their filthie lucre, that they never could attaine unto any kinde of civilitie or good behaviour. The shepherds of that region live a miserable, toilsome, wretched and beggerly life: they are a rude people, and (as a man may say) borne and bred to theft, deceit, and brutish manners. Their young men may goe a wooing to divers maides, till such time as they have sped of a wife. Yea, the father of the maide most friendly welcommeth her suiter: so that I thinke scarce any noble or gentleman among them can chuse a virgine for his spouse: albeit, so soone as any woman is married, she is quite forsaken of all her suiters; who then seeke out other new paramours for their liking. Concerning their religion, the greater part of these people are neither Mahumetans, Jewes, nor Christians; and hardly shall you finde so much as a sparke of pietie in any of them. They have no churches at all, nor any kinde of prayers, but being utterly estranged from all godly devotion, they leade a savage and beastly life: and if any man chanceth to be of a better disposition (because they have no law-givers nor teachers among them) he is constrained to follow the example of other mens lives & maners. All the Numidians being most ignorant of naturall, domesticall, & commonwealth-matters, are principally addicted unto treason, trecherie, murther, theft, and robberie. This nation, because it is most slavish, will right gladly accept of any service among the Barbarians, be it never so vile or contemptible. For some will take upon them to be dung-farmers, others to be scullians, some others to bee ostlers, and such like servile occupations. Likewise the inhabitants of Libya live a brutish kinde of life; who neglecting all kindes of good artes and sciences, doe wholy apply their mindes unto theft and violence. Never as yet had they any religion, any lawes, or any good forme of living; but alwaies had, and ever will have a most miserable and distressed life. There cannot any trechery or villanie be invented so damnable, which for lucres sake they dare not attempt. They spend all their daies either in most lewd practises, or in hunting, or else in warfare: neither weare they any shooes nor garments. The Negros likewise leade a beastly kinde of life, being utterly destitute of the use of reason, of dexteritie of wit, and of all artes. Yea they so behave themselves, as if they had continually lived in a forrest among wilde beasts. They have great swarmes of harlots among them; whereupon a man may easily conjecture their manner of living: except their conversation perhaps be somewhat more tolerable, who dwell in the principall townes and cities: for it is like that they are somewhat more addicted to civilitie. [. . .]

Fynes Moryson, *An Itinerary Containing His Ten Yeeres Travell*

(1617). Reprinted in Andrew Hadfield, ed., *Amazons, Savages and Machiavels: Travel and Colonial Writing in English, 1550–1630: An Anthology* (Oxford: Oxford University Press, 2001), pp. 169–70

Fynes Moryson (1566–1630) was probably the first professional English travel writer. He persuaded Peterhouse College, Cambridge, where he was a student, to fund his travels and he spent much of the 1590s travelling in Europe, Africa and the Near East. He spent some time in Ireland, then dedicated the rest of his life to publishing his account of his travels. Moryson is rude about most people, but is especially critical of the Irish and the Turks. He sees the Turks as a cruel and dangerous military nation (see above, **pp. 10–11**).

Certaine positions of religion and the due conferring of rewards and punishments make the Turkes bold adventure their persons and carefully performe all duties in

Warr. By blinde religion they are taught, that they mount to heaven without any impediment, who dye fighting for their Country and the Law of Mahomet. And that a Stoicall Fate or destiny governes all humane affaires, so as if the tyme of death be not come, a man is no lesse safe in the Campe then in a Castle, if it be come, he can be preserved in neither of them, and this makes them like beasts to rush uppon all daungers even without Armes to defend or offend, and to fill the ditches with their dead Carkases, thincking to overcome by number alone, without military art. Againe all rewards as the highest dignityes, and the like given continually by the Emperor to the most valiant and best deserving, make them apt to dare any thing. And in like sort severe punishments never failing to be inflicted on all offendors, more specially on such as brawle and fight among themselves, who are punished according to the quality of the offence, sometymes with death, and also such as breake martiall discipline, sometymes punishing him with death that pulls but a bunch of grapes in a Vineyard. I say these punishments never failing to be inflicted uppon offendors, make the soldiers formerly incouraged by rewards no lesse to feare base Cowardise, brawling, fighting or any breach of discipline, and keepe them in awe, as they keepe all other Subjects and enemyes under feare of their sword hanging over them. And the forme of this State being absolute tyranny, since all things must be kept by the same meanes they are gotten, the State gotten and mantayned by the sword, must needs give exorbitant Priviledges or rather meanes of oppression to all the Soldiers who (as I formerly have shewed) are not themselves free from the yoke of the same Tyranny which they exercise over others, while the superiors oppressing their inferiors are themselves grinded to dust by greater men, and the greatest of all hold life and goods at the Emperors pleasure, uppon an howers warning, among whome happy are the leane, for the fatt are still drawne to the shambles. The poorest man may aspire to the highest dignityes, if his mynde and fortune will serve him, but uppon those high pinnacles, there is no firme abiding, and the same Vertue and Starr, that made him rise, cannot preserve him long from falling. The great men most ravenously gape for treasure, and by rapine gett aboundance, but when they have it, all that cannot be made portage, must be hidden or buryed, for to build a fairer house, to have rich household stuff, or to keepe a good table, doth but make the Puttock[1] a prey to the Eagle. [. . .]

Thomas Coryat, *Coryat's Crudities* (1611), London

Thomas Coryat (1577–1617) was also a traveller who, like Moryson, spent a considerable time wandering through Europe, Africa and the Near East. His work is far more eccentric than Moryson's, and Coryat frequently represents himself as a fool, although the reader is always conscious that a more astute intelligence is actually at work. Coryat's encounter with the Venetian courtesans

---

1 [Hadfield's note.] A buzzard or kite, which are largely scavengers; in falconry terms, an ignoble bird, despite its size.

is a case in point. Coryat is both attracted to and repelled by the seductive but dangerous women he encounters. The overall point of his description is that excessive liberty is dangerous for all its attractions. Coryat's description of the courtesans shows why it is so easy for Iago to undermine Othello's faith in his wife (see below, **pp. 138–47**, and the essay by Jardine, **pp. 84–91**).

[VENETIAN WOMEN]

There is one thing used of the Venetian women, and some others dwelling in the cities and townes subject to the Signiory of Venice, that is not to be observed (I thinke) amongst any other women in Christendome: which is so common in Venice, that no woman whatsoever goeth without it, either in her house or abroad; a thing made of wood, and covered with leather of sundrey colors, some with white, some redde, some yellow. It is called a Chapiney, which they weare under their shoes. Many of them are curiously painted; some also I have scene fairely gilt so uncomely a thing (in my opinion) that it is pitty this foolish custom is not cleane banished and exterminated out of the citie. There are many of these Chapineys of great heigth, even half a yard high, which maketh many of their women that are very short, seeme much taller then the tallest women we have in England. Also I have heard that this is observed amongst them, that by how much the nobler a woman is, by so much the higher are her Chapineys. All their Gentlemen, and most of their wives and widowes that are of any wealth, are assisted and supported eyther by men or women when they walke abroad, to the end they may not fall. They are borne up most commonly by the left arme, otherwise they might quickly take a fall [. . .] For both I my self, and many other strangers (as I have observed in Venice) have often laughed at them for their vaine Chapineys [. . .]

[THE COURTESANS]

But since I have taken occasion to mention some notable particulars of their women, I will insist further upon that matter, and make relation of their Cortezans also, as being a thing incident and very proper to this discourse, especially because the name of a Cortezan of Venice is famoused over all Christendome [. . .] The woman that professeth this trade is called in the Italian tongue Cortezana, which word is derived from the Italian word cortesia that signifieth courtesie. Because these kinde of women are said to receive courtesies of their favourites [. . .] As for the number of these Venetian Cortezans it is very great. For it is thought there are of them in the whole City and other adjacent places, as Murano, Malomocco, &c. at the least twenty thousand, whereof many are esteemed so loose, that they are said to open their quivers to every arrow. A most ungodly thing without doubt that there should be a tolleration of such licentious wantons in so glorious, so potent, so renowned a city. For me thinks that the Venetians should be daylie afraid least their winking at such uncleannesse should be an

Figure 1 Thomas Coryat meets a Venetian courtesan. From Thomas Coryat, *Coryat's Crudities* (1611). By permission of the British Library (C32e9, opp. p. 262).

occasion to draw down upon them God's curses and vengeance from heaven, and to consume thier city with fire and brimstone, as in times past he did Sodome and Gomorrha. But they not fearing any such thing doe graunt large dispensation and indulgence unto them, and that for these two causes [. . .] For they thinke that the chastity of their wives would be the sooner assaulted, and so consequently they should be capricornified[1] (which of all the indignities in the world the Venetian cannot patiently endure) were it not for these places of evacuation. But I marvaile how that should be true though these Cortezans were utterly rooted out of the City. For the Gentlemen do even coope up their wives alwaies within the walles of their houses for feare of these inconveniencies, as much as if there were no Cortezans at all in the City. So that you shall very seldome see a Venetian

---

1 i.e. cuckolded and so made to wear the (metaphorical) horns of the foolish husband.

Gentleman's wife but either at the solemnization of a great marriage, or at the Christning of a Jew, or late in the evening rowing in a Gondola. The second cause is for that the revenues which they pay unto the Senate for their tolleration, doe maintaine a dozen of their galleys (as many reported unto me in Venice) and so save them a great charge.

Christopher Marlowe, *The Jew of Malta* (c.1590). Reprinted in *The Complete Plays*, ed. Mark Thornton Burnett (London: Everyman, 1999), pp. 489–90

Christopher Marlowe (1564–93) is arguably the most important dramatist before Shakespeare, famous for the grand, often controversial subjects of his poetry and plays. *The Jew of Malta* is a work that both uses racial stereotypes and shows how important they are in determining peoples' perceptions of other peoples. The Turk, Ithamore, acts as the willing servant of the evil Jew, Barabas. The extract included here shows Ithamore boasting of his villainous deeds against Christians, a passage designed to pander to an audience's prejudices and perhaps force them to consider how much they really know of other peoples.

BARABAS But tell me now, how hast thou spent thy time?	
ITHAMORE Faith, master,	
In setting Christian villages on fire,	
Chaining of eunuchs, binding galley-slaves.	
One time I was an ostler at an inn,	210
And in the night-time secretly would I steal	
To travellers' chambers, and there cut their throats:	
Once at Jerusalem, where the pilgrims kneeled,	
I strowèd powder on the marble stones,	
And therewithal their knees would rankle so,	215
That I have laughed a-good to see the cripples	
Go limping home to Christendom on stilts.	
BARABAS Why, this is something. Make account of me	
As of thy fellow; we are villains both:	
Both circumcisèd, we hate Christians both.	220
Be true and secret, thou shalt want no gold.	

Robert Greene, *Selimus, Emperor of the Turks* (1594). Reprinted in Daniel J. Vitkus, ed., *Three Turk Plays from Early Modern England* (New York: Columbia University Press, 2000), pp. 68–70

Robert Greene (c.1558–92), prolific pamphleteer, writer of prose fiction and playwright, famous for attacking Shakespeare as an 'upstart crow'. Greene wrote a vast amount of work, including a wide array of different types of play. Shakespeare knew his work as he used Greene's romance *Pandosto* as the key source for *The Winter's Tale*. In *Selimus*, Greene represents the Ottoman Empire very much as Moryson (see **pp. 24–5**) represents it in his travel writing. Selimus, the usurping emperor, is shown to be cruel and ruthless in getting what he wants. In the extract reproduced here Selimus reveals his true character as a selfish tyrant. It is possible that Shakespeare was deliberately reacting to such plays in his portrait of Othello.

SCENE 2.
SELIMUS' ENCAMPMENT NEAR ADRIANOPLE.[1]

Enter SELIMUS, SINAM BASSA, OTTRANTE, OCCHIALI, *and Soldiers.*

SELIMUS: Now Selimus, consider who thou art.
　　Long hast thou marched in disguisèd attire,
　　But now unmask thyself and play thy part
　　And manifest the heat of thy desire;
　　Nourish the coals of thine ambitious fire.　　　　　　5
　　And think that then thy empire is most sure
　　When men for fear thy tyranny endure.
　　Think that to thee there is no worse reproach
　　Than filial duty in so high a place.
　　Thou oughtst to set barrels of blood abroach　　　　10
　　And seek with sword whole kingdoms to displace.
　　Let Mahound's laws be locked up in their case,
　　And meaner men and of a baser spirit
　　In virtuous actions seek for glorious merit.
　　I count it sacrilege for to be holy　　　　　　　　　15
　　Or reverence this threadbare name of 'good.'
　　Leave to old men and babes that kind of folly,
　　Count it of equal value with the mud:
　　Make thou a passage for thy gushing flood
　　By slaughter, treason, or what else thou can;　　　20
　　And scorn religion—it disgraces man.
　　My father Bajazet is weak and old,
　　And hath not much above two years to live.
　　The Turkish crown of pearl and Ophir gold
　　He means to his dear Acomat to give;　　　　　　　25
　　But ere his ship can to her haven drive,
　　I'll send abroad my tempests in such sort
　　That she shall sink before she get the port.

1　Edirne, Turkey.

Alas, alas, his highness' agèd head
Is not sufficient to support a crown.   30
Then Selimus, take thou it in his stead,
And if at this thy boldness he dare frown
Or but resist thy will, then pull him down:
For since he hath so short a time t'enjoy it,
I'll make it shorter, or I will destroy it.   35
Nor pass I what our holy votaries
Shall here object against my forward mind:
I reck not of their foolish ceremonies,
But mean to take my fortune as I find.
Wisdom commands to follow tide and wind,   40
And catch the front of swift Occasion[2]
Before she be too quickly overgone.
Some man will say I am too impious,
Thus to lay siege against my father's life,
And that I ought to follow virtuous   45
And godly sons; that virtue is a glass
Wherein I may my errant life behold
And frame myself by it in ancient mold.
Good sir, your wisdom's overflowing wit
Digs deep with learning's wonder-working spade: 50
Perhaps you think that now forsooth you sit
With some grave wizard in a prattling shade.
Avaunt such glasses! Let them view in me
The perfect picture of right tyranny.

William Shakespeare, *Titus Andronicus* (c.1594), ed. Jonathan Bate
(London: Thompson, 2000, rpt of 1995), pp. 158–60 (Act II, Scene 1, lines
500–23)

Titus Andronicus was probably Shakespeare's first tragedy. The play, original to
Shakespeare, shows the struggle between the Romans and the Goths for
ascendancy in Rome after a series of disastrous conflicts leave the city vulnerable to invasion. Aaron is a Moor in the service of the Goths who becomes the
lover of the queen, Tamora. The resemblance to the cultural position of Othello
is clear. Aaron is a very different character from Shakespeare's other Moor,
however, exhibiting the calculating and grotesque stage evil of characters such
as Selimus and Ithamore. In creating Othello, Shakespeare was consciously moving away from the stereotype of the savage exotic villain. I have included Aaron's

---

2   The goddess Occasion was bald except for a long forelock that hung down over her face. This hair
    had to be seized when possible to earn good fortune.

AARON

> Now climbeth Tamora Olympus' top,   500
> Safe out of fortune's shot, and sits aloft,
> Secure of thunder's crack or lightning flash,
> Advanced above pale envy's threatening reach.
> As when the golden sun salutes the morn
> And, having gilt the ocean with his beams,   505
> Gallops the zodiac in his glistering coach
> And overlooks the highest-peering hills,
> So Tamora.
> Upon her wit doth earthly honour wait,
> And virtue stoops and trembles at her frown.   510
> Then, Aaron, arm thy heart and fit thy thoughts
> To mount aloft with thy imperial mistress,
> And mount her pitch whom thou in triumph long
> Hast prisoner held, fettered in amorous chains
> And faster bound to Aaron's charming eyes   515
> Than is Prometheus tied to Caucasus.
> Away with slavish weeds and servile thoughts!
> I will be bright, and shine in pearl and gold
> To wait upon this new-made empress.
> To wait, said I? – to wanton with this queen,   520
> This goddess, this Semiramis, this nymph,
> This siren that will charm Rome's Saturnine
> And see his shipwreck and his commonweal's.

2

Interpretations

Critical History

Othello appears to have been one of Shakespeare's most popular and frequently performed plays, from the first recorded performance to present-day screen and television productions.[1] There is also a wealth of critical analysis of the play, which has inspired varied and often vigorously expressed responses, indicating just how important the work has been for both audiences and readers. *Othello* has generally been regarded as one of Shakespeare's finest achievements but also as a scandalous play which has caused extreme discomfort for audiences and readers. Such contradictory responses have led to critics trying to deal with the play in a variety of ways. Some readers felt that Shakespeare had made an error in casting a Moor as his central character because only white characters could be tragic heroes (see Rymer below, **pp. 44–7**). Other critics have argued that Shakespeare was simply reflecting the attitudes and values of his contemporaries and so should not be dealt with too harshly if he produced what we think of as an offensive racist portrait of a black character (see Newman below, **pp. 74–8**). Others have argued that Shakespeare was deliberately exposing the racism of his fellow countrymen in representing a black tragic hero (see Hunter and Hadfield below, **pp. 66–70** and **92–3**). A more extreme response, but one which has a logical consistency, is that the play should no longer be performed. The danger, of course, is that critics' responses can be determined by their own sense of what Shakespeare was, or should have been, doing in the play. My own view is that it is hard to imagine that *Othello* was not written to produce some sort of reaction in an audience and cannot just be read as a routine work reflecting Elizabethan attitudes.[2]

1   Useful stage histories are provided in Virginia Mason Vaughan, *Othello: A Contextual History* (Cambridge: Cambridge University Press, 1994), pt 2; Julie Hankey, ed., *Othello* (Bristol: Bristol Classical Press, 1987); Marvin Rosenberg, *The Masks of Othello: The Search for the Identity of Othello, Iago and Desdemona by Three Centuries of Actors and Critics* (Newark, Del.: University of Delaware Press, 1993, rpt of 1961); Martin L. Wine, *Othello: Text and Performance* (Basingstoke: Macmillan, 1984).
2   Those interested in the conception of race in Elizabethan England should read Kim F. Hall, *Things of Darkness: Economies of Race and Gender in Early Modern England* (Ithaca, NY: Cornell University Press, 1995).

The earliest surviving evidence of a performance of *Othello* is an entry in the accounts of Edmund Tilney, Master of the Revels in 1604: 'By the Kings plaiers. Hallamas Day being the first of November. A play in the Banketinge house att Whithall called The Moor of Venis. Shaxberd.'[3] *Othello* must have been one of the first plays performed before James I by his newly acquired company, the King's Men, for whom Shakespeare wrote. This is an indication of the rising status of Shakespeare and his theatre company. However, we should not immediately assume that *Othello* necessarily made a huge impact on James. Plays and other performances were required on many diverse public occasions such as important weddings, visits of monarchs or other civic dignitaries, important dates in the calendar, and they were not always greeted with enthusiasm by the king or his court. On one occasion the impatient James stood up during a performance and demanded that the actors stopped speaking and got on with the dance that followed each performance. On another, when his brother-in-law the King of Denmark visited, the audience was described by a courtier as being far too inebriated to stand up let alone concentrate on the play.

Nevertheless, there are records of a number of performances of *Othello* at court and in the public theatres in the early seventeenth century. It was performed again at court in 1612/13 when James's daughter, Elizabeth, married the Elector Palatine, suggesting that at least some of the audience at court saw it as an appropriate play for such an event (although it is hard to see how a work in which the bridegroom eventually smothers the bride would have made for especially happy viewing!). There was a further court performance at Hampton Court in December 1636. It was also acted on the public stage at the Globe Theatre by the King's Men in April 1610, and later that year at Oxford, and at the Blackfriars Theatre in November 1629 and May 1635.[4]

Othello was also published three times in the early seventeenth century, which further indicates that it was a play in demand. The first quarto (a small and cheaply produced book made by folding a sheet of paper twice, hence its title) appeared in 1622, and a second one in 1630. It was also included in the folio edition (a much more expensive, larger type of book, formed by folding the pages just once) of Shakespeare's works in 1623. Plays were still not always published at this date (there is a large list of works lost for ever of which only the titles remain), and the folio edition of Shakespeare's works was only the second such text to be published, after Ben Jonson's trailblazing folio of his poetry and plays was produced in 1616.

In line with other contemporary textual scholarship of Shakespeare, many textual critics claim that the quarto and folio versions of the play need to be read as separate works and not collated as one play. The tendency of previous editors was to assume that there was one correct version of a Shakespeare play, and they would try to construct what they thought was the play that Shakespeare

3   Quoted in Norman Sanders, ed., *Othello* (Cambridge: Cambridge University Press, 1984), p. 1. The Master of the Revels was in charge of drama performed at court, and was also partly responsible for checking that what was performed in the public theatres was not scandalous or liable to censorship.
4   For details see *Othello*, ed. Norman Sanders (Cambridge: Cambridge University Press, 1984), p. 1.

had intended to write. Usually editors would construct a very long play including all the lines from the folio and quarto versions that only appeared once. This meant that some plays, such as *Hamlet*, would become extended to four or five hours if performed in total. It is now much more common for editors to suggest that plays existed in two distinct versions, and were revised by Shakespeare, so that it is difficult to assume that they can be combined as one play. This has been the case with *King Lear*, which is labelled as a history in the quarto text of 1608 and a tragedy in the 1623 folio. Some editors see these as two versions which must not be confused, as they are quite separate in meaning.[5]

The quarto and folio texts of *Othello* do not differ as much as those of *Hamlet* and *King Lear*, but they do show distinct differences which have occasioned much textual and critical debate. It is possible that Shakespeare did revise the text and this may have meant that two distinct versions of *Othello* were performed in the early seventeenth century. The folio version emphasises the sexual references in the play, Brabantio's obsession with Othello's conquest of his daughter (see below, **pp. 120–1, 125**), and foregrounds the role of Emilia.[6]

Comments on the first performances of the play are, as with most early modern drama, sparse. However, one record of a performance does survive. When the King's Men produced *Othello* in Oxford in 1610, a witness noted that the play made most of the crowd weep with pity: most notably, the actor who played Desdemona 'moved us especially in her death when, as she lay on her bed, her face itself implored the pity of the audience'.[7] Subsequent critics have often reacted strongly to Desdemona, some, invariably male critics, blaming her for her alleged foolhardiness in trying to argue the case of Michael Cassio. Others have seen her as one of Shakespeare's most tragic heroines, and the role of Desdemona became even more prominent when women were finally allowed to appear on stage after the Restoration (see Jardine below, **pp. 84–91**).

Othello was a popular favourite on the Restoration stage, where, in Virginia Mason Vaughan's words, it 'satisfied Restoration appetites for amorous intrigue and exotic language', as well as representing a series of contemporary social concerns (class, race and gender relationships).[8] The first sustained critical analysis of *Othello* was Thomas Rymer's *A Short View of Tragedy* (1693). Rymer (1641–1713) was an unsuccessful dramatist who had become a critic. His writings are notable for their desire to apply the stringent demands of neo-classicism to English drama, especially the demand that all plays obey the unities. The theory of the unities was a critical development of Aristotle's rule that drama had to possess a unified sense of action. In the seventeenth century a number of French critics argued that a good play should possess a unity of place (the action should

5   See William Shakespeare, *The Complete Works*, ed. Gary Taylor and Stanley Wells (Oxford: Oxford University Press, 1988).
6   For discussion see Scott McMillin, 'The *Othello* Quarto and the "Foul-Paper" Hypothesis', *Shakespeare Quarterly* 51 (2000), pp. 67–85; E. A. J. Honigmann, *The Texts of 'Othello' and Shakespearean Revision* (London: Nelson, 1996).
7   Cited in *Othello*, ed. Sanders, p. 38.
8   Vaughan, *Othello: A Contextual History*, pp. 100–1. See also Rosenberg, *Masks of Othello*, pp. 18–20.

all take place in a single location); a unity of time (that the action seen on stage should take place in the two or three hours that it took to perform the work, or, if that was not possible, then a day); as well as the unity of action. Obviously most English drama would be found wanting, as writers had not adhered to such rules in the way that contemporary French dramatists such as Jean Racine (1639–99) had done, Shakespeare being a key example, as most of his plays obeyed none of the unities.[9]

Rymer was an established critic of considerable reputation in the 1690s, having already written on Aristotle's *Poetics* and previous tragedy in *The Tragedies of the Last Age Consider'd* (1678) before he wrote the more polemical *A Short View of Tragedy*. This work became notorious for his attack on Shakespeare because he did not obey the rules that Rymer wished to see imposed on drama. No play serves to illustrate Rymer's method more clearly than his comments on *Othello*. Rymer suggests that *Othello*, although highly regarded by many critics, is a bad play because it refuses to observe the natural hierarchies of race, sex and class, as well as violating the demands of proper tragedy in having the plot hinge on silly details such as the problem of the lost handkerchief. Rymer was – quite justly – ridiculed for his views. Nevertheless, his comments show how popular the play was on the Restoration stage. They also illustrate the feeling of discomfort that the play has induced in subsequent audiences and writers and so set the agenda for much of what has followed. For Rymer, it was against nature that Othello, a black warrior, could be a tragic hero and a woman of Desdemona's class could fall in love with him (see Hunter's essay below, **pp. 66–70**). Just as the plot of a play had to obey certain rules of decorum, so did the characters within it.

Although there was considerable opposition to Rymer's prescriptive view of tragedy, the stage history and critical history of *Othello* show how the play was modernised and made less barbarous in line with a more loosely interpreted version of neo-classical principles. The more vulgar and crude lines of the play were omitted, notably Othello's references to the coarse sexuality of goats and monkeys as well as his spying on his wife (see below, **pp. 148–55, 161–3**). Desdemona was also made rather more lady-like with the willow song being removed because it was not deemed suitable for a properly tragic heroine.

Othello was tremendously popular in the eighteenth century and there is a record of a performance in London in nearly every year. In the eighteenth and nineteenth centuries *Othello* became one of the key plays in which major actors could demonstrate their pre-eminence, not just in the title role, but also playing Iago or even Cassio. The list of major actors who played Othello or Iago reads like a *Who's Who* of the English and American stages between 1700 and 1900: David Garrick, Charles Macklin, Spranger Barry, William Charles Macready, Tommaso Salvini, Henry Irving, and so on. The same is the case in the twentieth century when Laurence Olivier, Paul Robeson, John Gielgud, Bob Hoskins, Willard White and Ian McKellen are just a few of the actors who have played Othello or Iago. The role of Desdemona is more problematic and she has often

---

9 An exception is *The Tempest* (1611/12), which is consciously modelled on the unities.

been cast as a more insipid heroine than the text justifies. Nevertheless the role has been played successfully by numerous distinguished and popular actors including Helena Faucit Martin, Ellen Terry, Maggie Smith and Penelope Wilton.

One of the most important performances of Othello in the eighteenth century was that of Thomas Betterton, who acted the part from 21 May 1703 until 15 September 1709 (see the comments by Richard Steele below, **pp. 95–7**). Betterton, like many of the actors who followed him, was notable for the passion he brought to the role, portraying Othello as a man who had lost control when pushed too far. A significant failure was the Othello of David Garrick (1717–79), the most important English actor of the middle to late eighteenth century, who enjoyed a number of triumphs in Shakespeare's other plays. His naturalistic style of acting was seen to be not grand enough to encompass the tragic stature of Othello, reducing him to a ridiculous figure. John Philip Kemble (1757–1827) was another significant failure in the role. Like Garrick, Kemble enjoyed considerable success in leading roles in other Shakespeare plays, but his Othello was seen to be excessively philosophical and unsympathetic.

Samuel Johnson's (1709–84) enthusiasm for *Othello* is representative of the play's critical reception in the eighteenth century (see below, **pp. 47–8**). Shakespeare was now becoming the most celebrated English writer of all time, a dramatist whose natural brilliance allowed him to break all the rules that critics like Rymer would try to impose on him.[10] Johnson reads *Othello* as a play that is not easy to analyse because it teaches the reader or viewer the inner truth of human nature and so needs little comment from the critic. The characters all represent recognisable human types produced by the supreme artist with the finest imagination. Johnson's views predict those of the Romantic critics, who generally regarded Shakespeare as a sublime author whose works went beyond rational rules and presented the viewer or reader with the terror of innate human experience.[11] In trying to express the power that the play held over the Romantic imagination, Samuel Taylor Coleridge (1772–1834) produced some of the best-known descriptions of *Othello*, famously describing Iago's soliloquy at the start of the play as 'the motive-hunting of motiveless malignity', a phrase that has been re-used, debated and set as a problem for students to consider ever since (see **pp. 48–50**).

In the nineteenth century, *Othello* continued to be one of Shakespeare's most frequently performed plays, appealing to a Romantic taste for the sublime excesses of the emotions and a Victorian taste for melodrama. The three most celebrated actors who played the title role were Edmund Kean, William Charles Macready and the Italian Tommaso Salvini (for an account of Macready's performance, see the comments by William Hazlitt below, **pp. 97–100**). Kean was praised especially for the range of emotional states he could represent on stage from insane jealousy to extreme grief. Salvini portrayed Othello as a much more

---

10 For a fuller analysis, see Gary Taylor, *Reinventing Shakespeare: A Cultural History from the Restoration to the Present* (London: Hogarth, 1989).

11 For more comment, see Jonathan Bate, ed., *The Romantics on Shakespeare* (Harmondsworth: Penguin, 1996).

sensual creature in the early scenes before placing emphasis on the Moor's over-whelming grief and sense of loss at his wife's infidelity and subsequent death. Iago came to prominence in Victorian productions as more weight was given to his role in precipitating the tragic action. Kean played a notable Iago as well as playing Othello and was seen by William Hazlitt as possessing 'an overactivity of mind that is dangerous to himself and others' (a comment that might be usefully com-pared with Coleridge's description of Iago as 'motiveless malignity'). Hazlitt con-tinued that Kean's Iago 'so far from hating his fellow creatures . . . is perfectly regardless of them, except as they may afford him food for the exercise of his spleen', demonstrating the self-contained nature of Iago that was obviously becoming more evident on the stage.[12]

A number of Victorian critics wrote on *Othello*. One of the most prominent was Edward Dowden (1843–1913), an Irish critic whose work had a great impact on the study of Shakespeare and the Romantic poets, both of whom he wrote about extensively. Dowden's comments (see **pp. 50–2**) represent the Victorian enthusiasm for the romantic plot of the play, seeing the passion of the lovers as doomed (he describes them as 'mutually attracted by the wonder and grace of unlikeness'). He is ambivalent about Othello, regarding him as a strange and exotic hero of noble stature whilst possessing a side which 'it were well that Desdemona had seen though she trembled'.

Perhaps the most influential comments on the play were those of A. C. Bradley (1851–1935), one of the most important ever critics of Shakespeare (see **pp. 52–4**). Bradley's *Shakespearean Tragedy* (1904) helped to cement the still current notion that *Hamlet, Macbeth, Othello* and *King Lear* are the greatest examples of Shakespeare's art. Bradley has often been seen as no more than a character critic in a Victorian tradition, and it is true that his criticism is largely based on the experience of the main characters in the world of the play in which they exist. However, his main aim was to establish an interpretation of tragedy's meaning in a modern world in which the reality of a deity was hard to perceive. His com-ments on *Othello* try to show how the play is the most claustrophobic of Shake-speare's great tragedies, and that the unbearable enclosed atmosphere marks it out as a particular dramatic experience within the Shakespeare canon. It should also be noted that Bradley universalises the experience of tragedy, which enables him to ignore the problems of racial and sexual identity that have troubled so many other critics.

While criticism of *Othello* in the first half of the twentieth century concentrated on the existential and formal questions of *Othello*'s particular status as a tragedy and the tragic design it expressed, more recent criticism has been much more grounded in historical research and has concentrated on questions of race, politics and sexual politics. Major critics such as G. Wilson Knight (1897–1985), T. S. Eliot (1888–1965), William Empson (1906–84) and F. R. Leavis (1895–1978) all wrote important essays on *Othello*, seeing the play, as previous critics had done, as possessing a unique place in the Shakespeare canon. Wilson Knight (see

---

12 Cited in *Othello*, ed. Sanders, p. 44.

pp. 55–7) concentrated on the poetic style of the play, contributing the often-used phrase 'The *Othello* music' to describe the particular style of Othello's language. Knight sees the play as a battle between the harmony that Othello desires and the chaos that results when his world view is shattered by Iago. William Empson (see **pp. 60–1**) analyses the variety of meanings of the word 'honest' in *Othello*, part of a larger series of studies into the problems of close reading and the nature of ambiguity in literature, showing how the major themes are contained in the smallest details. Both studies illustrate extremely well the desire of much criticism written in the first half of the twentieth century to connect close reading of tiny details to important metaphysical themes. F. R. Leavis (see **pp. 62–3**) and T. S. Eliot wrote essays that argued that Othello was largely to blame for his downfall, emphasising Shakespeare's choice of a black African as a tragic hero, but also suggesting that he was a gullible and naïve character. Studies of Iago, such as that by E. E. Stoll (see **pp. 57–9**), followed on from the thoughts of Coleridge and cast him as a devil, placing the play in a theological context. I have included extracts from the work of these critics as their comments on *Othello* formed the basis for most discussions of the play until relatively recently.

Marvin Rosenberg's influential *The Masks of Othello* (**pp. 63–6**) sought to examine the play from an actor's point of view (arguably a perspective lacking in so many of the analyses of the poetic language of the play and its existential significance). Rosenberg shows how difficult the roles of Othello and Desdemona are to act, principally because their characters seem so contradictory. It is important to note that the critical works of Eliot, Leavis, Stoll et al. tend to consider *Othello* as if it were a work to be read, a subtle long poem on the vicissitudes of human nature. In doing so they conspicuously ignore the stage tradition of the play, a deficiency that Rosenberg's work remedies. There have, of course, been many important stage versions of *Othello* in the twentieth century, leaving aside the numerous film versions of the play. Abraham Sofaer's Othello (1935) portrayed him as tender and reasonable, perhaps somewhat too distant and cold, a marked contrast to the passionate Othellos of the nineteenth century. More in line with the previous tradition were the versions of Frederick Valk and Orson Welles (see below, **pp. 104–7**), who represented Othello as a seething cauldron of suppressed violence ready to boil over. An important breakthrough was undoubtedly made when Paul Robeson, the first major black actor to play the part, was cast in the role. I have included a long section here because of the significance of this production, which raised the issue of the relationship between the colour of the actor's skin and of the role he plays (see below, **pp. 100–4**). In contrast, the very successful – albeit highly controversial – Othello of Laurence Olivier showed the character to be self-obsessed and egotistical, a pseudo-sophisticate ready to lapse back into the primitive state he claimed to have left behind. Olivier's version appears to have owed a great deal to an English critical tradition as exemplified by Leavis and Eliot.

Othello's story has been one closely bound up with the question of race and racism. At one time white producers and audiences found it impossible to envisage the possibility of a black actor playing the lead role in the play (see Virginia Mason Vaughan on Paul Robeson's Othello, **pp. 100–4** below). Now, as Celia

C. Daileader has argued in an important essay, black actors are seen in terms of how they might play Othello, regarded as the pinnacle of their careers.[13] The reversal is a neat one, but the racial attitudes have simply been inverted, rather than being rethought in any constructive manner. This is one reason why *Othello* is still such a challenging play.

G. K. Hunter's article '*Othello* and Colour Prejudice', **pp. 66–70**, marked a watershed in criticism of the play when it was published in 1967. Although controversies about black actors playing Othello and the nature of the racial politics of the play had been aired often enough before (see below, **pp. 100–4**), Hunter's was the first serious scholarly attempt to reconstruct the significance of Othello's pigmentation in Shakespeare's time. Hunter argues that Shakespeare works harder to expose racial prejudice than he does to reinforce it, and that the audience was forced not to see Othello as 'a stereotype nigger'. The tragedy is that Iago is able to transform the noble Othello into what his prejudices want him to be, an uncomfortable lesson that explains why *Othello* has never been an easy play to watch, especially for a white audience.

More recent criticism has often taken Hunter's essay as a key starting point. Karen Newman's sophisticated analysis '"And wash the Ethiop white"' (see **pp. 74–8**) links such racial prejudices to sexual ones, showing how *Othello* plays on an audience's fear of miscegenation, the mingling of races. Like Hunter, Newman sees Shakespeare as eager to challenge the 'ideologies of race and gender in early modern England', even if he was undeniably 'subject to the racist, sexist and colonialist discourses of the time'. The real transgression of the play is its sympathetic representation of the love of a white woman for a black man, one of the central taboos of Western society, with its attendant fear of the production of mixed-race children.

Feminist theory and analysis has also played a significant part in enabling critics to rethink and refigure the significance of the play. The most notable problem has been the neglect of the role of Desdemona, and, to a lesser extent, Emilia. Lisa Jardine's exploration of the relationship between *Othello* and the contemporary legal definition of 'defamation' places Desdemona rather than Othello centre stage (see **pp. 84–91**). Jardine shows how Othello murders Desdemona for supposed adultery rather than jealousy as is conventionally assumed. In exposing his wife to public accusations, Othello shows a stubborn conviction in the justice of his cause, making him similar to the numerous husbands in early modern England who also felt that they had the right to humiliate their wives before the communities in which they lived.

Jardine's essay illustrates the 'historicist turn' of much recent criticism. The two essays by McPherson and Hadfield (see **pp. 78–84, 92–3**) explore the significance of the Venetian setting of the play, McPherson exposing its darker side and Hadfield showing how its political system may have appealed to many English men and women at the turn of the seventeenth century. Venice was a byword for

---

13 'Casting Black Actors: Beyond Othellophilia', in Catherine M. S. Alexander and Stanley Wells, eds, *Shakespeare and Race* (Cambridge: Cambridge University Press, 2000), pp. 177–202.

liberty, a desirable quality in moderation, but a curse if experienced in excess. Terry Eagleton argues that *Othello* is a sceptical play which explores the ways in which reality is represented (see **pp. 70–4**). Eagleton's witty argument shows how the deluded Othello cannot distinguish the difference between illusion and reality, precisely what Freud suggested was the basis of all psychopathological problems.

A key development in the performance of *Othello* in the twentieth century has been the medium of film. *Othello* has been among the Shakespeare plays most frequently translated from stage to screen and television with versions appearing in 1922, 1952, 1956, 1965, 1966, 1990 and 1995. The most important of these are the versions by Orson Welles (1952), Sergei Yutkevich (1956), Stuart Burge (1965) and Oliver Parker (1995).[14] I have included an analysis of the Orson Welles film as the first of these and the most technically original and influential. The film is also significant in its representation of Desdemona and the relationship between her and her husband and the intrusive camera. Just as Paul Robeson's performance placed racial issues at the centre of the stage, so did Welles's film highlight the problem of gender relationships and the representation of the female characters in the play.[15]

It is intriguing to imagine how performances and criticism of *Othello* will develop in the future. It is hard to imagine that the play can ever be successfully separated from the explosive theme of race unless it is reduced to a dead historical monument of little interest to a contemporary audience. It is possible that it may be thought too offensive by some to ever be successfully produced. There have already been passionate arguments concerning the casting of black actors in the title role, with some objecting to a black Othello on the grounds that this is not historically accurate because there were no black actors in Jacobean England. The problem is that the stage, critical and film histories of the play cannot be forgotten or ignored when a new production of *Othello* is planned. It would be a cruel irony if a play designed to attack and overcome prejudice ends up being seen as a work that reinforces it. But then one does not have to read *Othello* as a liberal, enlightened play, and there are plenty of critical precedents for interpreting it as a more conservative or bigoted work. As this section reveals, literary criticism and stage history are not necessarily genteel and harmless pursuits.

---

14 For further details see Russell Jackson, ed., *The Cambridge Companion to Shakespeare on Film* (Cambridge: Cambridge University Press, 2000), passim.
15 See Vaughan, *Othello: A Contextual History*, ch. 10, for analysis. On the importance of gender criticism of *Othello*, see Lisa Jardine (**pp. 84–91** below).

Early Critical Reception

Thomas Rymer, *A Short View of Tragedy* (1693). Reprinted in Brian Vickers, ed., *Shakespeare: The Critical Heritage, Vol. 2, 1693–1733* (London: Routledge, 1974), pp. 26–30, 54.

Rymer's comments have been ridiculed by other critics since he wrote them. He has been attacked for trying to reduce a complex play to a simple fable, his almost wilfully naïve readings of passages, his snobbishness and desire to fit every work into an inappropriate template, but, above all, for his derogatory conception of Othello and stubborn refusal to see any merit whatsoever in the play. Rymer is important, however, for showing the excesses of neo-classical interpretations of Shakespeare after the Restoration and in the early eighteenth century, which tried to refine and polish the rude genius of Shakespeare. His comments on Othello's wooing of Desdemona (see below, **pp. 45–6**) express an incredulity that anyone could be so foolish as to believe that the match between the couple could ever work. Note also the contrast Rymer draws between the sensible comments of Horace, the classical authority, and the ridiculous assumptions made by Shakespeare. Whatever our feelings about Rymer's comments, he does anticipate the exasperation expressed by such scrupulous modern readers as T. S. Eliot and F. R. Leavis.

From all the Tragedies acted on our English Stage, *Othello* is said to bear the Bell away. The *Subject* is more of a piece, and there is indeed something like—there is, as it were, some phantom of—a *Fable*. The *Fable* is always accounted the *Soul* of Tragedy, and it is the *Fable* which is properly the *Poets* part [. . .]

This Fable is drawn from a Novel compos'd in Italian by *Giraldi Cinthio*, who also was a Writer of Tragedies, and to that use employ'd such of his Tales, as he judged proper for the Stage. But with this of the *Moor*, he meddl'd no farther.

Shakespeare alters it from the Original in several particulars, but always, unfortunately, for the worse. He bestows a name on his *Moor*, and styles him *the Moor of Venice*: a Note of pre-eminence which neither History nor Heraldry can allow him. *Cinthio*, who knew him best, and whose creature he was, calls him simply a *Moor*. We say *the Piper of Strasburgh*; *the Jew of Florence*; and, if you please, *the Pindar of Wakefield*: all upon Record, and memorable in their Places. But we see no such Cause for the *Moor*'s preferment to that dignity. And it is an affront to all Chroniclers and Antiquaries to top upon 'em a *Moor* with that mark of renown who yet had never fain within the Sphere of their Cognisance.

Then is the *Moor's Wife*, from a simple Citizen in *Cinthio*, dress'd up with her Top knots and rais'd to be *Desdemona*, a Senators Daughter. All this is very strange, and therefore pleases such as reflect not on the improbability. This match might well be without the Parents' Consent [. . .]

The Fable.

Othello, *a Blackamoor Captain, by talking of his Prowess and Feats of War makes* Desdemona, *a Senators Daughter, to be in love with him and to be married to him, without her Parents' knowledge. And having preferred* Cassio *to be his Lieutenant (a place which his Ensign* Iago *sued for)* Iago, *in revenge, works the* Moor *into a Jealousy that* Cassio *Cuckolds him: which he effects by stealing and conveying a certain Handkerchief which had at the* Wedding *been by the* Moor *presented to his Bride. Hereupon* Othello *and* Iago *plot the Deaths of* Desdemona *and* Cassio. Othello *Murders her, and soon after is convinced of her Innocence. And as he is about to be carried to Prison, in order to be punish'd for the Murder He kills himself.*

What ever rubs or difficulty may stick on the Bark, the Moral, sure, of this Fable is very instructive.

I. First, This may be a caution to all Maidens of Quality how, without their Parents consent, they run away with *Blackamoors* [. . .]

Secondly, This may be a warning to all good Wives that they look well to their Linnen.

Thirdly, This may be a lesson to Husbands, that before their Jealousie be Tragical the proofs may be Mathematical.

Cinthio affirms that *She was not overcome by a Womanish Appetite but by the Vertue of the Moor.* It must be a good-natur'd Reader that takes *Cinthio*'s word in this case, tho' in a Novel. *Shakespeare*, who is accountable both to the *Eyes* and to the *Ears*, and to convince the very heart of an Audience, shews that *Desdemona* was won by hearing *Othello* talk.

> Othello.—*I spake of most disastrous chances,*
> *Of Moving accidents, by flood and field;* [. . .] [1.3.134 ff]

This was the Charm, this was the philtre, the love-powder that took the Daughter of this Noble Venetian. This was sufficient to make the *Black-amoor* White and reconcile all, tho' there had been a Cloven-foot into the bargain [. . .]

Shakespeare in this Play calls 'em the *supersubtle Venetians*, yet examine throughout the Tragedy, there is nothing in the noble *Desdemona* that is not below any Countrey Chamber-maid with us.

And the account he gives of their Noblemen and Senate can only be calculated for the latitude of *Gotham*.

The Character of that State is to employ strangers in their Wars. But shall a Poet thence fancy that they will set a Negro to be their General, or trust a *Moor* to defend them against the *Turk*? With us a *Black-amoor* might rise to be a Trumpeter: but *Shakespeare* would not have him less than a Lieutenant-General. With us a *Moor* might marry some little drab, or Small-coal Wench: *Shakespeare* would provide him the Daughter and Heir of some great Lord or Privy-Councellor, and all the Town should reckon it a very suitable match [. . .]

Nothing is more odious in Nature than an improbable lye; and certainly never was any Play fraught like this of *Othello* with improbabilities.

The *Characters* or Manners, which are the second part in a Tragedy, are not less unnatural and improper than the Fable was improbable and absurd.

Othello is made a Venetian General. We see nothing done by him nor related concerning him that comports with the condition of a General—or, indeed, of a Man—unless the killing himself to avoid a death the Law was about to inflict upon him. When his Jealousy had wrought him up to a resolution of's taking revenge for the suppos'd injury, he sets *Iago* to the fighting part to kill *Cassio*, and chuses himself to murder the silly Woman his Wife, that was like to make no resistance.

His Love and his Jealousie are no part of a Souldiers Character, unless for Comedy.

But what is most intolerable is *Iago*. He is no *Black-amoor* Souldier so we may be sure he should be like other Souldiers of our acquaintance. Yet never in Tragedy nor in Comedy nor in Nature was a Souldier with his Character; take it in the Authors own words:

> Emilia.—*some Eternal Villain,*
> *Some busie, and insinuating Rogue,*
> *Some cogging, couzening Slave, to get some Office.* [4.2.131 ff]

Horace Describes a Souldier otherwise:

> *Impiger, iracundus, inexorabilis, acer.*[1]

Shakespeare knew *his* Character of *Iago* was inconsistent. In *this* very Play he pronounces,

> *If thou deliver more or less than Truth,*
> *Thou are no Souldier.*— [2.3.210 ff]

This he knew, but to entertain the Audience with something new and surprising, against common sense and Nature, he would pass upon us a close, dissembling, false, insinuating rascal instead of an open-hearted, frank, plain-dealing Souldier,

---

1 Horace, *Ars Poetica*, 121: 'impatient, passionate, ruthless, fierce'.

a character constantly worn by them for some thousands of years in the World [. . .]

Nor is our Poet more discreet in his Desdemona. He had chosen a Souldier for his Knave, and a Venetian Lady is to be the Fool. This Senator's Daughter runs away to (a Carriers Inn) the *Sagittary*, with a *Black-amoor*; is no sooner wedded to him but the very night she Beds him is importuning and teizing him for a young smock-fac'd Lieutenant, *Cassio*; and tho' she perceives the *Moor* Jealous of *Cassio*, yet will she not forbear, but still rings *Cassio*, *Cassio* in both his Ears.

Roderigo is the Cully of *Iago*, brought in to be murder'd by *Iago*, that *Iago*'s hands might be the more in Blood, and be yet the more abominable Villain—who without that was too wicked on all Conscience, and had more to answer for than any Tragedy, or Furies, could inflict upon him. So there can be nothing in the *characters* either for the profit, or to delight an Audience.

The third thing to be consider'd is the *Thoughts*. But from such *Characters* we need not expect many that are either true, or fine, or noble.

And without these—that is, without sense or meaning—the fourth part of Tragedy, which is the *expression*, can hardly deserve to be treated on distinctly. The verse rumbling in our Ears are of good use to help off the action. In the *Neighing* of an Horse or in the *growling* of a Mastiff there is a meaning, there is as lively expression and, may I say, more humanity than many times in the Tragical flights of *Shakespeare* [. . .]

What can remain with the Audience to carry home with them from this sort of Poetry for their use and edification? How can it work, unless, instead of settling the mind, and purging our passions, to delude our senses, disorder our thoughts, addle our brain, pervert our affections, hair our imaginations, corrupt our appetite, and fill our head with vanity, confusion, *Tintamarre* and Jingle-jangle beyond what all the Parish Clarks of *London*, with their *old Testament* farces and interludes in *Richard the Second*'s time, cou'd ever pretend to? Our only hopes for the good of their Souls can be, that these people go to the Playhouse as they do to Church, to sit still, look on one another, make no reflection, nor mind the Play more than they would a Sermon.

There is in this Play some burlesk, some humour, and ramble of Comical Wit; some shew, and some *Mimickry* to divert the spectators: but the tragical part is, plainly, none other than a Bloody Farce, without salt or savour.

Samuel Johnson, *The Plays of Shakespeare* (1765). Reprinted in *Selections from Johnson on Shakespeare*, ed. Bertrand H. Bronson, with Jean M. O'Meara (New Haven, Conn.: Yale University Press, 1986), pp. 358–9

Johnson, one of the most significant commentators on Shakespeare, has a much more positive conception of *Othello* than Rymer, above. Johnson shares a similar value system to that of Rymer, and he is clearly troubled by Shakespeare's rough style and lack of literary polish. However, he regards Shakespeare's insight into human nature as his principal merit, and so is prepared to celebrate the natural genius of his art despite its unrefined style and presentation. Johnson finds, as have many subsequent critics (see below, **pp. 50, 59, 67–8**), the process by which Iago undermines Othello's faith in Desdemona to be terrifying and convincing.

The beauties of this play impress themselves so strongly upon the attention of the reader, that they can draw no aid from critical illustration. The fiery openness of Othello, magnanimous, artless, and credulous, boundless in his confidence, ardent in his affection, inflexible in his resolution, and obdurate in his revenge; the cool malignity of Iago, silent in his resentment, subtle in his designs, and studious at once of his interest and his vengeance; the soft simplicity of Desdemona, confident of merit, and conscious of innocence, her artless perseverance in her suit, and her slowness to suspect that she can be suspected, are such proofs of Shakespeare's skill in human nature, as, I suppose, it is vain to seek in any modern writer. The gradual progress which Iago makes in the Moor's conviction, and the circumstances which he employs to inflame him, are so artfully natural, that, though it will perhaps not be said of him as he says of himself, that he is "a man not easily jealous," yet we cannot but pity him when at last we find him "perplexed in the extreme."

There is always danger lest wickedness conjoined with abilities should steal upon esteem, though it misses of approbation; but the character of Iago is so conducted, that he is from the first scene to the last hated and despised.

Even the inferiour characters of this play would be very conspicuous in any other piece, not only for their justness but their strength. Cassio is brave, benevolent, and honest, ruined only by his want of stubbornness to resist an insidious invitation. Rodorigo's suspicious credulity, and impatient submission to the cheats which he sees practised upon him, and which by persuasion he suffers to be repeated, exhibit a strong picture of a weak mind betrayed by unlawful desires, to a false friend; and the virtue of Aemilia is such as we often find, worn loosely, but not cast off, easy to commit small crimes, but quickened and alarmed at atrocious villanies.

The scenes from the beginning to the end are busy, varied by happy interchanges, and regularly promoting the progression of the story; and the narrative in the end, though it tells but what is known already, yet is necessary to produce the death of Othello.

Samuel Taylor Coleridge, 'Notes on the Tragedies' (published 1836–9) and **Table Talk** (1835). Reprinted in *Coleridge's Shakespeare Criticism*, ed. Thomas Middleton Raysor, 2 vols. (London: Constable, 1930): Vol. I, pp. 49,125; Vol. II, pp. 350–1

Coleridge follows Johnson as one of Shakespeare's most perceptive and important critics. Coleridge has coined a number of key expressions which

have helped define the way in which the play has been read, notably his observation that Iago is a 'motiveless malignity'. Coleridge's critical strength is to
combine subtle and brilliant close reading of individual lines and phrases with
telling larger judgements. Like most Romantic critics, Coleridge responds to
the sublime tragic beauty of Shakespeare's writing, seeing his major works
expressing the essence of human nature in its rawest state. And like Johnson
and unlike Rymer, he is convinced that Iago's plot to destroy Othello is both
authentic and powerful. It is also worth noting Coleridge's conception of
Othello's character. Coleridge sees him as a Moor, not an African, possibly in
line with the play's original design (see above, **pp. 21–4**), and he argues that
Shakespeare's characterisation is designed to make the audience sympathetic
to Othello.

I.

In real life how do we look back to little speeches, either as presentimental [of], or
most contrasted with, an affecting event. Shakespeare, as secure of being read
over and over, of becoming a family friend, how he provides this for *his readers*,
and leaves it to them.

> [I. iii. 319–20.
> *Iago*. Virtue! a fig! 'tis in ourselves that we are thus or thus.]

Iago's passionless character, all *will* in intellect; therefore a bold partisan here of a
truth, but yet of a truth converted into falsehood by absence of all the modifica-
tions by the frail nature of man. And the *last sentiment*—

> [. . . our raging motions, our carnal stings, our unbitted lusts; whereof I
> take this, that you call love, to be a sect or scion]—

There lies the Iagoism of how many! And the repetition, "Go make money!"—a
pride in it, of an anticipated dupe, stronger than the love of lucre.

> [I. iii. 377–8.
> *Iago*. Go to, farewell, put money enough in your purse: Thus do I ever
> make my fool my purse.]

The triumph! Again, "put money," after the effect has been fully produced.
The last speech, [Iago's soliloquy,] the motive-hunting of motiveless malignity—
how awful! In itself fiendish; while yet he was allowed to bear the divine image,
too fiendish for his own steady view. A being next to devil, only *not* quite
devil—and this Shakespeare has attempted—executed—without disgust, without
scandal!

II.

[. . .] Othello's *belief* not jealousy; forced upon him by Iago, and such as any man would and must feel who had believed of Iago as Othello. His great mistake that *we* know Iago for a villain from the first moment. [III.iii.154–80]

Proofs of the contrary character in Othello.

[But in considering the essence of the Shakespearian Othello, we must perseveringly place ourselves in his situation, and under his circumstances. Then we shall immediately feel the [. . .] solemn agony of the noble Moor [. . .] Othello had no life but in Desdemona:—the belief that she, his angel, had fallen from the heaven of her native innocence, wrought a civil war in his heart. She is his counterpart; and, like him, is almost sanctified in our eyes by her absolute unsuspiciousness, and holy entireness of love. As the curtain drops, which do we pity the most?]

III.

Character of Othello.—Othello must not be conceived as a negro, but a high and chivalrous Moorish chief. Shakspeare learned the spirit of the character from the Spanish poetry, which was prevalent in England in his time. Jealousy does not strike me as the point in his passion; I take it to be rather an agony that the creature, whom he had believed angelic, with whom he had garnered up his heart, and whom he could not help still loving, should be proved impure and worthless. It was the struggle *not* to love her. It was a moral indignation and regret that virtue should so fall:—"But yet the *pity* of it, Iago!—O Iago! The *pity* of it, Iago!" In addition to this, his honour was concerned: Iago would not have succeeded but by hinting that his honour was compromised. There is no ferocity in Othello; his mind is majestic and composed. He deliberately determines to die; and speaks his last speech with a view of showing his attachment to the Venetian State, though it had superseded him.

Edward Dowden, *Shakespere: A Critical Study of His Mind and Art* (London: C. Kegan Paul & Co., 1879, rpt of 1875), pp. 230–3

Dowden (1843–1913), a major Victorian critic, was born in Cork and became Professor of English at the fiercely Protestant Trinity College, Dublin. He wrote mainly on nineteenth-century poetry and Shakespeare. Dowden is a far less incisive critic that Coleridge, but his comments on the play are interesting for the light they shed on Victorian conceptions of *Othello*. Dowden is sympathetic to Desdemona and Othello, and sees Shakespeare as the creator of a tragic love story which should elicit the sympathy of the audience. Note how he sees Othello as an exotic creature who captures Desdemona's heart through his strange nature and his air of adventure. Dowden's comments might be read in terms of the development of the British Empire in Victorian Britain. For Dowden, Othello appears most like a Indian prince, noble and proud, with a dark side, as the last line of the extract here indicates.

The tragedy of Othello is the tragedy of a free and lordly creature taken in the toils, and writhing to death. In one of his sonnets, Shakspere has spoken of

> Some fierce thing replete with too much rage
> Whose strength's abundance weakens his own heart.

Such a fierce thing, made weak by his very strength, is Othello. There is a barbaresque grandeur and simplicity about the movements of his soul. He sees things with a large and generous eye, not prying into the curious or the occult. He is a liberal acceptor of life, and with a careless magnificence wears about him the ornament of strange experience; memories of

> Antres vast, and desarts idle,
> Rough quarries, rocks, and hills whose heads touch heaven,

memories of "disastrous chances, of moving accidents by flood and field." There is something of grand innocence in his loyalty to Venice [. . .] Othello, a stranger, with tawny skin and fierce traditions in his blood, is fascinated by the grave senate, the nobly ordered life (possessing a certain rich colouring of its own), and the astute intelligence of the City of the Sea. At his last moment, through the blinding sandstorm of his own passion, this feeling of disinterested loyalty recurs to Othello, and brings him a moment's joy and pride. His history has been, indeed, a calamitous mistake; like the base Indian, he has thrown away "a pearl richer than all his tribe." But there is one fact with which the remembrance of him may go down to men, one fact which will rescue from complete deformity and absurd unreason the story of Othello:—

> Set you down this;
> And say, besides, that in Aleppo once,
> Where a malignant and a turban'd Turk
> Beat a Venetian, and traduc'd the State,
> I took by the throat the circumcised dog,
> And smote him, thus.

With this loyalty to Venice, there is also an instinctive turning towards the barbaric glory which he has surrendered. He is the child of royal ancestry: "I fetch my life and being from men of royal siege." All the more joyous on this account it is to devote himself to the service of the State. And thus Othello has reached manhood, and passed on to middle life.

Then in the house of Brabantio this simple and magnificent nature found his fate. Desdemona, moving to and fro at her house-affairs, or listening with grave wonder, and eager, restrained sympathy to the story of his adventurous life, became to him, at first in an unconscious way, the type of beauty, gentleness, repose, and tender womanhood. And Desdemona, in her turn, brought up amidst the refinements and ceremonies of Venetian life, watching each day the same gondolas glide by, hearing her father's talk of some little new law of the Duke, found in the Moor strangeness and splendour of strong manhood, heroic simplicity, the charm of one who had suffered in solitude, and on whose history compassion might be lavished. Thus, while Brutus and Portia were indissolubly bound together by their likeness, Desdemona and Othello were mutually attracted by the wonder and grace of unlikeness. In the love of each there was a romantic element; and romance is not the highest form of the service which imagination renders to love. For romance disguises certain facts or sees them, as it were, through a luminous mist; but the highest service which the imagination can render to the heart is the discovery of every fact, the hard and bare as well as the beautiful; and, to effect this, like a clear north wind it blows all mists away. There was a certain side of Othello's nature which it were well that Desdemona had seen, though she trembled.

A. C. Bradley, *Shakespearean Tragedy: Lectures on* Hamlet, Othello, King Lear, Macbeth (London: Macmillan, 1918, rpt of 1904), pp. 176–82

Bradley, as I have argued above (see **p. 40**), helped to create our modern conception of Shakespeare as the author of four of the world's greatest tragedies. Bradley responds to the claustrophic terror that *Othello* instills in the audience, an element many previous critics underplayed or ignored. He makes a significant point when he stresses the important omission of a sub-plot. He sees this as the defining tragic significance of the play in the Shakespeare canon. Bradley's criticism can seem impressionistic and he has less of an editor's eye for detail than Johnson and Coleridge. However, the grand sweep of his ideas helps not only to give a sense of the powerful effect that Shakespeare's plays exercise on audiences and readers, but also to explain why Shakespeare might have come to assume his pre-eminent literary status.

What is the peculiarity of *Othello*? What is the distinctive impression that it leaves? Of all Shakespeare's tragedies, I would answer, not even excepting *King Lear*, *Othello* is the most painfully exciting and the most terrible. From the moment when the temptation of the hero begins, the reader's heart and mind are held in a vice, experiencing the extremes of pity and fear, sympathy and repulsion, sickening hope and dreadful expectation.

Evil is displayed before him, not indeed with the profusion found in *King Lear*, but forming, as it were, the soul of a single character, and united with an intellectual superiority so great that he watches its advance fascinated and appalled. He sees it, in itself almost irresistible, aided at every step by fortunate accidents and the innocent mistakes of its victims. He seems to breathe an atmosphere as fateful as that of *King Lear*, but more confined and oppressive, the darkness not of night but of a close-shut murderous room. His imagination is excited to intense activity, but it is the activity of concentration rather than dilation [. . .]

(1) [. . .] *Othello* is not only the most masterly of the tragedies in point of construction, but its method of construction is unusual. And this method, by which the conflict begins late, and advances without appreciable pause and with accelerating speed to the catastrophe, is a main cause of the painful tension just described. To this may be added that, after the conflict has begun, there is very little relief by way of the ridiculous. Henceforward at any rate Iago's humour never raises a smile. The clown is a poor one; we hardly attend to him and quickly forget him; I believe most readers of Shakespeare, if asked whether there is a clown in *Othello*, would answer No.

(2) In the second place, there is no subject more exciting than sexual jealousy rising to the pitch of passion; and there can hardly be any spectacle at once so engrossing and so painful as that of a great nature suffering the torment of this passion, and driven by it to a crime which is also a hideous blunder. Such a passion as ambition, however terrible its results, is not itself ignoble; if we separate it in thought from the conditions which make it guilty, it does not appear despicable; it is not a kind of suffering, its nature is active; and therefore we can watch its course without shrinking. But jealousy, and especially sexual jealousy, brings with it a sense of shame and humiliation. For this reason it is generally hidden; if we perceive it we ourselves are ashamed and turn our eyes away; and when it is not hidden it commonly stirs contempt as well as pity. Nor is this all. Such jealousy as Othello's converts human nature into chaos, and liberates the beast in man; and it does this in relation to one of the most intense and also the most ideal of human feelings. What spectacle can be more painful than that of this feeling turned into a tortured mixture of longing and loathing, the 'golden purity' of passion split by poison into fragments, the animal in man forcing itself into his consciousness in naked grossness, and he writhing before it but powerless to deny it entrance, gasping inarticulate images of pollution, and finding relief only in a bestial thirst for blood? This is what we have to witness in one who was indeed 'great of heart' and no less pure and tender than he was great. And this, with what it leads to, the blow to Desdemona, and the scene where she is treated as the inmate of a brothel, a scene far more painful than the murder scene, is another cause of the special effect of this tragedy.[1]

(3) The mere mention of these scenes will remind us painfully of a third cause; and perhaps it is the most potent of all. I mean the suffering of Desdemona. This is, unless I mistake, the most nearly intolerable spectacle that Shakespeare offers us. For one thing, it is *mere* suffering; and, *ceteris paribus* [other things being equal], that is much worse to witness than suffering that issues in action. Desdemona is helplessly passive. She can do nothing whatever. She cannot retaliate even in speech; no, not even in silent feeling. And the chief reason of her helplessness only makes the sight of her suffering more exquisitely painful. She is helpless because her nature is infinitely sweet and her love absolute. I would not challenge Mr. Swinburne's statement that we *pity* Othello even more than Desdemona; but

---

1 [Bradley's note.] The whole force of the passages referred to can be felt only by a reader. The Othello of our stage can never be Shakespeare's Othello, any more than the Cleopatra of our stage can be his Cleopatra.

we watch Desdemona with more unmitigated distress.[2] We are never wholly uninfluenced by the feeling that Othello is a man contending with another man; but Desdemona's suffering is like that of the most loving of dumb creatures tortured without cause by the being he adores.

(4) Turning from the hero and heroine to the third principal character, we observe (what has often been pointed out) that the action and catastrophe of *Othello* depend largely on intrigue. We must not say more than this. We must not call the play a tragedy of intrigue as distinguished from a tragedy of character. Iago's plot is Iago's character in action; and it is built on his knowledge of Othello's character, and could not otherwise have succeeded. Still it remains true that an elaborate plot was necessary to elicit the catastrophe; for Othello was no Leontes, and his was the last nature to engender such jealousy from itself.[3] Accordingly Iago's intrigue occupies a position in the drama for which no parallel can be found in the other tragedies; the only approach, and that a distant one, being the intrigue of Edmund in the secondary plot of *King Lear*. Now in any novel or play, even if the persons rouse little interest and are never in serious danger, a skillfully-worked intrigue will excite eager attention and suspense. And where, as in *Othello*, the persons inspire the keenest sympathy and antipathy, and life and death depend on the intrigue, it becomes the source of a tension in which pain almost overpowers pleasure. Nowhere else in Shakespeare do we hold our breath in such anxiety and for so long a time as in the later Acts of *Othello*.

(5) One result of the prominence of the element of intrigue is that *Othello* is less unlike a story of private life than any other of the great tragedies. And this impression is strengthened in further ways. In the other great tragedies the action is placed in a distant period, so that its General significance is perceived through a thin veil which separates the persons from ourselves and our own world. But *Othello* is a drama of modern life; when it first appeared it was a drama almost of contemporary life, for the date of the Turkish attack on Cyprus is 1570.[4] The characters come close to us, and the application of the drama to ourselves (if the phrase may be pardoned) is more immediate than it can be in *Hamlet* or *Lear*. Besides this, their fortunes affect us as those of private individuals more than is possible in any of the later tragedies with the exception of *Timon*. I have not forgotten the Senate, nor Othello's position, nor his service to the State; but his deed and his death have not that influence on the interests of a nation or an empire which serves to idealise, and to remove far from our own sphere, the stories of Hamlet and Macbeth, of Coriolanus and Antony. Indeed he is already superseded at Cyprus when his fate is consummated, and as we leave him no vision rises on us, as in other tragedies, of peace descending on a distracted land.

(6) The peculiarities so far considered combine with others to produce those feelings of oppression, of confinement to a comparatively narrow world, and of dark fatality, which haunt us in reading *Othello* [. . .] In *Othello*, after the temptation has begun, it is incessant and terrible.

---

2   Algernon Charles Swinburne (1837–1909), poet and critic.
3   Leontes, the jealous king in *The Winter's Tale*.
4   Bradley is referring to the Battle of Lepanto (see Chronology).

Modern Criticism

G. Wilson Knight, 'The *Othello* Music' (1930), in *The Wheel of Fire:*
Interpretations of Shakespearean Tragedy (London: Routledge, 1993, rpt. of
1930), pp. 97–100

Wilson Knight was a prolific Shakespeare critic who wrote thirteen books on
Shakespeare. His most influential works are *The Wheel of Fire* (1930), *The
Imperial Theme* (1931) and *The Crown of Life* (1955). Knight tried to steer critical
analysis of Shakespeare away from a concentration on character study towards
a reading of a play's poetic metaphors and the overall sweep of its language.
Knight called his critical method 'spatial'. His work can be read alongside other
Shakespearian critics of the 1930s and 1940s who also concentrated on the
larger themes and patterns of language in the plays. However, Knight was keen
not to sever his critical method from an understanding of the plays as performances, as he felt many of his contemporaries did. Knight himself was a noted
flamboyant performer. His reading of *Othello* coined the term 'the *Othello*
music' and attempted to understand how the play's language worked to express
its tragic themes. Knight is also notably more sympathetic to Othello than many
other critics (see Leavis, **pp. 62–3**).

In *Othello* we are faced with the vividly particular rather than the vague and
universal. The play as a whole has a distinct formal beauty: within it we are ever
confronted with beautiful and solid forms. The persons tend to appear as warmly
human, concrete [. . .] It is true that Iago is here a mysterious, inhuman creature of
unlimited cynicism: but the very presence of the concrete creations around, in
differentiating him sharply from the rest, limits and defines him. *Othello* is a story
of intrigue rather than a visionary statement [. . .]

 Othello is dominated by its protagonist. Its supremely beautiful effects of style
are all expressions of Othello's personal passion. Thus, in first analysing Othello's
poetry, we shall lay the basis for an understanding of the play's symbolism: this
matter of style is, indeed, crucial, and I shall now indicate those qualities which

clearly distinguish it from other Shakespearian poetry. It holds a rich music all its own, and possesses a unique solidity and precision of picturesque phrase or image, a peculiar chastity and serenity of thought. It is, as a rule, barren of direct metaphysical content. Its thought does not mesh with the reader's: rather it is always outside us, aloof. This aloofness is the resultant of an inward aloofness of image from image, word from word. The dominant quality is separation, not, as is more usual in Shakespeare, cohesion. Consider these exquisite poetic movements:

> O heavy hour!
> Methinks it should be now a huge eclipse
> Of sun and moon, and that the affrighted globe
> Should yawn at alteration. (v. ii. 97)

Or,

> It is the very error of the moon;
> She comes more near the earth than she was wont,
> And makes men mad. (v. ii. 107)

These are solid gems of poetry which lose little by divorce from their context [. . .] In these two quotations we should note how the human drama is thrown into sudden contrast and vivid, unexpected relation with the tremendous concrete machinery of the universe, which is thought of in terms of individual heavenly bodies: 'sun' and 'moon'. The same effect is apparent in:

> Nay, had she been true,
> If Heaven would make me such another world
> Of one entire and perfect chrysolite,
> I'd not have sold her for it. (v. ii. 141)

Notice the single word 'chrysolite' with its outstanding and remote beauty: this is typical of *Othello*.

The effect in such passages is primarily one of contrast. The vastness of the night sky, and its moving planets, or the earth itself—here conceived objectively as a solid, round, visualized object—these things, though thrown momentarily into sensible relation with the passions of man, yet remain vast, distant, separate, seen but not apprehended; something against which the dramatic movement may be silhouetted, but with which it cannot be merged. This poetic use of heavenly bodies serves to elevate the theme, to raise issues infinite and unknowable. Those bodies are not, however, implicit symbols of man's spirit [. . .] they remain distinct, isolated phenomena, sublimely decorative to the play [. . .] Images in *Macbeth* are continually vague, mastered by passion; apprehended, but not seen. In Othello's poetry they are concrete, detached; seen but not apprehended. We meet the same effect in:

> Like to the Pontic sea,
> Whose icy current and compulsive course
> Ne'er feels retiring ebb, but keeps due on
> To the Propontic and the Hellespont,
> Even so my bloody thoughts, with violent pace,
> Shall ne'er look back, ne'er ebb to humble love,
> Till that a capable and wide revenge
> Swallow them up. Now, by yond marble heaven,
> In the due reverence of a sacred vow
> I here engage my words. (III. iii. 454)

This is a strongly typical speech. The long comparison, explicitly made [. . .] is another example of the separateness obtaining throughout *Othello*. There is no fusing of word with word, rather a careful juxtaposition of one word or image with another. And there are again the grand single words, 'Propontic' 'Hellespont', with their sharp, clear, consonant sounds, constituting defined aural solids typical of the *Othello* music: indeed, fine single words, especially proper names, are a characteristic of this play – Anthropophagi, Ottomites, Arabian trees, 'the base Indian', the Egyptian, Palestine, Mauretania, the Sagittary, Olympus, Mandragora, Othello, Desdemona. This is a rough assortment, not all used by Othello, but it points the Othello quality of rich, often expressly consonantal, outstanding words. Now Othello's prayer, with its 'marble heaven', is most typical and illustrative. One watches the figure of Othello silhouetted against a flat, solid, moveless sky: there is a plastic, static suggestion about the image.

E. E. Stoll, 'Iago', in *Shakespeare and Other Masters* (Cambridge, Mass.: Harvard University Press, 1940), pp. 254–7

Stoll (1874–1959) was a critic who reacted strongly against the influence of Bradley (see above, **pp. 52–4**) and his emphasis on reading Shakespeare's plays as character studies. Stoll was especially scornful of any criticism which attempted to offer insights into the minds of the protagonists in drama and he was noted for his acerbic and combative style. Instead he argued for a criticism based on the theatrical qualities of drama, making the case that this was what had really mattered to sixteenth- and seventeenth-century playwrights. Stoll's analysis of Iago illustrates the elements of his critical method: a concentration on the action and purpose of the play, as well as the effect it has on an audience, not the interior life of the character. Note how Stoll refuses to read the section of the play he analyses (the end of Act 1, Scene 3) as a 'slice of life', trying to persuade the reader that it is better read as a self-conscious work of art.

When, after the hearing before the Senate, Desdemona is by Othello given in charge to 'honest Iago,' we both start at the danger and are also impressed by the confidence the dishonest man inspires; and thereupon the plot thickens, as after the departure of the others and in response to the whimpering of his catspaw and creditor, 'what shall I do?' the villain, dropping into prose after the high poetry of the Council, but still speaking a poetry of his own, tells the gull, both openly and mysteriously, what it is he shall do and what will come to pass. It is a notable scene, in which Iago talks half to Roderigo like a bulldozing swindler, half to himself like the infernal angel that he is as well, looking into the seeds of time and saying which grain shall grow, which shall not. In either capacity he utters more of his atheistic-Satanic philosophy, not only of life but of love, and as if from the podium or the tripod:

> O villainous! I have look'd upon the world for four times seven years; and since I could distinguish betwixt a benefit and an injury, I never found man that knew how to love himself [. . .]
>
> Virtue! a fig! 'tis in ourselves that we are thus or thus [. . .] but we have reason to cool our raging motions, our carnal stings, our unbitted lusts, whereof I take this that you call love to be a sect or scion. [. . .]
>
> It is merely a lust of the blood and a permission of the will. [1.3.312–36].

And in the long speech beginning with the last-quoted sentence, the oracle is fairly rapt in a tragicomic 'enthousiasmos' as he sways and fluctuates, in both thought and word, from Desdemona's changing to Roderigo's drowning, from that to putting money in his purse and back again, the note of prophecy or destiny continually asserting itself:

> The food that to him now is luscious as locusts, shall be to him shortly as bitter as coloquintida. She must have change for youth; when she is sated with his body, she will find the error of her choice; she must have change, she must; therefore put money in thy purse. [. . .] If sanctimony and a frail vow betwixt an erring barbarian and a supersubtle Venetian be not too hard for my wits and all the tribe of hell, thou shalt enjoy her; therefore make money. A pox of drowning thyself! it is clean out of the way. Seek thou rather to be hang'd in compassing thy joy than to be drown'd and go without her. [348–62]

And after that:

> If thou canst cuckold him, thou cost thyself a pleasure, me a sport. There are many events in the womb of time which will be delivered. Traverse! go, provide thy money. [369–72]

And then, as a finishing touch for the swindler:

> Go to; farewell. Do you hear, Roderigo? (What say you?) No more of drowning, do you hear? [377–9]

This is not a slice of life, or any that I know of; the gull has had wit enough to complain of Iago's bleeding his purse at the beginning and these reiterated orders to replenish it after his unblushing avowal of duplicity would make even an idiot prick up his ears. It is no probable imposture, but is the poetry — for such it is, though not in verse, and not like Othello's, ample, noble, highly colored — is the poetry or rhapsody rather than the reality of deluding and diddling [. . .] this is art of a higher order, and is of value to the structure as an exhibition of Iago's personal prestige and dominance [. . .] Money, the villain intimates, opens every door; and under the hypnotic spell Roderigo is not free to consider what is behind the words. In the effect on us the chief value of the speech reposes — in the lyric elevation and prophetic exhilaration of a humorous swindler: sneering, gloating demon and vulgar cheat in one. Its very texture is lyrical, with its repeated themes and inverted phrases — 'she must have change for youth [. . .] she must have change, she must' — and yet the verbal rhythm, as always in Shakespeare, is true prose rhythm, such in quality as only Shakespeare ever framed. The high style is not out of keeping with the low in the scheme of alternation, for a grimly comic effect is intended. 'Shall be to him shortly as bitter as coloquintida,' which spurtles as from a darting and forked tongue, blends well enough with 'If thou wilt needs damn thyself do it a more delicate way than drowning.' And if there is a finishing touch for the swindler there is another afterwards for the 'black angel' as he rises into a paean of unholy triumph —

Thus do I ever make my fool my purse, — [382]

and in hatred lifts up his eyes to hell and night. The demon in the scene heightens expectation [. . .] and the comedian is not entirely diverting. Logically or poetically, though not psychologically, Iago is one of Shakespeare's most consistent characters; unlike most of them he has a 'philosophy,' or point of view, of which we have had some inkling, already; and now his portentous figure fully appears. The ending of the scene is at the same time both lyrical and intensely dramatic. The final, blood-curdling couplet

I have't. It is engend'red. Hell and night
Must bring this monstrous birth to the world's light. [402–3]

was prepared for by the quiet-disquieting, oracular words

There are many events in the womb of time which will be delivered. [370–1]

He is Satan, though without a God.

William Empson, 'Honest in *Othello*', in *The Structure of Complex Words* (London: Chatto & Windus, 1951), pp. 218–49: pp. 218, 224–5

Empson (1906–84) was one of the most influential critics of the twentieth century. He wrote books on a variety of themes from the Renaissance to contemporary literature, as well as poetry. His most important critical works are *Seven Types of Ambiguity* (1930), *The Structure of Complex Words* (1951), from which this extract is taken, and *Milton's God* (1961). Empson attempted to show how apparently tiny details, missed by ordinary readers and professional critics alike, often had profound implications affecting not simply the ways in which we might read particular literary works, but also perceive culture, society and politics in general. His work is characterised by dogged and often brilliant readings which scrupulously analyse individual words and relate their range of possible meanings in a general context to those in the work in question. Empson's analysis of the word 'honest' in *Othello* is one of his most celebrated essays.

The fifty-two uses of *honest* and *honesty* in *Othello* are a very queer business; there is no other play in which Shakespeare worries a word like that. *King Lear* uses *fool* nearly as often but does not treat it as a puzzle, only as a source of profound metaphors. In *Othello* divergent uses of the key word are found for all the main characters; even the attenuated clown plays on it; the unchaste Bianca, for instance, snatches a moment to clarion that she is more honest than Emilia the thief of the handkerchief, and with all the variety of use the ironies on the word mount up steadily to the end. Such is the general power of the writing that this is not obtrusive [. . .] Everybody calls Iago honest once or twice, but with Othello it becomes an obsession; at the crucial moment just before Emilia exposes Iago he keeps howling the word out. The general effect has been fully recognised by critics, but it looks as if there is something to be found about the word itself.

What Shakespeare hated in the word, I believe, was a peculiar use, at once hearty and individualist, which was then common among raffish low people but did not become upper-class till the Restoration; here as in Iago's heroic couplets the play has a curious effect of prophecy. But to put it like this is no doubt to over-simplify; the Restoration use, easy to feel though hard to define, seems really different from its earlier parallels, and in any case does not apply well to Iago. I want here to approach the play without taking for granted the previous analysis. But I hope it has become obvious that the word was in the middle of a rather complicated process of change, and that what emerged from it was a sort of jovial cult of independence. At some stage of the development (whether by the date of *Othello* or not) the word came to have in it a covert assertion that the man who accepts the natural desires, who does not live by principle, will be fit for such warm Yes of *honest* as simply "generous" and "faithful to friends", and to believe this is to disbelieve the Fall of Man. Thus the word, apart from being complicated, also came to raise large issues, and it is not I think a wild fancy to suppose that Shakespeare could feel the way it was going [. . .]

[. . .] There is an aspect of Iago in which he is the [. . .] "honest fellow", who is good company because he blows the gaff [. . .] much the clearest example of it is in the beginning of the second act, when he is making sport for his betters. While Desdemona is waiting for Othello's ship, which may have been lost in the tempest, he puts on an elaborate piece of clowning to distract her; and she takes his real opinion of love and women for a piece of hearty and good-natured fun. Iago's kind of honesty, he feels, is not valued as it should be; there is much in Iago of the Clown in Revolt, and the inevitable clown is almost washed out in this play to give him a free field. It is not, I think, dangerously far-fetched to take almost all Shakespeare's uses of *fool* as metaphors from the clown, whose symbolism certainly rode his imagination and was explained to the audience in most of his early plays [. . .]

IAGO: *O wretched fool,*
   That lov'st to make thine Honesty, a Vice!
   Oh monstrous world! Take note, take note (O World)
   To be direct and honest is not safe.
   I thank you for this profit, and from hence
   I'll love no Friend, sith Love breeds such offence.
OTH.: *Nay stay; thou should'st be honest.*
IAGO: *I should be wise; for Honesty's a Fool,*
   And loses that it works for.
OTH.:   *By the world,*
   I think my wife be honest, and think she is not. [3.3.378–87]

What comes out here is Iago's unwillingness to be the Fool he thinks he is taken for; but it is dramatic irony as well, and that comes back to his notion of *honest*; he is fooled by the way his plans run away with him; he fails in knowledge of others and perhaps even of his own desires.

Othello swears *by the world* because what Iago has said about being honest in the world, suggesting what worldly people think, is what has made him doubtful; yet the senses of *honest* are quite different—chastity and truth-telling. Desdemona is called a supersubtle Venetian, and he may suspect she would agree with what Iago treats as worldly wisdom; whereas it was her simplicity that made her helpless; though again, the fatal step was her lie about the handkerchief. *Lov'st* in the second line (Folios) seems to me better than *liv'st* (Quarto), as making the frightened Iago bring in his main claim at once; the comma after *lioness* perhaps makes the sense 'loves with the effect of making' rather than 'delights in making'; in any case *love* appears a few lines down. *Breeds* could suggest sexual love, as if Iago's contempt for that has spread to his notions of friendship; Othello's marriage is what has spoilt their relations (Cassio 'came a-wooing with' Othello, as a social figure, and then got the lieutenantship). In the same way Othello's two uses of *honest* here jump from 'loving towards friends, which breeds honour' to (of women) 'chaste'. It is important I think that the feminine sense, which a later time felt to be quite distinct, is so deeply confused here with the other ones.

F. R. Leavis, 'Diabolic Intellect and the Noble Hero' (1952), in *The Common Pursuit* (Harmondsworth: Penguin, 1978, rpt of 1952), pp. 136–59: pp. 138, 151–2

Leavis (1895–1978), like Empson, was a literary and cultural critic of immense influence who helped to shape the study of English literature as a discipline, especially in his capacity as editor of the journal *Scrutiny* (1932–53). Leavis also wrote on literature and culture from the Renaissance to the twentieth century, his most important works being *Revaluation* (1936), *The Great Tradition* (1948) and *D. H. Lawrence: Novelist* (1955). Leavis wrote a number of influential essays on Shakespeare but never a complete book. His essay on *Othello* made the case that Othello was a lesser tragic hero than Shakespeare's other major protagonists. It is not one of Leavis's most incisive pieces of writing but the essay did spark a major controversy and is also important as an example of the sort of attitude that later critics such as Hunter and Newman (see below, **pp. 66–70, 74–7**) were anxious to refute.

The plain fact that has to be asserted [. . .] is that in Shakespeare's tragedy of *Othello* Othello is the chief personage – the chief personage in such a sense that the tragedy may fairly be said to be Othello's character in action. Iago is subordinate and merely ancillary. He is not much more than a necessary piece of dramatic mechanism – that at any rate is a fit reply to the view of Othello as necessary material and provocation for a display of Iago's fiendish intellectual superiority. Iago, of course, is sufficiently convincing as a person; he could not perform his dramatic function otherwise [. . .]

For even, or rather especially, in that magnificent last speech of his Othello does tend to sentimentalize; though to say that and no more would convey a false impression, for the speech conveys something like the full complexity of Othello's simple nature, and in the total effect the simplicity is tragic and grand. The quiet beginning gives us the man of action with his habit of effortless authority:

> Soft you; a word or two before you go.
> I have done the State some service, and they know't.
> No more of that. I pray you in your letters,
> When you shall these unlucky deeds relate,
> Speak of me as I am; nothing extenuate,
> Nor set down aught in malice . . . [5.2.336–41]

Othello really is, we cannot doubt, the stoic-captain whose few words know their full sufficiency: up to this point we cannot say he dramatizes himself, he simply *is*. But then, in a marvellous way (if we consider Shakespeare's art), the emotion works itself up until in less than half-a-dozen lines the stoic of few words is eloquently weeping. With

Then must you speak
Of one that loved not wisely but too well, [341–2]

the epigrammatic terseness of the dispatch, the dictated dispatch, begins to quiver. Then, with a rising emotional swell, description becomes unmistakably self-dramatization – self-dramatization as un-self-comprehending as before:

Of one not easily jealous, but being wrought,
Perplex'd in the extreme; of one whose hand,
Like the base Indian, threw a pearl away
Richer than all his tribe; of one whose subdued eyes,
Albeit unused to the melting mood,
Drop tears as fast as the Arabian trees
Their medicinal gum. [342–9]

Contemplating the spectacle of himself, Othello is overcome with the pathos of it. But this is not the part to die in: drawing himself proudly up, he speaks his last words as the stern soldier who recalls, and re-enacts, his supreme moment of deliberate courage:

Set you down this;
And say besides, that in Aleppo once,
Where a malignant and a turban'd Turk
Beat a Venetian and traduced the state,
I took by the throat the circumcised dog
And smote him, thus. [Stabs himself.] [349–53]

It is a superb *coup de théâtre*.

As, with that double force, a *coup de théâtre*, it is peculiarly right ending to the tragedy of Othello. The theme of the tragedy is concentrated in it – concentrated in the final speech and action as it could not have been had Othello 'learnt through suffering'. That he should die acting his ideal part is all in the part: the part is manifested here in its rightness and solidity, and the actor as inseparably the man of action. The final blow is as real as the blow it re-enacts, and the histrionic intent symbolically affirms the reality: Othello dies belonging to the world of action in which his true part lay.

Marvin Rosenberg, *The Masks of Othello: The Search for the Identity of Othello, Iago and Desdemona by Three Centuries of Actors and Critics* (Newark, Del.: University of Delaware Press, 1993, rpt of 1961), pp. 5–7, 209–10

An extract from Rosenberg's book is included here because he was influential in establishing ways in which the play might be performed on stage in the 1960s and 1970s. Rosenberg examines the play as it might appear to both actors and audiences and tries to help readers understand the different problems to be solved and questions that need to be asked before a successful production can be staged. He looks at characters as they might appear on stage.

From the beginning, men wept at *Othello*. A rare "review" from 1610 tells how, when Shakespeare's company went down to Oxford to play the tragedy, the actors "drew tears not only by their speech, but also by their action. Indeed Desdemona, though always excellent, moved us especially in her death when, as she lay on her bed, her face itself implored the pity of the audience" [see above, p. 37].

So Shakespeare's own actors achieved an effect that would be many, many times repeated: they moved an audience beyond attention and involvement to compassion, and "drew tears." How did the playwright do it? What was his artistic design? Centuries of critics and actors have tried to answer; and in their answers the outlines of the essential character problems may be seen.

First, the problem of Othello. Basically, it is this: how can he be both noble and a murderer? What kind of sympathy, what empathy, can he evoke? His act of killing is somewhat less calculating, less brutal, than that of Cinthio's Moor [see above, **pp. 19–21**]; but there is still calculation and brutality in it, and the playwright's vision in him of man's murderous passion is far more terrifying than anything in the original. Is the Moor who commits his crime, on Iago's urging, as noble as he—and everyone else—says he is? Or, to consult some critics, is he perhaps an insecure, oversexed soldier, experienced in adultery—with Emilia, among others—who is more than ready, even eager, to believe wrong of his wife? Is he a self-deceived impostor, fooling himself as well as all the others? What about his romantic tales: the antres vast, the cannibals, and the men whose heads grow beneath their shoulders? Or the magical handkerchief—protected by a witch's curse—woven by a Sybil from hallowed silk dyed in an ancient liquor made of maiden's hearts? Is this all lying and boasting? When he stops the brawling night clash with Brabantio, when he puts down the riot in Cyprus, does he command, or bluster? Then Iago deceives him—too easily? Is he a fool? Is he a neurotic eager to be deceived? Once deceived, and his surface disintegrates, what is to be made of the violence that erupts from the centre of his being? The turbid sexual fantasies that sweep him into his "trance"? The stormy assaults on Desdemona, and then the killing? Is this the inner shape of a barbarian? Of Anyman? What is the meaning of his dark skin?

As many problems are found in Desdemona by actors—and especially by critics. How different she is from Cinthio's pious Disdemona, who fears "that I shall prove a warning to young girls not to marry against the wishes of their parents, and that the Italian ladies may learn from me not to wed a man whom nature and habitude of life estrange from us." Desdemona declares her faith in marriage to the death, and even in a faint reprise beyond it. Yet she too is partly responsible for the catastrophe. She has taken the initiative in marriage, has virtually proposed to Othello; she has deceived her father, has eloped against his wishes with a man of another race and color. She is certainly not "proper"; and she too is touched with the erotic ambience of the play: when she listens to Iago's rowdy jokes on the Cyprus quay, when she lets Emilia discuss the virtues of adultery, in her love play with Othello, and in her undressing and bedroom scenes. She "meddles" in her husband's business, presses him to reinstate his dismissed officer—presses him at the worst moment, when he most needs understanding. Finally, she lies to him, and destroys their hope of love. Is this quite a heroine? Or, as some critics have suggested, is she perhaps to be scorned for her filial ingratitude, for her lies, for her forwardness, for her spinelessness? Is there something "unnatural" in her love? Does she deserve what happened to her? Conversely, is she perhaps the very essence of goodness? A symbol of divinity? A Christ figure? Can any of this explain why audiences would weep for her, as they did at Oxford?

Most complex of all for actors and critics is the Iago problem. This villain is much more dangerous than Cinthio's. He not only betrays the Moor and the Captain (Cassio); he injures everyone in his vicinity. How can so evil a man be plausible? How can he win the confidence of so apparently noble a man as Othello? And more important, what is his motivation? Why should any man hurt others so much? Is he simply a dramatic mechanism? A symbol of the devil? The devil himself? Or is he in fact a good man who has been provoked to revenge by wrongs done him? Was he unfairly denied promotion by Othello? Cuckolded by him? By Cassio? Why is his language so charged with erotic allusions: the lascivious wordplay directed at Brabantio, at Roderigo, even at Desdemona; the insidious, then blatant images of carnality, nakedness, and intercourse with which he overwhelms Othello; and, most of all, the brooding sexual fantasy that pervades his soliloquies? Does he really lust after Desdemona? Is he driven by a repressed homosexual attachment to Othello? Finally, how can a character who does so much wrong involve audiences so deeply in his fate? [. . .]

It seems to me as dangerous to rob Desdemona of her human frailty as it is to steal her essential goodness from her. Fortunately for the long life of Shakespeare's play, she no more personifies divinity than deceit. If she were not much more than either, we would not care what she was. But we care intensely for this young, passionate woman who ran away secretly from her father's house to the arms of her lover, who has a healthy desire to be with her husband on her wedding night, who cries when she is struck, and who fears death terribly. Divinity is beyond our pity; but we weep for the mortal woman who was Desdemona.

To come away from her tragic experience remembering her as either a saint or sinner is to abstract from the complex weave of the character a few small threads of behavior, meaningless out of the pattern, and find in them the design of the whole. Desdemona indeed tells a lie, as Othello commits a murder; but we never think of Othello as an assassin—it is Shakespeare's art to make us feel Othello is a good man driven to kill, as he meant us to feel Desdemona is a fine woman, a fair woman, a sweet woman driven by fear and love to untruth.

This, certainly, is the interpretation that best unites the prevailing critical perception of her essential goodness with the franker humanity that great actresses have brought to her. Both aspects contribute to a central character purpose in the living theater. Here, in the play's natural home, where meanings are determined by what reaches the brain and emotions through the eye and ear, where the bits and pieces of Desdemona's behavior are absorbed into a total, tangible artistic image, we first see her as a young, still playful, utterly devoted wife, whose character is being changed and shaped by her love for her husband. We see this love urge her rebellion against her father, her hazardous trip to Cyprus, her lies, her dying attempt to save Othello. We see it mature her, as it kills her. Our *seeing* is of the utmost importance: the way she looks always toward Othello, the way she surrounds him with her affection, her unspoken happiness in his presence. Her love, like her honor, must be always apparent, for it defines her.

G. K. Hunter, 'Othello and Colour Prejudice' (1967), in Dramatic Identities and Cultural Tradition: Studies in Shakespeare and His Contemporaries (Liverpool: Liverpool University Press, 1978), pp. 31–59: pp. 31–2, 45–6, 53, 54–6

Hunter is a critic who has produced a number of important studies of Renaissance culture and drama. This essay was the first serious attempt to examine Elizabethan attitudes to race and so try to establish what the play might have meant to a contemporary audience rather than relying on later productions of *Othello* to establish its meaning. Hunter's essay prefigures much later historically informed readings of the play which have become increasingly important (see Newman, **pp. 74–8**, McPherson, **pp. 78–84**, Jardine, **pp. 84–91**, Hadfield, **pp. 92–3**). Hunter suggests that Shakespeare was sympathetic to his protagonist and was trying to establish that a black man from North Africa could be as noble and impressive as a white man (in contrast, see Leavis, **pp. 62–3**). Critics have debated this issue ever since.

It is generally admitted today that Shakespeare was a practical man of the theatre: however careless he may have been about maintaining consistency for the exact *reader* of his plays, he was not likely to introduce a theatrical novelty which would only puzzle his audience; it does not seem wise, therefore, to dismiss his theatrical innovations as if they were unintentional. The blackness of Othello is a case in point. Shakespeare largely modified the story he took over from Cinthio: he made a tragic hero out of Cinthio's passionate and bloody lover; he gave him a royal origin, a Christian baptism, a romantic *bravura* of manner and, most important of all, an orotund magnificence of diction [see above, **pp. 55–7**]. Yet, changing all this, he did not change his colour, and so produced a daring theatrical novelty—a black hero for a white community—a novelty which remains too daring for many recent theatrical audiences. Shakespeare cannot merely have carried over the colour of Othello by being too lazy or too uninterested to meddle with it; for no actor, spending the time in 'blacking-up', and hence no producer, could be indifferent to such an innovation, especially in that age, devoted to 'imitation' and hostile to 'originality'. In fact, the repeated references to Othello's colour in the play and the wider net of images of dark and light spread across the diction, show that Shakespeare was not only not unaware of the implication of his hero's colour, but was indeed intensely aware of it as one of the primary factors in his play. I am therefore assuming [. . .] that the blackness of Othello has a theatrical purpose, and I intend to try to suggest what it was possible for that purpose to have been.

Shakespeare intended his hero to be a black man—that much I take for granted; what is unknown is what the idea of a black man suggested to Shakespeare, and what reaction the appearance of a black man on the stage was calculated to produce. It is fairly certain, however, that some modern reactions are not likely to have been shared by the Elizabethans. The modern theatre-going European intellectual, with a background of cultivated superiority to 'colour problems' in other continents, would often choose to regard Othello as a fellow man and to watch the story—which could so easily be reduced to its headline level: 'sheltered white girl errs: said, "Colour does not matter"'—with a sense of freedom from such prejudices. But this lofty fair-mindedness may be too lofty for Shakespeare's play, and not take the European any nearer the Othello of Shakespeare than the lady from Maryland quoted in the Furness New Variorum edition: 'In studying the play of *Othello*, I have always *imagined* its hero a white man.' Both views, that the colour of Othello does not matter, and that it matters too much to be tolerable, err, I suggest, by over-simplifying. Shakespeare was clearly deliberate in keeping Othello's colour; and it is obvious that he counted on some positive audience reaction to this colour; but it is equally obvious that he did not wish the audience to dismiss Othello as a stereotype nigger [. . .]

[. . .] It is in such terms that the play opens. We hear from men like us of a man not like us, of 'his Moorship', 'the Moor', 'the thick-lips', 'an old black ram', 'a Barbary horse', 'the devil', of 'the gross clasps of a lascivious Moor'. The sexual fear and disgust that lie behind so much racial prejudice are exposed for our derisive expectations to fasten upon them. And we are at this point bound to agree with these valuations, for no alternative view is revealed. There is, of course, a certain comic *brio* which helps to distance the whole situation, and neither Brabantio, nor Iago nor Roderigo can wholly command our identification. None the less we are drawn on to await the entry of a traditional Moor figure, the kind of person we came to the theatre expecting to find.

When the second scene begins, however, it is clear that Shakespeare is bent to ends other than the fulfilment of these expectations. The Iago/Roderigo relationship of I. i is repeated in the Iago/Othello relationship of the opening of I. ii; but Othello's response to the real-seeming circumstance with which Iago lards his discourse is very different from the hungrily self-absorbed questionings of Roderigo. Othello draws on an inward certainty about himself, a radiant clarity about his own well-founded moral position. This is no 'lascivious Moor', but a great Christian gentleman, against whom Iago's insinuations break like water against granite. Not only is Othello a Christian, moreover; he is the leader of Christendom in the last and highest sense in which Christendom existed as a viable entity, crusading against the 'black pagans'. He is to defend Cyprus against the

Turk [. . .] It was the fall of Cyprus which produced the alliance of Lepanto [see above, p. 15], and we should associate Othello with the emotion that Europe continued to feel—till well after the date of *Othello*—about that victory [. . .]

Shakespeare has presented to us a traditional view of what Moors are like, i.e. gross, disgusting, inferior, carrying the symbol of their damnation on their skin; and has caught our over-easy assent to such assumptions in the grip of a guilt which associates us and our assent with the white man representative of such views in the play—Iago. Othello acquires the glamour of an innocent man that we have wronged, and an admiration stronger than he could have achieved by virtue plainly represented [. . .]

[. . .] *Othello* has *something* of the structure of a morality play, with Othello caught between Desdemona and Iago, the good angel and the evil angel. Iago is the master of appearances, which he seeks to exploit as realities; Desdemona, on the other hand, cares nothing for appearances (as her 'downright violence and storm of fortunes/May trumpet to the world'), only for realities; Othello, seeing appearance and reality as indissoluble cues to action, stands between the two, the object of the attentions and the assumptions of both. The play has something of this morality structure; but by giving too much importance to this it would be easy to underplay the extent to which Othello becomes what Iago and the society to which *we* belong assumes him to be [. . .]

The dramatic function of Iago is to reduce the white 'reality' of Othello to the black 'appearance' of his face, indeed induce in him the belief that all reality is 'black', that Desdemona in particular, 'where I have garnered up my heart'

> . . . that was fresh
> As Dian's visage, is now begrimed and black
> As mine own face. [3.3.389–91]

Thus in the bedroom scene (v. ii) Othello's view of Desdemona is one that contrasts

> that whiter skin of hers than snow
> And smooth as monumental alabaster [5.2.4–5]

with the dark deeds her nature requires of her.

> Put out the light, and then put out the light, [7]

he says; that is, 'let the face be as dark as the soul it covers'; and then murder will be justified.

This intention on Shakespeare's part is made very explicit at one point, where Othello tells Desdemona,

> Come, swear it, damn thyself; lest, being like one of heaven, the devils themselves should fear to seize thee; therefore be double-damn'd—swear thou art honest. (IV. ii. 36 ff.)

What Othello is asking here is that the white and so 'heavenly' Desdemona should damn herself black [. . .]

The dark reality originating in Iago's soul spreads across the play, blackening whatever it overcomes and making the deeds of Othello at last fit in with the prejudice that his face at first excited. Sometimes it is supposed that this proves the prejudice to have been justified. There is a powerful line of criticism on *Othello* [. . .] that paints the Moor as a savage at heart, one whose veneer of Christianity and civilization cracks as the play proceeds, to reveal and liberate his basic savagery: Othello turns out to be in fact what barbarians *have* to be.

This view, however comforting to our sense of society and our prejudices, does not find much support in the play itself. The fact that the darkness of 'Hell and night' spreads from Iago and then takes over Othello—this fact at least should prevent us from supposing that the blackness is inherent in Othello's barbarian nature. Othello himself, it is true, loses faith not only in Desdemona but in that fair quality of himself which Desdemona saw and worshipped: ('for she had eyes and chose me'). Believing that she lied about the qualities she saw in him it is easy for him to believe that she lies elsewhere and everywhere. Once the visionary quality of *faith*, which made it possible to believe (what in common sense was unbelievable) that she *chose* him—once this is cancelled, knowingness acquires a claim to truth that only faith could dispossess; and so when Iago says

> I know our country disposition well:
> In Venice they do let God see the pranks
> They dare not show their husbands. [3.3.204–6]

Othello can only answer 'Dost thou say so?' Once faith is gone, physical common sense becomes all too probable:

> Foh! one may smell in such a will most rank,
> Foul disproportion, thoughts unnatural. [236–7]

The superficial 'disproportion' between black skin and white skin conquers the inward, unseen 'marriage of true minds'. Similarly with the disproportion between youth and age: 'She must change for youth'; being sated with his body she will find the error of her choice. The tragedy becomes [. . .] a tragedy of the loss of faith. And, such is the nature of Othello's heroic temperament, the loss of faith means the loss of all meaning and all value, all sense of light:

> I have no wife.
> O insupportable! O heavy hour!
> Methinks it should be now a huge eclipse
> Of sun and moon, and that the affrighted globe
> Did yawn at alteration. [5.2.96–9]

Universal darkness has buried all.

But the end of the play is not simply a collapse of civilization into barbarism, nor a destruction of meaning. Desdemona *was* true, faith *was* justified, the appearance was not the key to the truth. To complete the circle we must accept, finally and above all, that Othello was not the credulous and passionate savage that Iago has tried *to* make him, but that he was justified in his second, as in his first, self-defence:

> For nought I did in hate, but all in honour.[5.2.292]

The imposition of Iago's vulgar prejudices on Othello ('These Moors are change-able in their wills', etc.) is so successful that it takes over not only Othello but almost all the critics. But Iago's suppression of Othello into the vulgar prejudice about him can only be sustained as the truth if we ignore the end of the play. The wonderful recovery here of the sense of ethical meaning in the world, even in the ashes of all that embodied meaning [. . .] It is in fact a marvellous *stretto* [rapid summary] of all the themes that have sounded throughout the play.

Terry Eagleton, 'Nothing', from *William Shakespeare* (Oxford: Blackwell, 1986), pp. 64–70

Eagleton is a prolific Marxist critic who has written numerous books on English and Irish literature, politics and philosophy. His short, provocative book on Shakespeare used new critical methods to inspire debate and to make sure that innovative ways of reading did not remain confined to the academy. Eagleton combines a keen sense of history with insights derived from deconstruction, a mode of criticism that reads every text as part of a linguistic and cultural system that determines the ways in which an author can speak or write, but also shows ways in which what we assume to be the truth is often a delusion. The aim is to enable us to read more closely, carefully and critically. Eagleton's essay also owes much to feminist theory and shows how assumptions of male superiority – often as much unconscious as conscious – have blinded readers to the true issues explored in Shakespeare's play.

There is some evidence that the word 'nothing' in Elizabethan English could mean the female genitals.[1] [. . .] a woman appears to have nothing between her legs, which is as alarming for men as it is reassuring. On the one hand, this apparent lack in the female confirms the male's power over her; on the other hand, it stirs in

---

1   [Eagleton's note.] See E. A. M. Colman, *The Dramatic Use of Bawdy in Shakespeare* (London, 1974), pp. 15–18; and David Wilberns, 'Shakespeare's nothing', in M. Schwartz and C. Kahn (eds), *Representing Shakespeare* (Baltimore, 1980). There is some controversy over how common this sexual connotation of the word was. It would certainly seem to be present in Hamlet's crude remarks to Ophelia before 'The Mousetrap', and possibly also in the title *Much Ado About Nothing*, which, since 'ado' can mean 'copulation', may be doubly suggestive. It need not be supposed, however, that when Lear asks Cordelia what she can say to win his favour, she replies 'female genitals, my lord'.

him unconscious thoughts of his own possible castration, reminding him that his own being may not be as flawlessly complete as he had imagined. The sight of an external lack may stimulate a sense of vacancy within himself, which he can plug, paradoxically, with the woman idealized as fetish: if woman has nothing between her legs then she is a desexualized Madonna, whose purity of being can protect him totemically against the chaos which the female nothing threatens. Desdemona oscillates for Othello between these two impossible roles: 'But I do love thee,' he says of her, 'and when I love thee not/Chaos is come again' (III.ii.92–3). If the female nothing were simple absence, it would pose no problem; but there is in fact no simple absence, since all absence is dependent for its perceptibility upon presence. It is, then, a void which cannot help being powerfully suggestive [. . .] The woman's nothing is of a peculiarly convoluted kind, a yawning abyss within which man can lose his virile identity. This modest nothing begins to look like some sublimely terrifying all; and indeed this is the riddle of woman, that though for patriarchy she is in one sense mere deficiency or negation – non-man, defective man – she also has the power to incite the tumultuous 'everything' of desire in man himself, and so to destroy him. How does it come about that this sweet nothing can become a sinister everything?

Paranoid jealousy like Othello's is convinced that a simple nothing – the mistress's lack of fidelity – is, in fact, an abysmal one, a nameless depth beneath the smooth surface of her outward appearance. When Iago cunningly replies 'Nothing' to Othello's request to know what ails him, his comment is ironically exact; but he speculates rightly that Othello will promptly read some dreadful something into this temptingly blank text. This indeed is the classic condition of paranoia, which discerns an oppressively systematic significance in every contingent detail, 'over-reading' the world as Othello over-reads the stolen handkerchief. The closest thing to paranoia, Freud commented dryly, is philosophy; and both are characterized by what he named 'epistemophilia', a pathological obsession with hunting down hidden knowledge, plucking out the heart of a mystery so as to master and possess it. Since there is in fact no heart to the mystery – indeed in *Othello* no mystery at all – this drive for power and knowledge must be endlessly frustrated. Systematically mistrusting appearances, the paranoiac cannot accept that everything lies open to view, that the world just is the way it is with no secret essence, that what he is seeing are not appearances but, amazingly, the real thing.

Sexual jealousy [. . .] is fundamentally a crisis of interpretation. Othello insists voyeuristically on seeing, observing, obtaining the 'ocular proof' of his wife's supposed adultery; but the irony of this naive trust in brute fact is that perception is itself a text, requiring interpretation before it means anything at all. And since interpretation is both partial and interminable, 'seeing the facts' is more likely to complicate the issue than to resolve it. Reality itself, things as they are, is thus a kind of blank, needing to be signified before it becomes anything determinate; there is a 'nothing' at the very core of the world, a pervasive absence infiltrating the whole of experience, which can be abolished only by the supplementary benefit of language. The problem, however, is that language itself can be a sort of nothing, as with Iago's insinuating fictions, punching a gaping hole in reality and inducing you to believe in what is not in fact there. For the sexually jealous, the entire world seems struck sickeningly empty of meaning, as it is for Leontes in *The Winter's Tale*:

> Is whispering nothing?
> Is leaning cheek to cheek? Is meeting noses?
> Kissing with inside lip? [. . .]
> Why, then the world and all that's in't is nothing;
> The covering sky is nothing; Bohemia nothing;
> My wife is nothing; nor nothing have these nothings
> If this be nothing.
> (I.ii.284–6, 293–6)

The whole world becomes the female genitals; female sexuality is either in one place – the male's private possession – or it is everywhere [. . .]

[. . .] If Othello could 'go beyond' Iago's duplicitous text rather than fall helpless prisoner to its letter then, paradoxically, he would see reality as it is, join signifier and signified together appropriately. Only a certain creative excess of interpretation could restore him to the norm. As it is, he conforms himself obediently to Iago's empty signifiers, filling them with the imaginary signifieds of Desdemona's infidelity.

It is in the nature of paranoid jealousy to overwhelm its object in this way, as a signifier without a referent, a monstrous hermeneutical inflation ('exsufflicate and blown surmises', as Othello calls it in his customary jargon) which feeds off itself without the frailest rooting in reality. Jealousy is a tyrannical language which manipulates the world to suit its own ends, an absolutist law which bends the evidence in its own interests: 'Trifles light as air/Are to the jealous confirmation strong/As proofs of holy writ' (III.iii.326–7). Othello thinks at first that this chain of empty signifiers can be arrested by concrete evidence:

> No, Iago;
> I'll see before I doubt; when I doubt, prove;
> And, on the proof, there is no more but this –
> Away at once with love or jealousy!
> (III.iii.193–6)

But since the hypothesis of jealousy rigs the very evidence against which it tests itself, this claim turns out to be purely circular. 'I swear 'tis better to be much abus'd/Than but to know't a little' (III.iii.340–1), Othello cries later – the torment being that to know only something (and who knows more?) is to know that this implies something else of which you are ignorant. Knowledge stretches out to infinity, each present piece of evidence suggesting another which is necessarily absent. Anything definite is thus also unavoidably ambiguous, and sexual jealousy merely intensifies this common state of affairs, reading volumes into a simple handkerchief [. . .] Within the double bind of patriarchy, there is no way in which Desdemona can behave 'properly' towards Cassio without being continually open to the suspicion of behaving 'improperly', no firm borderline between courtesy and lechery. For the woman, to be free is always to be too free; to render an exact, socially dutiful love to Cassio is to risk transgressing the norm. The woman is a constantly travestied text, perpetually open to misreading; she is a stumbling-block in the path of lucid interpretation, unable to be proper without promiscuity, frigid when judicious, never warm without being too hot [. . .]

The unpalatable implication of all this is that jealousy is not a form of sexual desire: sexual desire is a form of jealousy. If a woman is capable of being faithful then she is also eternally capable of being unfaithful, just as a word which can be used to speak truth can always be used to deceive. Othello contemplates the possibility of 'nature erring from itself', but this possibility is structural to Nature itself. To desire someone is to see them as an 'other' which one lacks; cannot speak of desiring that which one possesses. What we desire, then, can never by definition be fully possessed, and the possibility of losing the desired object entirely is thus built into the passion itself. 'Poor and content is rich, and rich enough', Iago remarks, 'But riches fineless is as poor as winter/To him that ever fears he shall be poor' (III.iii.176–8). If to have is to be able to lose, however, then all possession becomes a source of anxiety. This is obvious in the fact that Othello only really comes to desire his wife intensely once he begins to suspect that she is unfaithful to him. His previous 'love' for her is the sheerest narcissism: he wins Desdemona by military boasting, and is agreeably flattered by her admiration for his skill as a professional butcher. To suspect that she is adulterous is to credit her with an identity autonomous of his own, which snaps the narcissistic circuit and begins to undermine his own identity. Much of his jealousy is no more than this self-regarding fear that his own magnificently replete selfhood is collapsing from the inside, as the female nothing, the green girl who gasped at his tall tales, becomes a sinisterly independent something. But if such lack and autonomy are logical to all desire, then all desire is a kind of monstrosity or perversion. Woman is that which man can never possess, that which eludes his mastery and so breeds in him a feverish activity of 'over-interpretation'. Inflated signifiers, slanderous misreadings, infinite webs of text and tortuous *aponas* ('I think my wife be honest, and I think she is not') would seem to go 'naturally' with erotic love. It is in the nature of such Eros to override the measure, generate delusion, squint at its object. *Othello* is not a play about sexual deviancy, but about the deviancy of sex.

This is not, however, to justify the cynicism of an Iago. If Othello in the end is unable to distinguish between delusion and reality, Iago has severed them too rigorously all along. 'I am not what I am' signals not a crisis of identity but a smug self-affirmation: Iago is the exact opposite of whatever he appears to be, which is a consistent enough way of possessing oneself. Appearances for Iago are just empty rituals to be pragmatically manipulated: 'I must show out a flag and sign of love,/Which is indeed but sign' (I.i.157–8). But nothing for Shakespeare is *but* sign: the signifier is always active in respect of its meaning, not some hollow container to be discarded at will. Iago is one of a long line of possessive individualists in Shakespeare who locate reality only in bodily appetite, believing that they can exploit signs and forms from the outside while remaining themselves unscathed by the consequent mystification. Whereas Othello lives straight out of an imaginary self-image, his very being indissociable from rhetoric and theatricality, Iago scorns such burnished discourse as 'mere prattle, without practice'. But both Othello's histrionic 'bombast' and Iago's brisk materialism miss the measure. Othello starts off with a wholly 'imaginary' relation to reality: his rotund, mouth-filling rhetoric signifies a delusory completeness of being, in which the whole world becomes a signified obediently 'reflecting back the imperious signifier of the self. Even Desdemona becomes his 'fair warrior', as though he can grasp nothing which he has not first translated into his own military idiom. From this deceptively secure standpoint, Othello is then pitched violently into the 'symbolic order' of desire, where signifier and signified never quite coincide. The problem, then, is how to recognize, unlike the cynically naturalistic Iago, that signs and illusions are structural to reality – that all experience, because driven by desire, has an inescapable dimension of fantasy and mystification – without falling prey to the tragic lunacy of an Othello, for whom appearance and reality come to merge into a seamless whole. Iago fails to see that all bodily appetite is caught up in discourse and symbolism, which are not 'superstructural' pieties but part of its inward form. Othello knows this too well, and comes to mistake the sign for the reality. How does one distinguish between taking appearances for reality, and acknowledging the reality of appearances? Failing to make such a distinction, *Othello* suggests, is a psychopathological condition; but it also suggests, more alarmingly, that this psychopathology may be intrinsic to everyday life.

Karen Newman, ' "And wash the Ethiop white": Femininity and the Monstrous in *Othello*', in Jean E. Howard and Marion F. O'Connor, eds, *Shakespeare Reproduced: The Text in History and Ideology* (London: Routledge, 1987), pp. 151–3, 157–9, 161–2

Newman's essay develops the themes explored in those by Eagleton (see **pp. 70–4**) and Hunter (see **pp. 66–70**), combining a discussion of race with a feminist approach to the play. Newman is especially interested in the question of miscegenation, the production of children of mixed race, and the consequent fear that pure and stable identities might be undermined, thus threatening notions of white supremacy. In doing so, Newman has moved the debate over *Othello* beyond the question of whether Shakespeare was sympathetic to Othello, the central issue considered by Hunter, while still considering that issue. Newman argues that both Othello and Desdemona are regarded as monstrous in subtly intertwined ways. Like Eagleton, Newman wants readers to challenge conventional modes of thinking and so open up new ways of reading the play.

For the white male characters of the play, the black man's power resides in his sexual difference from a white male norm. Their preoccupation with black sexuality is not an eruption of a normally repressed animal sexuality in the "civilized" white male, but of the feared power and potency of a different and monstrous sexuality which threatens the white male sexual norm represented in the play most emphatically by Iago. For however evil Iago reveals himself to be, as Spivak pointed out[1] [. . .] Iago enjoys a privileged relation with the audience. He possesses what can be termed the discourse of knowledge in *Othello* and annexes not only the other characters, but the resisting spectator as well, into his world and its perspective. By virtue of his manipulative power and his superior knowledge and control over the action, which we share, we are implicated in his machinations and the cultural values they imply. Iago is a cultural hyperbole; he does not oppose cultural norms so much as hyperbolize them.

Before the English had wide experience of miscegenation, they seem to have believed [. . .] that the black man had the power to subjugate his partner's whiteness, to make both his "victim" and her offspring resemble him, to make them both black, a literal blackness in the case of a child, a metaphorical blackness in the case of a sexual partner. So in *Othello*, Desdemona becomes "thou black weed" (IV. iii. 69) and the white pages of her "goodly book" are blackened by writing when Othello imagines "whore" inscribed across them. At IV. iii, she explicitly identifies herself with her mother's maid Barbary whose name connotes blackness. The union of Desdemona and Othello represents a sympathetic identification between femininity and the monstrous which offers a potentially subversive recognition of sexual and racial difference.

Both the male-dominated Venetian world of *Othello* and the criticism the play has generated have been dominated by a scopic economy which privileges sight, from the spectacular opposition of black and white to Othello's demands for ocular proof of Desdemona's infidelity. But Desdemona *hears* Othello and loves him, awed by his traveler's tales of the dangers he had passed, dangers which emphasize his link with monsters and marvels. Her responses to his tales are perceived as voracious – she "devours" his discourses with a "greedy ear," conflating the oral and aural, and his language betrays a masculine fear of a cultural femininity which is envisioned as a greedy mouth, never satisfied, always seeking increase, a point of view which Desdemona's response to their reunion at Cyprus reinforces. Desdemona is presented in the play as a sexual subject who hears and desires, and that desire is punished because the non-specular, or non-phallic sexuality it displays is frightening and dangerous. Instead of a specular imaginary, Desdemona's desire is represented in terms of an aural/oral libidinal economy which generates anxiety in Othello, as his account to the Senate of his courtship via fiction betrays – Othello fears Desdemona's desire because it invokes his monstrous difference from the sex/race code he has adopted, or, alternatively, allies her imagined monstrous sexual appetite with his own.

Thomas Rymer, a kind of critical Iago, claims the moral of *Othello* is first, "a caution to all maidens of Quality how, without their parents' consent, they run away with Blackamoors," an instruction which he follows with the version of his Italian source, Cinthio [see above, **pp. 19–21**] [. . .] Desdemona is punished for her desire: she *hears* Othello and desires him, and her desire is punished because it threatens a white male hegemony in which women cannot be desiring subjects.

1 [Newman's note.] Bernard Spivak, *The Allegory of Evil* (New York: Columbia University Press, 1958), pp. 415ff.

When Desdemona comes to tell her version of their wooing, she says: "I saw Othello's visage in his mind." The allusion here is certainly to her audience's prejudice against the black "visage" that both the Senators and Shakespeare's audience see in Othello, but Desdemona "saw" his visage through hearing the tales he tells of his past, tales which, far from washing the Moor white as her line seems to imply, emphatically affirm Othello's link with Africa and its legendary monstrous creatures. Rymer's moral points up the patriarchal and scopic assumptions of his culture which are assumed as well in the play and most pointedly summed up by Brabantio's open quoted lines: "Look to her, Moor, have a quick eye to see:/She has deceiv'd her father, may do thee" (I. iii. 292–3). Fathers have the right to dispose of their daughters as they see fit, to whom they see fit, and disobedience against the father's law is merely a prelude to the descent into hell and blackness the play enacts [. . .] Desdemona's desire threatens the patriarchal privilege of disposing daughters and in the play world signals sexual duplicity and lust.

The irony, of course, is that Othello himself is the instrument of punishment; he enacts the moral Rymer and Cinthio point, both confirming cultural prejudice by his monstrous murder of Desdemona and punishing her desire which transgresses the norms of the Elizabethan sex/race system. Both Othello and Desdemona deviate from the norms of the sex/race system in which they participate from the margins. Othello is not, in Cinthio's words, "da noi," one of "us," nor is Desdemona. Women depend for their class status on their affiliation with men – fathers, husbands, sons – and Desdemona forfeits that status and the protection it affords when she marries outside the categories her culture allows. For her transgression, her desire of difference, she is punished not only in a loss of status, but even of life. The woman's desire is punished, and ultimately its monstrous inspiration as well. As the object of Desdemona's illegitimate passion, Othello both figures monstrosity *and* at the same time represents the white male norms the play encodes through Iago, Roderigo, Brabantio. Not surprisingly, Othello reveals at last a complicitous self-loathing, for blackness is as loathsome to him as [. . .] any male character in the play, or ostensibly the audience.

At IV. i., Iago constructs a drama which Othello is instructed to interpret, a scene rich in its figurations of desire and the monstrous. Cast by Iago as eavesdropper and voyeur, Othello imagines and thus constitutes a sexual encounter and pleasure that excludes him, and a Desdemona as whore instead of fair angel. Cassio's mocking rehearsal of Bianca's love is not the sight/site of Desdemona's transgression, as Othello believes, but its representation; ironically this theatrical representation directed by Iago functions as effectively as would the real. Representation for Othello is transparent. The male gaze is privileged; it constructs a world which the drama plays out. The aptly and ironically named Bianca is a cypher for Desdemona whose "blackened whiteness" she embodies. Plots of desire conventionally figure woman as the erotic object, but in *Othello* the iconic center of the spectacle is shifted from the woman to the monstrous Othello whose blackness charms *and* threatens, but ultimately fulfills the cultural prejudices it represents. Othello is both hero and outsider because he embodies not only the norms of male power and privilege represented by the white male hegemony which rules Venice, a world of prejudice, ambition, jealousy, and the denial of difference, but also the threatening power of the alien: Othello is a monster in the Renaissance sense of the word, a deformed creature like the herm-aphrodites and other strange spectacles which so fascinated the early modern period. And *monstrum*, the word itself, figures both the creature and its move-ment into representation, for it meant as well a showing or demonstration, a *representation* [. . .]

Was Shakespeare a racist who condoned the negative image of blacks in his culture? Is Desdemona somehow guilty in her stubborn defense of Cassio and her admiring remark "Ludovico is a proper man?" [. . .] Readers preoccupied with formal dramatic features claim such questions are moot, that the questions themselves expose the limits of moral or political readings of texts because they raise the specters of intention or ignore the touted transcendence of history by art. But as much recent poststructuralist and/or political criticism has demon-strated, even highly formalist readings are political, inscribed in the discourses both of the period in which the work was produced and of those in which it is consumed.

The task of a political criticism is not merely to expose or demystify the ideological discourses which organize literary texts, but to *reconstitute* those texts, to reread canonical texts in noncanonical ways which reveal the contin-gency of so-called canonical readings, which disturb conventional interpretations and discover them as partisan, constructed, made rather than given, natural, and inevitable. Such strategies of reading are particularly necessary in drama because the dramatic immediacy of theatrical representation obscures the fact that the audience is watching a highly artificial enactment of what, in the case of *Othello*, a non-African and a man has made into a vision of blackness and femininity, of passion and desire in the other, those marginal groups which stand outside culture and simultaneously within it.

Shakespeare was certainly subject to the racist, sexist, and colonialist dis-courses of his time, but by making the black Othello a hero, and by making Desdemona's love for Othello, and her transgression of her society's norms for women in choosing him, sympathetic, Shakespeare's play stands in a contestatory relation to the hegemonic ideologies of race and gender in early modern England. Othello is, of course, the play's hero only within the terms of a white, elitist male ethos, and he suffers the generic "punishment" of tragedy, but he is nevertheless represented as heroic and tragic at a historical moment when the only role blacks played on stage was that of a villain of low status. The case of Desdemona is more complex because the fate she suffers is the conventional fate assigned to the desir-ing woman. Nevertheless, Shakespeare's representation of her as at once virtuous and desiring, and of her choice in love as heroic rather than demonic, dislocates the conventional ideology of gender the play also enacts.

We need to read Shakespeare in ways which produce resistant readings, ways which contest the hegemonic forces the plays at the same time affirm. Our critical task is not merely to describe the formal parameters of a play, nor is it to make claims about Shakespeare's politics, conservative or subversive, but to reveal the discursive and dramatic evidence for such representations, and their counterparts in criticism, as representations.

David McPherson, 'Othello and the Myth of Venice', in Shakespeare, Jonson, and the Myth of Venice (Newark, Del.: University of Delaware Press, 1990), pp. 81–4, 86–90

McPherson subjects *Othello* to a scrupulous historical analysis in his book, *Shakespeare, Jonson and the Myth of Venice* (1990). McPherson shows how the Venetian setting of the play is not simply an exotic backdrop, but deliberately chosen by Shakespeare who wishes to explore a number of themes in his tragedy. The essay should be read alongside the contemporary description of Venice in the Contemporary Documents section above (see **pp. 25–8**). McPherson shows how important the myth of Venetian liberty was for Renaissance Englishmen, with its attendant promise of the lascivious vice of Venetian women.

IAGO

"I know our country disposition well," says Iago in the temptation scene: "In Venice they do let [God] see the pranks / They dare not show their husbands; their best conscience, / Is not to leave's undone, but keep's unknown" (3.3.201–04). He is craftily using the dark side of the myth of *Venezia-città-galante*.[1]

As he gives voice to the Myth, he is in a sense a product of it. Foreign critics of Venice claimed that the large conscience that Venice had below the navel resulted from the education given the young men in the city, and Iago has been shaped by this education. William Thomas complains:

> But surely many of them trade and bring up their children in so much liberty that one is no sooner out of the shell but he is hail fellow with father and friend, and by that time he cometh to twenty years of age, he knoweth as much lewdness as is possible to be imagined. For his greatest exercise is to go amongst his companions to this good woman's house and that, of which in Venice are many thousands of ordinary less than honest.[2]

Amelot de la Houssaye asserts, ". . . 'tis a common thing to see the Father courting his Concubine, and treating the other instruments of his Debauchery in the presence of his Son, who perhaps learns the act, before he understands the evil . . .".[3] [Maximillien] Mission even claims that mothers had been known to conclude the financial agreements with their sons' courtesans.[4]

Iago is a true son of his native land, or at least of the negative stereotype of his

---

1   Venice was seen as a centre of pleasure and liberty. See the comments by Thomas Coryat, **pp. 25–8** above.
2   William Thomas, *Historie of Italie* (1549), p. 82.
3   *The History of the Government of Venice* (1677), p. 266.
4   In *Navigantium atque Itinerantium Biblioteca*, ed. John Harris (London, 1705), II, p. 656.

native land. Because his own mind is so inveterately pornographic, he is able to use pornography to manipulate other characters. Othello is only the most notable of these; Iago also uses this weapon on Brabantio. The magnifico first answers to the "terrible summons" of Iago and Roderigo in the opening scene sleepily and confusedly; but he becomes more attentive after Iago's graphic imagery of the old black ram tupping the white ewe and the devil making a grandsire of him. On discovering Roderigo's name, however, Brabantio's interest wanes; and he is unimpressed by the gull's relatively polite protestations. We may imagine that he is even considering going back to bed. To the rescue, Iago's pornography: ". . . you'll have your daughter cover'd with a Barbary horse, you'll have your nephews neigh to you; you'll have coursers for cousins, and gennets for germane" (1.1.111–13). Brabantio, his interest caught, inquires, "What profane wretch art thou?" Iago typically answers with yet another graphic sexual image: ". . . your daughter and the Moor are [now] making the beast with two backs."

Iago nearly always uses sexual imagery to manipulate Roderigo. He urges Roderigo, "And though he in a fertile climate dwell,/Plague him with flies" (1.1.70–71). The main effect of his steamy imagery is to make Roderigo angry enough to disturb Brabantio, but surely Roderigo is also imagining himself as dwelling in the fertile climate instead of Othello. The same technique works in persuading Roderigo to join the first plot against Cassio. The Ancient re-creates the scene in which Cassio was kissing Desdemona's hand:

> Lechery, by this hand; an index and obscure prologue to the history of lust and foul thoughts. They met so near with their lips that their breaths embrac'd together. . . . When these [mutualities] so marshal the way, hard at hand comes the master and main exercise, th'incorporate conclusion. (2.1.257–63)

One does not have to be an experienced consumer of commercial pornography to recognize the pattern here: from foreplay to coition itself, from dalliance to climax.

It is as if Iago had merely been practicing on Roderigo; he uses pornography brilliantly to manipulate Othello. He ostensibly argues that he cannot arrange for Othello to "behold her topped" (3.3.396), but his word picture is so powerful that in effect Othello does "see" them in the act:

> It were a tedious difficulty, I think,
> To bring them to that prospect; damn them then,
> If ever mortal eyes do see them bolster
> More than their own! What then? How then?
> What shall I say? Where's satisfaction?
> It is impossible you should see this,
> Were they as prime as goats, as hot as monkeys,
> As salt as wolves in pride, and fools as gross
> As ignorance made drunk.
> (3.3.397–405)

That Iago's imagery has lodged in Othello's mind and is festering is indicated by
the Moor's later involuntary eruption "Goats, and monkeys!" (4.1.263).

Iago's greatest pornographic masterpiece, however, is his account of the night
he spent with Cassio. This dirty fiction is replete with dialogue, even:

> In sleep I heard him say, "Sweet Desdemona,
> Let us be wary, let us hide our loves";
> And then, sir, would he gripe and wring my hand;
> Cry, "O sweet creature!" then kiss me hard,
> As if he pluck'd up kisses by the roots
> That grew upon my lips; [then] laid his leg
> [Over] my thigh, and [sigh'd], and [kiss'd], and then
> [Cried], "Cursed fate that gave thee to the Moor!"
> (3.3.419–26)

In sum, Iago's pornography does much to drive the plot, and Iago's pornographic habits of mind are more comprehensible against the background of the
negative stereotypes about the education of young men in Venice.

DESDEMONA

Vecellio tells a story that helps to explain how the reputation of Venice for courtesans rubbed off to some extent on the decent women of the city. He says that
some of the higher-class courtesans, when they had been the mistress of a noble
Venetian for a considerable time, often had the nerve to assume the last name of
their protector, and by this means occasionally convinced foreigners that they
were themselves members of the most noble families in Venice. Vecellio adds that
most of the foreigners who went around bragging that they had enjoyed the
favors of Venetian gentlewomen were victims of this confidence game, "since
commonly Venetian gentlewomen are very jealous of their honor and are mirrors
of honesty and modesty".[5]

Vecellio is guilty of special pleading, since Venetian gentlewomen were doubtless the main market for his book. Yet he is not altogether off the mark. Venetian
wives could not possibly have strayed much because they were watched so warily.
If wives and daughters were indeed kept virtual prisoners, as most travelers
believed, then it is easy to understand Desdemona's naiveté.

For Desdemona is extremely naive. We can believe that she has been faithful
and has never even thought of straying. But it is difficult to suspend disbelief when
she asks, "Dost thou in conscience think—tell me, Emilia—/That there be women
do abuse their husbands/In such gross kind?" (4.3.61–63). This is staggeringly
naive.

How are we to reconcile this naiveté with the boldness that she displays in the
Senate scene? One way is to look toward the Venetian background of the play.

---

5   Cesare Vecellio, *De Gli Habiti antichi, et moderni di diverse parti del mondo* (Venice, 1590), Sig. S7.

The naiveté, as already pointed out, is explicable in light of the idea that wives and daughters were kept cloistered. The boldness may be explicable in light of Venetian education for a few privileged women . . . [T]he humanist movement reached a tiny proportion of aristocratic Venetian women in the fifteenth century, and we may presume that the habit of giving a humanist education to an occasional daughter of the *Clarissimi* [Venetian aristocrats] continued into the sixteenth century as well. There was strong prejudice against educating women, of course; indeed, one malicious male accused a learned woman of incest and added that he agreed with the many wise men who held that an eloquent woman was never chaste. The Venetian Senate itself, however, chose Cassandra Fedele to pen an oration in honor of the visiting Queen of Poland in 1556.

We may doubt whether Shakespeare knew much about the education of Venetian women; but such information may sometimes be transmitted via lowbrow books (novellas) as well as by highbrow books (learned treatises). I have a suggestion as to one medium through which the idea of Venetian gentlewomen speaking eloquently might have reached Shakespeare. William Painter's *Palace of Pleasure* contains a story, "Two Gentlewomen of Venice," that features such an incident. The chances that Shakespeare might have read this story, and that it might have influenced his handling of 1.3, seem to me great enough to merit an extended examination of this novella and its possible relationships to the play.

The story, originally by Bandello, was translated into French and thence into English. We can be reasonably sure that Shakespeare had access to it because it comes in *The Palace of Pleasure* immediately after Painter's version of the Romeo and Juliet story, a version which (it is generally agreed) Shakespeare had probably read. Those aspects of the plot of "Two Gentlewomen" that are relevant to my arguments may be summarized as follows:

> Two noble Venetians marry wives who are long-time friends. Each falls
> in love with the other's wife, but the "subtill dames" pull the old bed
> trick (doubled): each man is sleeping with his own wife, but thinks he is
> committing adultery. One night during a commotion caused by some-
> one else the two Venetians are apprehended—nearly nude and in the
> wrong beds—by the Officers of Night. Thrown into adjacent cells, they
> compare notes; each decides that he is a cuckold. Despondent and desir-
> ing to commit a kind of suicide, they falsely confess to have murdered
> the Duke's nephew. But the Duke figures out that their confession is
> false. To arrive at the truth publicly he condemns the gentlemen to
> death, though he has no intention of carrying out the sentences. The two
> wives then ask for a public hearing before the Council and there, in
> order to save their husbands' lives, they confess their trickery. One of
> the wives, Mistress Isotta, delivers an eloquent oration before the Coun-
> cil in which she argues at great length that all the turmoil is due to the
> infidelity of their husbands—that it is just as bad for husbands to be
> unfaithful as it is for wives to do so. The husbands gladly endure this
> energetic and protracted feminist lecture because they are so happy to
> discover they are not cuckolds after all. The couples are reconciled.

Painter calls attention to the speech by special mention in the heading:

> *Two gentlemen of Venice were honourably deceived of their Wyves,*
> *whose notable practises, and secret conference for atchievinge their*
> *desire, occasioned divers accidentes, and ingendred double benefit:*
> *wherein also is recited an eloquent oration, made by one of them, pro-*
> *nounced before the Duke and the state of that Cittye. [. . .]*[6]

The stage is set for Mistress Isotta's speech by the ravings of her jealous husband, who somewhat resembles Othello after the latter's transformation:

> Anselmo more angry and impacient then Girolamo, brake out into sutch
> furie, as had it not ben for the majesty of the place, and the Companye of
> People to have stayed him, woulde have kylled them: and seyng he was
> not able to hurt them, he began to utter the vylest Woords, that he
> possibly could devise agaynst them. (p. 146)

We think of the scene (4.2.24–94) in which Othello "bewhores" his wife as brutal, but at least it takes place in private rather than in public.

Mistress Isotta's eloquence in the face of her husband's bitter denunciation is
stressed by the narrator. At the outset we are told that she "conceived courage,
and cravinge licence of the Duke to speake, with merrye countenance and good
uttrance began [. . .] to say her mind" (p. 146). Similarly, at the close of the speech
we are told that the "Parents, Cosins, and Friends of the husbands and wyves
[. . .] greatly praysed the maner of their delivery, accoumpting the women to be
very wise, and mistresse Isotta to be an eloquent gentlewoman. [. . .]" (p. 152).

Isotta's speech may be eloquent, but it does not have the virtue of brevity. The
modern reader tends to want her to hurry up and get to the point. Desdemona, by
contrast, is admirably brief: she speaks only three times, for a total of some
twenty-seven verse lines, in the whole Council scene. Yet she, like Isotta, is (to my
mind) quite eloquent. The rhetorical balance in her first speech (1.3.180–89)
between the expressions of gratitude to her father and the pledges of fidelity to her
husband is admirable, and her argument is the stronger for being based on biblical
authority: "For this cause shall a man leave father and mother, and shall cleave to
his wife: and they twain shall be one flesh" [Matt. 19:5]. Skipping to her third
speech, we are impressed by the vividness of her metaphors:

> That I [did] love the Moor to live with him,
> My downright violence, and storm of fortunes,
> May trumpet to the world. My heart's subdu'd
> Even to the very quality of my lord.
> I saw Othello's visage in his mind,
> And to his honors and his valiant parts
> Did I my soul and fortunes consecrate.
> (1.3.248–54)

---

6   William Painter, *The Palace of Pleasure* (1566, 1575), ed. Joseph Jacobs (London, 1890).

Both Isotta and Desdemona are eloquent and bold in speaking out before a Venetian Council (Painter's Council and Shakespeare's may not be precisely the same body, technically speaking; but it would not be to the purpose here to go into the intricacies of Venetian polity). Isotta observes the proprieties of that era by apologizing that she, a mere woman, is addressing them:

> ... I will assay ... although it be not appropriate to our kind in publike place to declayme, nor yet to open sutch bold attempts, but that necessity of matter and oportunity of time, and place dothe bolden us to enter into these termes, whereof we crave a thousand pardons for our unkindely dealings, and render double thanks to your honours, for admitting us to speake. (pp. 146–47)

Desdemona too is apologetic to the Duke: "Most gracious Duke;/To my unfolding lend your prosperous ear,/And let me find a charter in your voice/T'assist my simpleness" (1.3.243–46). She does not bring up the issue of the alleged inappropriateness of women addressing the Council, but her allusion to her "simpleness" may hint at it. In any case, the boldness displayed by Isotta before an august body of Venetians may have suggested to Shakespeare the boldness that Desdemona displays before a similar Venetian body.

Which is the "real" Desdemona: the bold speaker before the Council, or the naive sheltered girl? If we look at her with the aid of the Myth of Venice, both Desdemonas are believable. Indeed, they are one and the same, and her character appears reasonably consistent throughout.

A Sense of Doom in *Othello*

The common thread connecting the political and sexual uses of the Myth in *Othello* is that both add a sense of impending doom. The fall of the real, as opposed to the fictional, Cyprus was not a possibility but a *fait accompli*; and the fall of the real Cyprus in a sense foreshadows the fall of Othello himself: both are attached to Venice but both meet their downfall—one through the machinations of the Turks, the other through the machinations of Iago—although both the island and the Moor are ripe for the picking. As for the sexual reputation of Venice, the characters seen against it are more understandable but also more helpless, more easily prey to the forces of their social environment.

Othello does not have anything like the same power in its sense of doom that the witches add to *Macbeth*, and yet there are parallels. Macbeth *has* free will and yet, paradoxically, he and the whole cast are in the grip of demonic powers; Othello, similarly, does not *have* to be jealous and yet, paradoxically, he and the whole cast are in the grip, to some extent, of a subtle kind of cultural determinism. As great and exceptional a hero as Othello is, he cannot singlehandedly battle the Myth of Venice and win.

Several critics have pointed out the striking similarities between portions of the plot of *Othello* and the structure of comedy. Yet we would never mistake the play for a comedy. Iago's dark predictions do more than anything to keep the tone from becoming too light, but we should not overlook the subtle contribution of the Venetian background toward the same end.

Lisa Jardine, '"Why should he call her whore?": Defamation and Desdemona's Case', in *Reading Shakespeare Historically* (London: Routledge, 1996), pp. 19–34, 162–70; pp. 25–31, 33–4, 165–70

Jardine is an intellectual historian and literary critic of the English Renaissance whose work is informed by a feminist perspective. Jardine's essay concentrates on the women in the play using evidence from court records to establish attitudes towards women in England around the year 1600 and so illuminate their position in Shakespeare's work. Jardine claims that Desdemona is publicly defamed by her husband, encouraging the audience to use their knowledge of marital and legal disputes to read the action of the play.

In *Othello* three women, of three distinct social ranks, figure prominently in the plot. Desdemona is the daughter of one of Venice's most senior and influential citizens. Bianca is a Venetian courtesan – a woman of substance who supports herself and her household by her liaisons with men of rank (notably Cassio, Othello's second-in-command).[1] Emilia is the wife of Othello's third-in-command, Iago, and personal maid to Desdemona.[2] As women playing active roles within the community the three are occupationally distinct. All three are wrongfully accused of sexual misdemeanour in the course of the play; all three, though unequal in their rank-power, are equally vulnerable to a *sexual* charge brought against them: although the incidents which provoke the slander may be presumed to be of separate and distinct types (as befits the differing social situations in which the three women find themselves), they yield the identical slur, the identical charge of sexual promiscuity – the most readily available form of assault on a woman's reputation.[3] Each takes the accusation (once made) extremely seriously; but the ways these accusations are dealt with by the women themselves have very different consequences, and this is crucial, I shall argue, for a 'historical' understanding of the outcome of the plot [. . .]

The Ecclesiastical Court records which survive for England in the early modern period contain a profusion of examples of cases in which individual women believed their reputations had been harmed by imputations of unchastity, and what they felt it necessary to do about them. To be more precise: the depositions

---

1   [Jardine's note.] Although the text is not explicit as to Bianca's place of origin, I would argue that it is crucial to the play that Bianca might be described as a 'whore of Venice' (the phrase used by Othello to insult Desdemona, and a popular Renaissance 'type'). Bianca has a household in Cyprus and is Cassio's established courtesan.

2   [Jardine's note.] This is an alteration of the source story, in which Emilia's rank is higher.

3   [Jardine's note.] Apart from the claim that Desdemona has committed adultery with Cassio, Emilia has been accused of adultery with Othello, and Bianca (although professionally a courtesan) is accused of running a bawdy house and whoring by Iago and Emilia.

laid in defamation cases in the Ecclesiastical Courts (throughout England, though I shall use the Durham records because of their comparative accessibility) show us how it was expected that a story would be shaped in relation to public accusations of unchastity – the sort of occasion, the nature of the accusation, the circumstances of the incident, and above all how these were put together as a 'convincing' tale for the presiding clerical official. Throughout the period, ordinary people who had been publicly accused of social misdemeanour sought restitution in the Ecclesiastical Courts (the courts which had jurisdiction over violations of acceptable practice in domestic, marital and sexual matters).[4] The offended party made depositions (sworn statements) which if substantiated in court led to the offender's doing public penance, paying a fine, or (in extreme cases) being excommunicated. The charges of adultery, whoring, bastard-bearing, scolding, petty theft, etc. were such, however, that if the defamation were allowed to stand the person defamed (the offended party of the records) stood in danger of being charged in their turn in the courts. In other words, the defamation, if it went unchallenged, could become an 'actuality'. I shall argue that we can use the evidence of the Ecclesiastical Court records to make good sense of what does and does not happen with regard to such accusations in *Othello*.[5]

One of the conclusions to emerge from these records is that 'when women defended their reputations through defamation suits in the ecclesiastical courts, they were more concerned with their reputation for chastity, not for submissiveness, obedience or being a good housewife. [. . .] [By contrast] [m]en worried about insults to their social position, their honesty or sobriety as well as about their sexual behaviour'.[6] In a sample survey of the York records, for example, 90 per cent of cases concerning a female plaintiff involved her sexual reputation.[7] Ritual sexual banter, including lewd mocking rhymes and fairly explicit romping at weddings, was an acceptable part of social practice.[8] But there was a point at which it was understood that lewd talk became defamation – when the accusation, circulating publicly, endangered the individual's reputation. The impact of defamation is most graphically illustrated by citing some cases (here taken from the Durham records).

On 26 October 1568, Margaret Nicolson ('singlewoman') made a deposition against Agnes, wife of Robert Blenkinsop, claiming that she, Margaret, had been defamed as follows:

---

4   [Jardine's note.] By 'ordinary' I mean to indicate the fact that the middling sort (women and men) had regular recourse to the ecclesiastical courts in this period.
5   [Jardine's note.] On defamation depositions see J. Sharpe, *Defamation and Sexual Slander in Early Modern England: The Church Court at York*, Borthwick Papers, 58, York, University of York and St Andrew's, 1980.
6   [Jardine's note.] S. Amussen, 'Gender, family and social order, 1560–1725', in A. Fletcher and J. Stevenson (eds), *Order and Disorder in Early Modern England*, Cambridge, Cambridge University Press, 1985, pp. 196–217, at p. 208.
7   [Jardine's note.] Sharpe, *Defamation*, p. 13.
8   [Jardine's note.] See M. Ingram, 'Ridings, rough music and mocking rhymes in early modern England', in B. Reay (ed.), *Popular Culture in Seventeenth Century England*, London, Croom Helm, 1985, pp. 166–97; Roper, ' "Going to church and street": weddings in Reformation Augsburg', *Past and Present*, 1985, vol. 106, pp. 62–101.

Hyte hoore, a whipe and a cart and a franc hoode, wales [woe is] me for the, my lasse, wenst [wilst thou] have a halpeny halter for the to goo up Gallygait and be hanged?[9]

On 7 December 1568, Ann Foster made a deposition against Elizabeth Elder:

That the wyfes of the Close wold say that she was a spanyell hoore.[10]

Here the *circulation* of the defamatory accusation is the substance of the accusation, but (by implication) it emanates from Elizabeth Elder [. . .]

A case in which the shaping of the tale is more obviously a crucial element is the one brought by Katherine Reid against Isabell Hynde, in 1569. Two depositions were made in this case, both on behalf of Katherine Reid, the woman against whom the defamation has been uttered. It will be clear that the accused woman, Isabell Hynde, is the more vulnerable of the two, and has no one (perhaps) to speak on her behalf The first deposition is made by Agnes Dods ('late wife of Edward Dods of Newcastle, shipwright, aged 23 years' [a widow?]):

> She saith that, the weik byfore Easter last past, one George Dawson and the said Isabell was in this examinate's house, what other certain day this deponent cannott depose, at what time the said Isabell spoke to a baster [bastard] litle boy of the said Isabell, which the said Georg bygatt of hir and put to this examinat to boor [board], thes words, 'Thow shall not caule Katherine Reid mother, for she caul me hoor, and I never maid fault but for this christen soull, and they wyll nott dytt [stop] ther mowethes with a bowell of wheit that wold say she had bore a barne in Chirton.' – She said the said Dawson, that shulde mary the said Katherin, was present.

Here the scenario is explicitly socially fraught: the slander is perpetrated by the unwed mother about her ex-lover's wife-to-be (in the presence of the woman with whom her child boards, while she herself works to support him). The second deposition shows how by repetition it is reinforced and becomes more serious. This deposition is made by Helinor Reid ('wife of John Reid of Newcastle, merchant, aged 26 years' [sister-in-law of Katherine Reid]):

> She saith that the said Katherine haith been sick these 2 last yeres, and for the most part this twelmonth haith bein in house with this examinat, hir brother's wyf. And that the said Kathren toke on very hevylye for that she had gotton knowled that the said Isabell had slandered hir, and that she had borne a barne in Chirton. Whereupon this deponent said

9   [Jardine's note.] *Depositions and other Ecclesiastical Proceedings from the Courts of Durham, extending from 1311 to the reign of Elizabeth*, London, The Publications of the Surtees Society, 1845, p. 89.
10   [Jardine's note.] *Depositions*, pp. 89.

'Suster Kathren, be of good cheir, and cast not your self downe again for any such talk; And, for ease of your myend, I wyll myself goo and question hir of hir words.' And therupon this examinat went to Mr Th. Clibborn house, and the wench Isabell was out a doores. And to [until] she came yn this deponent was opening the matter to hir dame. And at last the said Isabell came in, to whome hir dame Clibborn's wyfe said, 'Thou hast brought thyself in troble with this good wife's suster,' pointing to this examinat then present, and said, 'Thy Mr will not be in troble therwith.' And the said Isabell maid answer, 'What, Katherine Reid?' 'Yea,' saith this examinat, 'she will have you to answer the sklander that ye have maid upon hir, which was that she had borne a barne in Chirton.' And the said Isabell annswered, after many folish words, that that which she had sayd she wold say ytt again, for that she had one wytnes for hir.[11]

The point in invoking these depositions is not that they are 'documentary', but that as texts they are explicitly *purposive* – they shape the story told to a desired outcome. As this last example shows particularly clearly, they are told to the clerk so as to 'make a case': someone's good name has to be shown to have been damaged, by an accusation which must be shown to be false (what would happen to Katherine Reid's engagement, if Isabell Hynde's defamation were allowed to stand?). The apportioning of blame is constructed into the telling: the deponent for the person slandered acts as character witness for them, and endeavours to show that the slanderer is unreliable. What helps our understanding of the case against Desdemona in *Othello*, is that the depositions show how some ostensibly verbal incidents between individuals, as they spill over into the community space (the village green, the pump, outside the house) become recognised as events, which generate particular expectations on the part of the audience (for the local community is surely both onlookers and audience): whatever the audience thought heretofore, the event in question introduces competing versions of fault and blame, which must now be resolved in order that the individuals concerned may be reintegrated into the community.

In *Othello* the crisis point in the play's presentation of Desdemona comes in Act 4, scene 2, when Othello publicly defames Desdemona, and Emilia repeats and circulates the defamation (thus reinforcing and confirming it). The seriousness of the incident is explicit, in strong contrast to the earlier easy, casual impugning of Desdemona's honesty amongst male figures in the play, in private, and in her absence:

Othello. Impudent strumpet!
Desdemona. By heaven, you do me wrong.
Othello. Are not you a strumpet?
Desdemona. No, as I am a Christian:

11 [Jardine's note.] *Depositions*, pp. 90–1.

> If to preserve this vessel for my lord
> From any hated foul unlawful touch,
> Be not to be a strumpet, I am none.
> *Othello.* What, not a whore?
> *Desdemona.* No, as I shall be sav'd.
>   *Enter* EMILIA
> *Othello.* Is't possible?
> *Desdemona.* O heaven, forgiveness.
> *Othello.* I cry you mercy,
> I took you for that cunning whore of Venice,
> That married with Othello: you, mistress,
> That have the office opposite to Saint Peter,
> And keeps the gates in hell, ay, you, you, you!
> We ha' done our course; there's money for your pains,
> I pray you turn the key, and keep our counsel. [4.2.81–96]

When Othello accuses Desdemona of unchastity he sends Emilia away, giving her expressly to understand that the conversation between himself and his wife is to be private and intimate: 'Leave procreants[12] alone, and shut the door,/Cough, or cry hem, if anybody come' (4.2.28–9). It is her premature return which results in her overhearing Othello call Desdemona whore. But once the defamation has been accidentally uttered Emilia's outrage on her mistress's behalf consolidates it:

> *Emilia.* Alas, Iago, my lord hath so bewhor'd her,
> Thrown such despite, and heavy terms upon her,
> As true hearts cannot bear.
> *Desdemona.* Am I that name, Iago?
> *Iago.* What name, fair lady?
> *Desdemona.* Such as she says my lord did say I was?
> *Emilia.* He call'd her whore: a beggar in his drink
> Could not have laid such terms upon his callat. [4.2.117–23]

'Speak within doors', cautions Iago – 'speak lower; "you don't want the whole street to hear"', reads Ridley's note – underlining the fact that the charge has moved from the intimacy of the bedroom to the public space (4.2.146). And the very forms of Emilia's repetition of this 'slander' (4.2.135) indicate first, the seriousness of the accusation, and second, the necessity for formally rebutting it:

> *Emilia.* Why should he call her whore? who keeps her company?
> What place, what time, what form, what likelihood?(139–40)

This is technical defamation, which invites direct comparison with the cases in the Durham records. In historical and cultural terms this is the point in the play at

---

12 [Jardine's note.] 'Would-be copulators', according to Ridley's Arden note.

which Desdemona's culpability becomes an 'actual' issue, in the sense that the depositions in the Ecclesiastical Court records suggest: the verbal has been constituted as event in the community by virtue of the circumstances of utterance, its location in public space, the inclusion in its performance of persons not entitled to hear what is uttered in privacy or intimacy. Just as the tale is told so as to enhance these features of the alleged *causa diffamationis* in the records, so Act 4, scene 2 of *Othello is* shaped, I am suggesting, so that the audience at this point is party to a slander, 'audiently' uttered, and hears it repeated and circulated.

The point is reinforced in the play by what immediately follows: Emilia reminds Iago that (as the audience already knows) Othello was once suspected of sexual misdemeanour with Emilia ('it is thought abroad, that 'twixt my sheets/ He's done my office' (1.3.385–6; also 2.1.290–4)). But now she specifies that in that case she too was a victim of a defamation:

> *Emilia.* Why should he call her whore? who keeps her company?
>   What place, what time, what form, what likelihood?
>   The Moor's abus'd by some outrageous knave.
>   Some base notorious knave, some scurvy fellow; . . .
>   Oh, fie upon him! Some such squire he was,
>   That turn'd your wit, the seamy side without,
>   And made you to suspect me with the Moor. [139–49]

Unlike the noblewoman Desdemona, Bianca and Emilia understand the need actively to counter defamatory utterance against their reputation. In Act 5, scene 1 (and surely in deliberate juxtaposition with Desdemona's defamation?) Iago accuses the courtesan Bianca of keeping a bawdy house, and Emilia publicly calls her strumpet; Bianca's retaliation is immediate:

> *Iago.* This is the fruit of whoring, pray, Emilia,
>   Go know of Cassio where he supp'd to-night:
>   What, do you [Bianca] shake at that?
> *Bianca.* He supp'd at my house, but I therefore shake not.
> *Iago.* O, did he so? I charge you go with me.
> *Emilia.* Fie, fie upon thee, strumpet!
> *Bianca.* I am no strumpet, but of life as honest
>   As you, that thus abuse me.
> *Emilia.* As I? faugh, fie upon thee!
> *Iago.* Kind gentlemen, let's go see poor Cassio dress'd;
>   Come, mistress, you must tell 's another tale [5.1.115–24]

Bianca, in spite of her 'profession', retaliates against the slanderous 'strumpet'. Bianca is uncomfortably 'like' Desdemona at this point in the play: both women of independent spirit (and means), both Venetian women of some rank and status, both accused of being 'whores of Venice', when Venetian whores were a recognizable *topos* of literature and art, both associated negatively with Cassio's Florentine manners and 'proper manhood'. Textually a critic might note their 'equivalence'; but there are considerable consequences to their occupying entirely different rank positions in the community, with differing sets of social relations.

I am proposing that Desdemona's case is altered from this point forward in the play – in the telling of the tale of Desdemona's relations with a community which includes the play's audience – not because of any alteration in Desdemona's own conduct, but because she has been publicly designated 'whore' in terms damaging enough to constitute a substantial threat to her reputation. From this point on there is no casual innuendo, no lewd comment on Othello's wife's behaviour or supposed sexual appetite. Desdemona's two remaining scenes focus on her now supposedly culpable sexuality, culminating in her suffocation on her bed, in a state of undress – a whore's death for all her innocence.

Desdemona's defamation has no substance at all; at the moment of her own death Emilia testifies to her mistress's chastity: 'Moor, she was chaste, she lov'd thee, cruel Moor,/So come my soul to bliss, as I speak true' (5.2.250–1). Yet in spite of her private protestations of innocence, Desdemona does nothing formally to restore her now 'actually' impugned reputation. It might be said that she does nothing because she does not know of what she is accused (reminding us that calling your wife 'whore' is common abuse, whatever the offence): 'If haply you my father do suspect/An instrument of this your calling back [to Venice],/Lay not your blame on me', she says, whilst begging Othello forgiveness on her knees (4.2.45–7). She cannot even bring herself to utter the word used against her ('Am I that name, Iago?' 'What name, fair lady?' 'Such as she says my lord did say I was?'; 'I cannot say "whore":/It does abhor me now I speak the word') [4.2.120–21, 163–64]. In striking contrast to the innocent Desdemona's inaction, the worldly Bianca recognises the affront, and its damaging consequences, and retaliates [. . .]

In conclusion, I want to suggest that if we allow a historical reading to s direct us towards substantial defamation as the crux of the plot in *Othello*, then we are also led towards a revised reading of the instrumentality of Othello's 'jealousy'.

I suggest that once the substantial defamation stands against Desdemona Othello murders her for adultery, not out of jealousy. If we retrace the play to Act 3, scene 3, we find jealousy contrasted both with ignorance of dishonour on the part of a husband, and with certainty. Jealousy is the humiliating condition of doubt in relation to your own honour and your wife's obedience. It is linked from the outset, by Iago, with 'good name':

> *Iago.* Good name in man and woman's dear, my lord;
>   Is the immediate jewel of our souls:
>   Who steals my purse, steals trash, 'tis something, nothing,
>   'Twas mine, 'tis his, and has been slave to thousands:
>   But he that filches from me my good name
>   Robs me of that which not enriches him,
>   And makes me poor indeed.
> *Othello.* By heaven I'll know thy thought.

Iago. You cannot, if my heart were in your hand,
   Nor shall not, whilst 'tis in my custody:
   O, beware jealousy;
   It is the green-ey'd monster, which doth mock
   That meat it feeds on. That cuckold lives in bliss,
   Who, certain of his fate, loves not his wronger:
   But O, what damned minutes tells he o'er
   Who dotes, yet doubts, suspects, yet strongly loves! . . .
Othello. Think'st thou I'ld make a life of jealousy?
   To follow still the changes of the moon
   With fresh suspicions? No, to be once in doubt,
   Is once to be resolv'd . . .
   I'll see before I doubt, when I doubt, prove,
   And on the proof, there is no more but this:
   Away at once with love or jealousy! [3.3.159–96]

Later in the scene Othello reiterates the view that cuckoldry is not theft until it is public knowledge ('Let him not know't, and he's not robb'd at all' (3.3.349)). And what he demands of Iago is knowledge, to end his doubt (and his jealousy):

Othello. Villain, be sure thou prove my love a whore,
   Be sure of it, give me the ocular proof . . .
   Make me to see't, or at the least so prove it,
   That the probation bear no hinge, nor loop,
   To hang a doubt on [3.3.365–72]

In the crafted narrative of the play, Othello's doubt is ended, and with it his jealousy, when a case of defamation is perpetrated against Desdemona and the case is not answered – 'She turn'd to folly, and she was a whore' (5.2.133).[13] From that point he acts with complete certainty of her guilt. 'It is the cause [the case, adultery]', he says, as he prepares to murder her (5.2.1–3), and as he murders her, his cross-examination is couched in the terms of the lawcourt: 'If you bethink yourself of any crime . . . solicit for it straight'; 'take heed of perjury'; 'confess'; 'O perjur'd woman'; 'He hath confess'd . . . That he hath . . . us'd thee . . . unlawfully' [5.2 *passim*]. In other words, doubt has given way to certainty – a certainty built not on 'ocular proof', nor even on the misinterpretation of his eavesdropping on Cassio, far less on the persistence of Iago's lies. Certainty, for Othello, the certainty that entitles the cuckolded husband to seek retribution upon his wife,[14] hinges on that substantial defamation perpetrated by Othello himself – who 'beinge a very suspicious man, haith some tyme audiently caulde . . . [his wife] "hore" '.

---

13 [Jardine's note.] And again 'Iago knows/That she with Cassio hath the act of shame/A thousand times committed; Cassio confess'd it' (5.2.211–13).
14 [Jardine's note.] For an English audience, Othello is none the less guilty of murder in killing his wife as retribution for her adultery, since English law specified that murder by a husband of his adulterous wife could only be excused if it took place in the first flush of anger.

Andrew Hadfield, 'The "gross clasps of a lascivious Moor": The Domestic and Exotic Contexts of *Othello*' (1998), in *Literature, Travel, and Colonial Writing in the English Renaissance, 1545–1625* (Oxford: Clarendon Press, 1998), pp. 232–6.

This extract is part of a larger study of English travel writing in the Renaissance and attitudes to foreign cultures and peoples. I argue, like McPherson (see **pp. 78–84**), that the Venetian setting is crucial to our understanding of the play. While McPherson concentrates on issues of sexuality, I suggest that the city's political institutions and the ways in which they were seen to preserve the liberty of its inhabitants were used by Shakespeare as a means of comparing contemporary England and Venice.

Venice demands to be read as England [. . .] Can Venice deal with problems which appear insurmountable in England and threaten the very foundations of the state? Is Venetian society in *Othello* more just than English society? Does it represent the ideal of civilized European liberty [. . .] or display the dangers of that liberty in the form of an excessive licentiousness, tempting but dangerous for Protestant Englishmen [. . .] In fact, formal justice in Venice appears to be exceptionally well administered, in line with the comments of [Sir Lewis] Lewkenor [see above, **pp. 8–9**] and [William] Thomas. When Brabantio brings his case before a special council meeting held on Othello and Desdemona's wedding night, to deal with the imminent Turkish threat to Cyprus, both his confidence that the Duke and councillors will 'feel this wrong, as 'twere their own' and his fear that if Othello and Desdemona's marriage is not annulled then Venetian liberty will be overturned, 'Bondslaves, and pagans, shall our statesmen be' (I. ii. 97–9), are shown to be unfounded.

The Duke's opening lines to the group who have burst into the council meeting emphasize the democratic nature of Venetian government, where matters of public importance are discussed openly, and equal respect is granted to both the alien Othello and the native Brabantio: 'Valiant Othello, we must straight employ you,/ Against the general enemy Ottoman;/[*To Brabantio*] I did not see you; welcome, gentle signior,/we lack'd your counsel and your help to-night' (I. iii. 48–51). The Venetian council is shown to be able to react quickly to events in order to defend itself. The fact that the Turkish fleet has changed course in order to deceive Venetian observers in Cyprus, and that Marcus Luccios, the first-choice general, is away in Florence, does not significantly reduce the effectiveness of the council's response to the crisis. Othello is included within the upper echelons of the Venetian state and defined against the common enemy, the Turks, by the Duke, a gesture he repeats in his 'round unvarnish'd tale' (l. 90), by identifying with European travellers against the bizarre races of his native Africa. In writing his own traveller's tale he gives the Venetians exactly what they want to hear. Although the Duke promises Brabantio that 'the bloody book of law' will be used against whoever has bewitched his daughter, the actual trial scene vindicates the newlyweds against the bigoted law of the father. The Duke refuses to accept Brabantio's assertions as proof. Both Othello and Desdemona are able to conduct a proper defence of their actions, with the result that a just outcome is swiftly reached before the council return to the problem of the defence of Cyprus.

There are, of course, limits to the solution, which hint at the tragedy to come; Desdemona's love for Othello is based on her perception of his inner self—'I saw Othello's visage in his mind' (l. 252)—which suggests that she may well have fallen 'in love with what she fear'd to look on' (l. 98), as her father asserted. Her lines also expose the problem of Othello's 'self', elaborately constructed to suit the role of a European adventurer, and his access to knowledge. At this stage in the play it seems likely that the couple will eventually have to deal with Brabantio's bitterness, which is expressed at great length and spills over into a feeble stoicism at odds with the resolution of the rest of the council: 'So let the Turk of Cyprus us beguile,/We lose it not so long as we can smile' (ll. 210–11), a reminder of the dangers which need to be faced as well as a foresight of the problem of 'turning Turk' in Cyprus. Moreover, the casual use of the metaphor 'tyranny' (ll. 197, 229) hints that, in the military garrison of Cyprus, Venice's democratic norms will not apply, closing off the possibility of open discussion and effective justice [. . .]

Venice in *Othello* is represented as a society which is liberal enough to accommodate citizens from other cultures—a necessary virtue in a city-state, which served as the economic and military bridge between Europe and the East[1]—and strong enough to control its own citizens who wished to undermine its democratic traditions, exactly as Contarini/Lewkenor and William Thomas saw the republic.[2] Cyprus does not possess these advantages, and is continually represented in contrast to the motherland. After the Turkish fleet has been destroyed Othello issues a proclamation ordering revelry, which is also to celebrate his marriage. The resulting 'full liberty' (II. ii. 9) is that of a carnival, not a settled state, a holiday from the rigours of military service rather than the institutional freedom enjoyed in the metropolis. The celebrations lead to the first important action in the tragedy, the drunken brawl which sees Michael Cassio demoted. Initially Othello is capable of dealing with the crisis, imposing his authority on the unruly soldiers and restoring order through military command, just as he separated Roderigo and Brabantio with his eloquence in Venice (I. ii. 59–61).

1 [Hadfield's note.] Lisa Jardine, *Worldly Goods* (London: Macmillan, 1996), 45–9, *passim*; Virginia Mason Vaughan, *Othello: A Contextual History* (Cambridge: Cambridge University Press, 1994), ch. 1.

2 [Hadfield's note.] [Gaspar] Contarini sees the respect for strangers and foreigners as one of Venice's main strengths *(The Commonwealth and Gouernment of Venice*, trans. Lewis Lewkenor (1599), fo. 105); yet the citizens were powerful enough to have a corrupt and tyrannous Duke, Marino Phalerio, beheaded (fo. 82). See also William Thomas, *Historie of Italie* (1549), fos. 81–2, 85, 103. Venice's ability to accept different citizens can be contrasted to Elizabeth I's notorious proclamation ordering the expulsion of 'Negroes and blackamoors' from the realm, *c*. January 1601, 3 years before *Othello* was probably first performed. See Ania Loomba, *Gender, Race, Renaissance Drama* (Manchester: Manchester University Press, 1989), p. 43; Eldred Jones, *Othello's Countrymen* (London: Oxford University Press, 1965), p. 5.

The Work in Performance

Virginia Mason Vaughan, '*Othello* on the English Stage
1604–1754' (1994), in *Othello: A Contextual History* (Cambridge: Cambridge
University Press, 1994), pp. 94–6.

Early records of productions of most Shakespeare plays are thin. The same is
true of *Othello*, although it is clear from what survives that it was frequently
performed throughout the seventeenth century.

[. . .] From its initial performance, sometime around 1604, until the closing of the
theatres in 1642, *Othello* was a popular commercial play and was also staged at
Court well into the reign of Charles I. It was performed at the Banquetting House
at Whitehall in 1604, for the Princess Elizabeth's wedding in 1612–13, and at
Hampton Court in 1636. Early on the lead was acted by the King's Company's
major tragedian, Richard Burbage, who (according to an elegy published at his
death) excelled in the role. After 1618, the Moor was played by Eyllaerdt
Swanston; Joseph Taylor was recognized for his rendition of Iago.

In 1648 members of the King's Company (Lowin, Taylor, and Pollard who had
known Shakespeare) tried to start acting again, but the government suppressed
their efforts. Associated with these old-timers were some younger actors, men
who had begun their careers in the 1630s playing women's roles. During the Civil
War the younger actors were allied with the Royalists; several fought with Prince
Rupert's forces. And when the theatres reopened in 1660, these actors – not
so young anymore – formed the new King's Company, managed by Thomas
Killegrew, a Royalist who had also participated in Charles II's exile. *Othello*
became part of its repertory.

The first Restoration Othello was Nicholas Burt, succeeded by Charles Hart in
the 1670s. The first Iago was Walter Clun. James Wright records in his *Historia
Histrionica* (1699) that Clun and Hart "were bred up Boys at the *Blackfriers*; and
Acted Women's Parts." If Wright was correct, they must have seen *Othello* in the
1630s, even if they were too young to perform in it, and therefore *they* represent

an unbroken line of tradition reaching back to Shakespeare's own acting company. At the same time, much had changed since the closing of the theatres. Burt and Hart's Othello may have echoed the resonant tones of Burbage, but as produced by Killegrew, the play was probably stamped by Interregnum experiences as well.

The illustration for Nicholas Rowe's edition (1709), which may reflect actual performances, depicts Othello as a black man dressed in the uniform of a British army officer; a tradition that continued throughout much of the eighteenth century. Francis Gentleman writes in *The Dramatic Censor* (1770) that while actor James Quin's "magpye" appearance – with black face under powdered wig – was absurd, it was nonetheless striking to see the contrast between Othello's gloved white hand and the blackness of his skin when he removed his gloves. Gentleman refers here to performances in the first half of the century; Quin last appeared as Othello at Covent Garden in 1751 and retired altogether in 1754. Given the continuous chain of *Othello* tradition, it is reasonable to assume that Shakespeare's Moor was meant to be black and that he was played black throughout the Restoration.

Sir Richard Steele, *The Tatler*, no. 167 (2 May 1710)

> Steele (1672–1729) was an important dramatist and essayist, responsible for establishing a number of literary periodicals, the most significant of which were *The Tatler* and *The Spectator*. Both of these contained a number of essays which helped to define cultivated eighteenth-century taste. Here Steele praises the performance of Thomas Betterton as Othello. Note that Steele's praise is based on Betterton's ability to bring Shakespeare convincingly to life through a proper expression of the passions that the character of Othello feels.

Having received Notice that the famous Actor Mr. *Betterton*[1] was to be interred this Evening in the Cloysters near *Westminster Abbey*, I was resolved to walk thither and see the last Office done to a Man whom I had always very much admired, and from whose Action I had received more strong Impressions of what is great and noble in Human Nature than from the Arguments of the most solid Philosophers or the Descriptions of the most charming Poets I have ever read. As the rude and untaught Multitude are no Way wrought upon more effectually than by seeing publick Punishments and Executions, so Men of Letters and Education feel their Humanity most forcibly exercised when they attend the Obsequies of Men who had arrived at any Perfection in Liberal Accomplishments. Theatrical Action is to be esteemed as such, except it be objected that we cannot call that an Art which cannot be attained by Art. Voice, Stature, Motion, and other Gifts must

---

1 Thomas Betterton, Restoration actor. For further details see Marvin Rosenberg, *The Masks of Othello: The Search for the Identity of Othello, Iago and Desdemona by Three Centuries of Actors and Critics* (Newark, Del.: University of Delaware Press, 1993, rpt of 1961), pp. 19–20.

Figure 2 The frontispiece to Nicholas Rowe's edition of *Othello* (1709). By permission of the Folger Shakespeare Library.

be very bountifully bestowed by Nature, or Labour and Industry will but push the unhappy Endeavourer in that Way the further off his Wishes [. . .]

I have hardly a Notion that any Performer of Antiquity could surpass the Action of Mr. *Betterton* in any of the Occasions in which he has appeared on our Stage. The wonderful Agony which he appeared in when he examined the Circumstance of the Handkerchief of *Othello*, the Mixture of Love that intruded upon his Mind upon the innocent Answers *Desdemona* makes, betrayed in his Gesture such a Variety and Vicissitude of Passions as would admonish a Man to be afraid of his own Heart, and perfectly convince him that it is to stab it to admit that worst of Daggers, Jealousy. Whoever reads in his Closet this admirable Scene will find that he cannot, except he has as warm an Imagination as *Shakespeare* himself, find any but dry, incoherent, and broken Sentences. But a Reader that has seen *Betterton* act it observes there could not be a Word added, that longer Speech had been unnatural, nay impossible to be uttered in *Othello*'s Circumstances. The charming Passage in the same Tragedy where he tells the Manner of winning the Affection of his Mistress was urged with so moving and graceful an Energy that, while I walked in the Cloysters, I thought of him with the same Concern as if I waited for the Remains of a Person who had in real Life done all that I had seen him represent.

William Hazlitt, 'Mr. Macready's Othello' (*The Examiner*, 13 October 1816)

Hazlitt (1778–1830) was an important journalist, critic and essayist of the Romantic era. Hazlitt was obviously disappointed because William Charles Macready's Othello was not as emotionally intense as he thought the part required. Note the difference between Hazlitt's assumptions and those of Steele (see above). Hazlitt expects a theatrical experience to go beyond the ordinary range of human emotion and transport the audience to heights of poetic vision and intensity. Steele expects an intelligent reconstruction of a noble heroism on stage.

We have to speak this week of Mr. Macready's Othello, at Covent-Garden Theatre, and though it must be in favourable terms, it cannot be in very favourable ones.[1] We have been rather spoiled for seeing any one else in this character, by Mr. Kean's performance of it, and also by having read the play itself lately.[2] Mr. Macready was more than respectable in the part; and he only failed because he attempted to excel. He did not, however, express the individual bursts of feeling, nor the deep and accumulating tide of passion which ought to be given to Othello. It may perhaps seem an extravagant illustration, but the idea which we think any

---

1 On William Charles Macready, see Virginia Mason Vaughan, *Othello: A Contextual History* (Cambridge: Cambridge University Press, 1994), ch. 7.
2 On Edmund Kean, see Rosenberg, *Masks of Othello*, ch. 4.

THE WORK IN PERFORMANCE   97

Figure 3 William Charles Macready as Othello. By permission of the Folger Shakespeare Library.

actor ought to have of this character, to play it to the height of the poetical conception, is that of a majestic serpent wounded, writhing under its pain, stung to madness, and attempting by sudden darts, or coiling up its whole force, to wreak its vengeance on those about it, and falling at last a mighty victim under the redoubled strokes of its assailants. No one can admire more than we do the force of genius and passion which Mr. Kean shews in this part, but he is not stately enough for it. He plays it like a gipsey, and not like a Moor. We miss in Mr. Kean not the physiognomy, or the costume, so much as the *architectural* building up of the part. This character always puts us in mind of the line—

'Let Afric on its hundred thrones rejoice.'[3]

It not only appears to hold commerce with meridian suns, and that its blood is made drunk with the heat of scorching skies; but it indistinctly presents to us all the symbols of eastern magnificence. It wears a crown and turban, and stands before us like a tower. All this, it may be answered, is only saying that Mr. Kean is not so tall as a tower: but any one, to play Othello properly, ought to look taller and grander than any tower. We shall see how Mr. Young will play it.[4] But this is from our present purpose. Mr. Macready is tall enough for the part, and the looseness of his figure was rather in character with the flexibility of the South: but there were no sweeping outlines, no massy movements in his action.

The movements of passion in Othello (and the motions of the body should answer to those of the mind) resemble the heaving of the sea in a storm; there are no sharp, slight, angular transitions, or if there are any, they are subject to this general swell and commotion. Mr. Kean is sometimes too wedgy and determined; but Mr. Macready goes off like a shot, and startles our sense of hearing. One of these sudden explosions was when he is in such haste to answer the demands of the Senate on his services: 'I do agnise a natural hardness,' &c. as if he was impatient to exculpate himself from some charge, or wanted to take them at their word lest they should retract. There is nothing of this in Othello. He is calm and collected; and the reason why he is carried along with such vehemence by his passions when they are roused, is, that he is moved by their collected force. Another fault in Mr. Macready's conception was, that he whined and whimpered once or twice, and tried to affect the audience by affecting a pitiful sensibility, not consistent with the dignity and masculine imagination of the character: as where he repeated, 'No, not much moved,' and again, 'Othello's occupation's gone,' in a childish treble. The only part which should approach to this effeminate tenderness of complaint is his reflection, 'Yet, oh the pity of it, Iago, the pity of it!' What we liked best was his ejaculation, 'Swell, bosom, with thy fraught, *for 'tis of aspick's tongues*.' This was forcibly given, and as if his expression were choked with the bitterness of passion. We do not know how he would have spoken the speech, 'Like to the Pontic sea that knows no ebb,' &c. which occurs just before,

---

3 Edward Young, *The Revenge* (1721), V, ii.
4 Charles Mayne Young, actor who played both Othello and Iago; see Rosenberg, *Masks of Othello*, pp. 120–1, 123.

for it was left out. There was also something fine in his uneasiness and inward starting at the name of Cassio, but it was too often repeated, with a view to effect. Mr. Macready got most applause in such speeches as that addressed to Iago, 'Horror on horror's head accumulate!' This should be a lesson to him. He very injudiciously, we think, threw himself on a chair at the back of the stage, to deliver the farewell apostrophe to Content, and to the 'pride, pomp, and circumstance of glorious war.' This might be a relief to him, but it distressed the audience.—On the whole, we think Mr. Macready's powers are more adapted to the declamation than to the acting of passion: that is, that he is a better orator than actor. As to Mr. Young's Iago, 'we never saw a gentleman acted finer.' Mrs. Faucit's Desdemona was very pretty. Mr. C. Kemble's Cassio was excellent.[5]

Virginia Mason Vaughan, *Othello: A Contextual History* (Cambridge: Cambridge University Press, 1994), pp. 181–2, 187–90, 197–8

Paul Robeson's Othello (1930, 1943) marked a watershed in productions of the play. There had been a few black actors cast as Othello before, but once Robeson was cast in the role the question of the race and identity of the leading actor assumed a new importance. Robeson's performance needs to be read alongside critical analyses of the play made at the same time. It is not until later that the issue of race assumes a burning intensity in critical discussions of *Othello*, a fact that helps to explain why debates are still often heated today.

Cultural assumptions – comprised of many forces, including Orientalism, racial Darwinism, and Anglo-Saxonism – were based on pejorative categories of racial difference, yet they made the debut of a black actor as Othello possible, if not inevitable. Once Othello had been identified as a role difficult for cold "Anglo-Saxon" temperaments and more suitable for those from southern climes, it was easier to conceive of a black actor in the role. Many potential viewers would still believe that no Negro could or should mix with white actors on a public stage [. . .] But some audiences were ready for a change, particularly when they watched a young African American actor enthrall audiences with his magnificent physique and singing voice in the 1928 production of *Showboat* at Drury Lane. Paul Robeson was not, of course, the first black man to enact Othello in a white cast to a white audience. During the nineteenth century, Ira Aldridge left the United States because of its segregated theatre and spent a long career acting Othello on the provincial stages of England and in Europe. But though Aldridge was acclaimed as the "African Roscius," he was barred from the United States and from the prime professional theatres of London, Drury Lane and Covent

5   On Helena Faucit Martin, see Vaughan, *Othello*, pp. 136–8. Charles Kemble is not to be confused with the more famous John Martin Kemble, the eighteenth-century actor who played Othello: see Rosenberg, *Masks of Othello*, pp. 43–4, *passim*.

Garden. It wasn't until 1930 that a black American actor would play Othello to a London audience in a major theatre, and only in 1943 was the color barrier broken on Broadway; both of these firsts featured Paul Robeson.

Although the 1930 and 1943 Robeson productions of *Othello* were haunted by fear of public reaction to an openly sexual relationship between a black man and a white woman, they bravely and openly presented an African American Moor. Even so, the reactions from some participants in the productions and from the critics who saw them indicate how and deeply engrained white racism had become [. . .]

[Robeson] knew that his race might affect English audiences negatively [. . .] *Othello*, he noted, "is a tragedy of racial conflict; a tragedy of honour rather than of jealousy . . . [I]t is because he is an alien among white people that his mind works so quickly, for he feels dishonour more deeply." As a victim of racial prejudice throughout his life, Robeson saw Othello as an underdog, a stranger in someone else's culture whose experience was by definition akin to his own. Othello, he contended,

> in the Venice of that time was in practically the same position as a coloured man in America to-day. He was a general, and while he could be valuable as a fighter he was tolerated, just as a negro who could save New York from a disaster would become a great man overnight.
>
> So soon, however, as Othello wanted a white woman, Desdemona, everything was changed, just as New York would be indignant if their coloured man married a white woman.[1]

This conviction informed his representation of Othello [. . .]

Robeson also felt alienated from his producer and director. [Martin] Duberman reports that both Robeson and his wife Eslanda concluded that [the producer] Ellen Van Volkenburg was a racist. She not only approved a set designed to Robeson's disadvantage, but she also "pasted a disfiguring beard and goatee on Robeson and until the final scene dressed him in unsuitably long Elizabethan garments (including tights, puffed sleeves, and doublets), instead of Moorish robes, which would have naturally entranced the dignity of his performance."[2]

Robeson's understandable lack of confidence was noted by reviewers and assessed according to their various preconceptions. Ashley Dukes wrote with a mixture of praise and reservation that

> Robeson brings to his part the special and sensational appeal of a Negro actor; he brings also a noble voice, a tremendous presence, and an infinite simplicity that is of the elemental forest and not at all of the world of Renaissance Europe as seen through the mind of Stratford. He brings an infinite humility, too; and that must detract from the rank and prestige

1 Paul Robeson, "My Fight for Fame. How Shakespeare Paved My Way to Stardom." *Pearson's Weekly*, 5 April 1930, p. 100.
2 Martin Bauml Duberman, *Paul Robeson* (New York: Knopf, 1989), p. 136.

of the man Othello, who will never lose an audience's affection from having his own share of vanity.[3]

James Agate argued in his review that Robeson "did not trust his power *as an actor* sufficiently; he certainly did not take the risk, with the result that all that Othello ought to be throughout the first two acts he was not." Agate then extended his critique beyond language to Robeson's stage presence: "He walked with a stoop, his body sagged, his hands appeared to hang below his knees, and his whole bearing, gait, and diction were full of humility and apology: the inferiority complex in a word." Agate summed up the performance in overtly and offensively racist terms: "This was nigger Shakespeare."[4] Herbert Farjeon noticed a similar lack of command: "He was the underdog from the start. The cares of 'Old Man River' were still upon him. He was a member of a subject race, still dragging the chains of his ancestors." "Shakespeare wrote this part," Farjeon concluded, "for a white man to play."[5] For Agate and Farjeon the color line had been violated; by definition Robeson was not fit to play the noble Moor.

If racism pervades these critiques in obvious ways, it appears more subtly in the reviewers who praised Robeson's performance. Believing fully in the concept of "the romantic Moor," they lauded Robeson's performance because he succeeded in presenting Othello as the truly primitive man he was meant to be. As a Negro (primitive man), Robeson could convey Othello's true character more faithfully than a white (nonprimitive) actor. The *Illustrated Sporting and Dramatic News*' "Captious Critic" praised Robeson as an Othello who "looms majestic, larger than human." This is why

> You may say that Robeson might fail with western and northern characters, that his triumph is merely because the simple nature of Othello is that of his own race, the race which boasts "the shadow'd livery of the burnished sun," that his "farewell" and "handkerchief" speeches are not delivered with full understanding and that, in general, where anything but emotion is wanted he falls below the best. Granted. But what is the theatre but a temple of emotion and who troubles himself about accuracy of impersonation, of obtuseness or intelligence of rendering, so long as the joy or fear or pity of the scene being acted enters the watcher's soul? This is the crown of Paul Robeson's effort, that you rejoice and grieve with his Othello. (7 June 1930)

This praise is accompanied by cartoon drawings of "The Ethiopian Moor" that caricature a black man with grossly thick lips and bugeyes, a monkey-like figure who surely suggests the "primitive." The subsequent page provides black and white illustrations from the production, but these are well-lighted close-ups,

3   Ashley Dukes, "The English Scene: Europe in London," *Theatre Arts Monthly* (August 1930), p. 645.
4   James Agate, *Brief Chronicles: A Survey of the Plays of Shakespeare and the Elizabethans in Actual Performance* (London: Cape, 1943), pp. 285–7.
5   Herbert Farjeon, *The Shakespearean Scene* (London: Hutchinson, n.d.), p.166.

Our Captious Critic

on "OTHELLO" (The Savoy Theatre).

I ADVISE all people who think Shakespeare no longer interesting on the stage to go to the Savoy Theatre to see "Othello." There you will see an in-effective Iago, a caricature of Cassio and a Desdemona who is, though pleasant, lacking the needed poise for this lofty stage. Yet go to this theatre none the less, because there you will see such an Othello as may never be found again, an Othello whose passion rises and falls with the ease of the wave, whose voice is rich music allied to language the wonder of the modern world; an Othello who, as no white man in this country has ever done in living memory, convinces you of the reality of his illusion concerning his wife, of his belief in the absolute necessity of killing her, of the shattering of his being through the dreadful thought. Your pity for Othello is as profound as his own grief ("The pity of it, Iago!") and overpowers your fears for Desdemona. You leave the theatre lamenting that you

The "honest" Ancient, who "hates the slime that sticks on filthy deeds"; Maurice Browne as Iago.

could not help the Moor to know the truth, not in order that he might refrain from the murder of innocence, but that he might retain the happy peace of his soul. You find yourself wondering if the actors of the past really could create those immense effects which loom gigantic on the historic sky and which you have always derided as fiction, when suddenly you encounter a man named Paul Robeson who justifies that tradition and himself looms majestic, "larger than human," before you on this modern stage.

Technically, this negro's Othello has defects, yet not since Irving has so tremendous a general effect been created by any acting. At the risk of seeming childish I will explain my meaning. On leaving the Lyceum after seeing Irving in "Faust," I had to compel myself to walk on sole and heel, so intensely had that tip-toeing Mephistopheles obtained possession of me. On leaving the Savoy Theatre the other day the "pity of it" hung like a cloud over all the city.

You may say that Robeson might fail with western and northern characters, that his triumph is merely because the simple nature of Othello is that of his own race, the race which boasts "the shadow'd livery of the burnished sun," that his "farewell" and "handkerchief" speeches are not delivered with full understanding and that, in general, where anything but emotion is wanted he falls below the best. Granted. But what is the theatre but a temple of emotion and who troubles himself about accuracy of impersonation, of obtuseness or intelligence of rendering, so long as the joy or fear or pity of the scene being acted enters the watcher's soul? This is the crown of Paul Robeson's effort, that you rejoice and grieve with his Othello.

Let us, lest great praise be thought blind praise, admit that there are times when this Othello seems to be repeating words he does not understand, like a schoolboy reading from a book, that he puts absurd emphasis on the word "Venetian" in his last speech of all, that he often stands awkwardly for so well built a man and often makes you too conscious of his hands. Yet the very head and front of his offending hath this extent, no more, and we succumb, as Desdemona did, to the simple nobility of his nature.

The play is acted, for some unexplained reason, on a series of steps and mostly on their upper and more distant parts. Beyond giving certain Venetian gentlemen a chance to strike attitudes with one foot on one step and one on another, these stairs seem a nuisance. The stage is built out over

the orchestra space, but is little used there by the actors for establishing a greater intimacy with the audience.

Mr. Maurice Browne's Iago is a man of no importance, who has more gift for talking than persuading. He is just about as devilish as a chartered accountant and seems to be planning his murders because that happened to be his job and a man must live, anyway. His voice is equally

Desdemona drops a tear; Peggy Ashcroft as the great captain's captain.

colourless whether he wishes to influence his victim by reason, affected passion or by maddening allusion to Desdemona's lechery. How great must be this Othello then, when his emotion can surge up so naturally, although its inspirer is himself so uninspired. "Honest Iago" almost suits this ancient of the Moor's, and "harmless" too, so puny seems his guile. It is a careful performance, lacking strength.

In this production poor Cassio becomes rather a brainless dandy than a smart and honest lieutenant, but from the point of view chosen Mr. Max Montesole acts efficiently and Mr. Ralph Richardson's Roderigo is also capable.

Miss Peggy Ashcroft, though she cannot contrive to be both dignified and natural, achieves the better half of the crowded Desdemona by being the latter. She cannot raise her scenes with Othello to their full height, because that slightly mannish note which is to be found in Shakespeare's heroines and which, though not admirable in itself, harmonises with his plays, is not within her compass. She is like light chamber music to the full orchestra of the Moor, but she wins our affections to the full, for, in Cassio's words, "indeed, she's a most fresh and delicate creature."

As Emilia, Miss Sybil Thorndike's quality is needed, and is forthcoming, for her outburst in the last scene, where the coarse-minded materialist discovers a death-defying devotion to the pale ghost who was once her mistress, and dies for that virtue in her.

It is to be presumed that if Shakespeare had known that his works would so long outlive their author he would have been as careful about his plots as he was about his characters and their poetry. Here we have a cool old soldier-like Iago and who, for motives which even he explains half-heartedly, plots a revenge which can only be kept secret by killing off most of the characters in the play. It was long odds, too, on Othello's strangling him on his first daring to hint at Desdemona's frailty—a consummation devoutly to be wished, as another illogical Shakespearean character remarked.

Two studies of the Ethiopian Moor at the Savoy / Paul Robeson as Othello beside himself with the green-eyed monster.

"Trifles, light as air, are to the jealous confirmation strong, as proof of Holy Writ." Paul Robeson and Maurice Browne.   *Iago puts Othello on the rack.*

Figure 4   'Our Captious Critic', with caricatures of Paul Robeson as Othello. From *The Illustrated Sporting and Dramatic News* (7 June 1930). By permission of the British Library (p. 2489 dea.)

depicting Robeson and Ashcroft on intimate terms. They hardly reflect what must have been the actual visual experience of the Savoy production [. . .]

Paul Robeson's Othello had tremendous repercussions for the twentieth-century's understanding of the play and the title role. It not only influenced the efforts of black actors such as James Earl Jones (who saw and admired Robeson's Moor), but also white actors such as Sir Laurence Olivier. But if

Robeson's interpretation of Othello had a lasting impact, it by no means closed the issue of race in *Othello* [. . .]

[. . .] When Sir Laurence Olivier chose total black body make-up for his National Theatre production in 1964–65, the decision aroused understandable controversy. The BBC/Time-Life production's casting of Anthony Hopkins in the title role also sparked negative reactions. And in 1987 I heard Sir Ian McKellen state in an interview with Michael Kahn at the Folger Shakespeare Theatre that he had no plans to essay the role of Othello, and that in our time, no white actor should. Two years later he attained great acclaim as Iago in an RSC production at The Other Place in Stratford.

Othello's blackness also became an issue in 1987 when Janet Suzman directed the first professional production of *Othello* in South Africa with a black actor in the title role. The Market Theatre production featured John Kani as Othello and Richard Haddon Haines as Iago. According to a newspaper report, Kani and Suzman believed that *Othello* "with its focus on the destruction of an interracial marriage, contains important messages for South Africans." In the program notes Suzman wrote: "The overtones, undercurrents and reverberations for our country are hauntingly evident" (*Washington Post*, 6 September 1987) [. . .]

Multiracial casting, now prominent in the urban theatres of England and the United States, is likely to affect *Othello* productions in the future. During the 1989–90 Folger Shakespeare Theatre season in Washington DC two African Americans – Andre Braugher as Iago and Avery Brooks as Othello – changed the racial dimensions of the play. The presence of a black Iago, for example, explained Othello's absolute trust in his Ensign; it became logical that he should believe a black comrade in arms before a white wife. But at the same time, it removed the issue of race as a factor in Iago's motivation, blurring the obvious racism the Ensign displays under Brabantio's window [. . .]

[. . .] The color prejudice Shakespeare depicted in Renaissance Venice still thrives. Still, the increasing prevalence of multiracial casting indicates that much has changed since Paul Robeson's "Ethiopian Moor" first spoke the Othello music in 1930 [. . .] Paul Robeson opened up *Othello* to new resonances, forcing audiences and critics alike to debate – if not to solve – the racial issues embedded in Shakespeare's text.

Patricia Tatspaugh, 'The Tragedies of Love on Film', in Russell Jackson, ed., *The Cambridge Companion to Shakespeare on Film* (Cambridge: Cambridge University Press, 2000), pp. 144–6

Orson Welles (1915–85) was a maverick and frequently brilliant filmmaker, especially in his youth. *Citizen Kane* (1941), made when Welles was only twenty-six, is often voted best film of all time by critics. His film of *Othello* (1952), made on location in Morocco, has received lavish praise as a visual interpretation of Shakespeare's play, especially for its imaginative use of scenery, camera angles and editing, but has been criticised as an inadequate representation of the pathos and grandeur of tragedy. Welles played Othello himself. There is a full account of the making of the film by the Irish actor Micheál MacLiammóir, who played Iago: *Put Money in Thy Purse* (1952).

In the pre-credit sequence, Welles establishes the formal tone, stately pace and visual images that will dominate his filmic adaptation of Shakespeare's tragedy. Cowled, chanting monks process behind the biers of Othello and Desdemona; mourning soldiers and villagers crowd against the castle wall; chained Iago is dragged through the crowd and imprisoned in an iron cage, which is raised high over a fortress wall; Emilia's casket joins the procession. The sequence anticipates the Venetians' affording Othello a Christian funeral and, presumably, the forgiveness implicit in the act. It also introduces a number of visual motifs: silhouettes and shadows; sequences shot from a number of angles; imagery of containment; contrasts between horizontal and vertical; significant architectural details. Welles relies on visual effects to amplify the heavily cut text and to contribute significantly to the presentation of Othello (Welles), Desdemona (Suzanne Cloutier) and Iago (Micheál MacLiammóir).

Welles's Othello is statuesque and controlled. His first words are the formal, measured speech to the senators, 'Most potent, grave, and reverend signors' (1.3.76 etc.); his reunion with Desdemona is coldly formal; he sends an emissary to summon the brawlers before him; and his face conveys little of the turmoil evoked by Iago. Welles's dignified Othello, whose long robes accentuate his noble stature, contrasts sharply with MacLiammóir's scrappy loner, his unbecoming costume inspired by Carpaccio. In his diary of the filming, *Put Money in Thy Purse* [1952], MacLiammóir describes Iago's appearance: 'hair falling wispishly to shoulders, small round hats of plummy red felt ... very short belted jackets, undershirt pulled in puffs through apertures in sleeves laced with ribbons and leather thongs, long hose, and laced boots'. MacLiammóir spits out Iago's words in a matter-of-fact manner. Whereas Othello fills a frame, Iago typically enters the frame from behind his target and adjusts his pace to accommodate that of the character he is manipulating. Two other visual images characterize Iago: he is seldom still, and he almost always gets the dominant physical position from which he literally looks down on Othello, as well as on Roderigo (Robert Coote) and Cassio (Michael Lawrence). Iago is diminished by Roderigo's cuddly white lapdog, who seems to comment ironically on Iago's disloyalty and to call attention to the ensign's mongrel appearance.

[. . .] Welles interpolates scenes to introduce and define the marriage. He films Othello and Desdemona in a gondola *en route* to the wedding, a brief glimpse of the secret ceremony and Desdemona, her loose blond hair arranged decoratively on the pillow, awaiting Othello for the consummation of their marriage. Their Cypriot bed figures in three other brief interpolated scenes: before the brawl, the couple, with lines transferred from Act 2 scene 1 ('If it were now to die/'Twere now to die most happy'); Othello, his rest disturbed by rioting. In Act 3 scene 3,

Figure 5 **Orson Welles as Othello. A still from *Othello*, dir. Orson Welles (1952). Films Marceau/Mercury Productions (courtesy of the Kobal Collection).**

seeking evidence for Desdemona's alleged adultery, Othello draws the curtains and looks at their bed.

Welles's script helps establish Desdemona's loyalty: on her own initiative she attends the Senate and she arrives at the brawl immediately after Othello. Despite the interpolated sequences, the bedroom shots and Desdemona's loyalty, Welles's film falls short of conveying the marriage as a love-match and the tragedy of love. The formality of concept and Welles's stately Othello raise the film to a lofty plain, but the sharp and moving visual images, which appeal primarily to the eye, undermine the tragic intent.

Throughout the film, shots of the empty cage foreshadow Iago's punishment and fit into a pattern of images that confine Desdemona and Othello. Desdemona's braided hair and, later, her snood, both decorated with pearls, signal her innocence. But they also anticipate the imagery of imprisonment in three key scenes. Desdemona's second plea for Cassio takes place in the armoury where Iago had, literally, disarmed Othello. Shot through a rack of spears, Desdemona seems to be behind bars. Separated from Emilia (Fay Compton) by a window grille with spikes on one side, Desdemona hums the willow song and discusses adultery with her companion (Act 4 scene 3). Immediately after, Othello, whose approach is filmed as shadows on stone walls, peers at Desdemona through another barred window. Nets and cages also help portray Iago's entrapment of Othello. But another set of images works in much the same way as do those which resonate with Desdemona's pearls, braids and snood. Othello's triumphant arrival at the fortress in Cyprus contrasts with his loss of command and Iago's confinement of his general to stony rooms and narrow stairwells. Welles encouraged MacLiammóir to play Iago as impotent and explained 'that's why he hates life so much'. MacLiammóir summarises Welles's view:

> No single trace of the Mephistophelean Iago is to be used: no conscious villainy; a common man, clever as a waggonload of monkeys, his thought never on the present moment but always on the move after the move after next: a business man dealing in destruction with neatness, method, and a proper pleasure in his work the honest Iago reputation is accepted because it has become almost the truth.

MacLiammóir's Iago is passionless, even somewhat mechanical, and he makes no concessions to companionability. Emilia makes clear her bitter disgust with him, especially in her delivery of ''Tis not a year or two shows us a man./They are all but stomachs, and we all but food;/They eat us hungerly, and when they are full,/They belch us' (3.4.99–102) and in her angry glance and quick departure when Iago dismisses her.

Stanley Wells, 'Shakespeare Production in England in 1989',
Shakespeare Survey 43 (1991), pp. 191–4

I have concluded this section with a full account of a relatively recent production of *Othello*, directed by Trevor Nunn, to give readers an idea of the ways in which the play has been interpreted on stage in recent years. The reader might want to ask whether modern settings enhance or diminish Shakespeare's play, whether they offer new insights or are simply used to bolster the director's reputation by seeming to depart from an established tradition of performance.

The Other Place, which had been put out of commission at the end of 1988, was pressed into service again when Trevor Nunn found himself free to direct a special production of *Othello* for a short run there and at the Young Vic in London [. . .]

Othello was played virtually complete, even including the second (though not the first) Clown episode, where the Clown was played, ironically, as a Soldier ('for me to say a soldier lies, 'tis stabbing'). With a short interval the performance lasted over four hours. (Were these texts really played in full to audiences of Shakespeare's time? And if so, must they not have formed some of the most intelligent, thoughtful, attentive, imaginative, and intellectually receptive audiences ever to have peopled the theatre?)

The setting was extremely simple: the audience sat round three sides of the playing area, the other side had a central entrance and, above, a slatted wall behind which Othello could lurk as he overlooked Cassio and Desdemona. Costumes and detailed properties created the impression of a predominantly military society, late nineteenth century in period and indeterminate in locality though with strong hints of American Civil War (reinforced by plangent music played on cornet and harmonium) and of *Death in Venice*.

A wealth of social detail – especially in the earlier part of the play – illuminated the characterization and played over and beneath the surface of the text to release its full emotional potential. Iago, a non-commissioned officer with a slightly plebeian accent, swigged beer from a bottle which he offered to a dandyish Roderigo who wiped its top with a handkerchief before drinking; military ritual signalled Othello's entrance; the Duke's court met in the early hours of the morning over brandy glasses around a baize-topped table; Brabanzio was a top-hatted Victorian paterfamilias, touching as he rejected Desdemona's tenders of affection on his departure; Iago pocketed a cigar left on the council table and finished off the remains of the brandy. A large telescope on a stand established the quay-side setting for Cyprus; Cassio gave Desdemona his overcoat to keep her warm; Emilia wiped the rain off a piece of baggage before sitting on it. Iago here was very much the conscious entertainer, making a great set-piece of 'She that was ever fair and never proud . . .' (2.1.151ff.); merriment rose to an almost hysterical climax followed by a long, long pause during which the overwrought Desdemona's anxiety rose to the surface in sobs; Cassio's attempts to console her provoked Iago's cynicism on 'He takes her by the palm . . .' The drinking scene took place indoors, with a couple of portable camp beds and washbasins into which Iago sloshed two bottles of wine simultaneously, adding brandy from a flask in Cassio's absence, tasting the mixture with a finger, then adding more brandy; this scene, too, worked up to a brilliant climax with the debagging of one of the company, after which Iago and his mates converged on Cassio with the same intention, to be thwarted by his assertion of a drunken authority. Othello entered to still the brawl with his shirt off but his men leapt instantly to attention; after his departure Cassio vomited into one of the basins, provoking Iago's 'What, are you hurt, Lieutenant?'; he slept on one of the camp beds during Iago's 'And what's he then that says I play the villain . . .', addressed challengingly to the audience. The 'temptation' scene had a double setting, a workmanlike table and camp chairs to the back for Iago and Othello, with further forward a little outdoor table and chairs for Emilia and Desdemona where they mixed lemonade which Desdemona gave jokingly without sugar to Othello; she sat cajolingly on his knee as she spoke with him of Cassio. The sound of cicadas was heard as Othello and Iago worked on their papers. Entering to tell Othello that his dinner was ready, Desdemona plonked a watch before him to remind him of the time, then dropped her handkerchief. They went off together; a moment later she returned, anxiously seeking what she had left behind, and sighed with relief when she found – the watch. It was a brilliantly ironic end to the first part.

Social detail dwindled in the second part as passion mounted, but the production remained rooted in naturalism; indeed, a fully written account of this production would read like a Victorian novel. Searching Desdemona's dressing table for evidence of Desdemona's infidelity, Othello found only the box of sweets with which Cassio had tried to cheer her up on the quayside. As he reviled her with the name of whore he made her stand on a table, pacing around her like a beast tormenting its prey. At 'Swear thou art honest' (4.1.40) he dragged her to a prie-dieu, and there, at the end of the willow scene, she knelt to say 'God me such uses send/Not to pick bad from bad, but by bad mend!', momentarily recalling Verdi's insertion of an 'Ave Maria' at this point. For the murder Othello wore an elaborate Moorish gown and carried a scimitar. He smothered her orgasmically on a large bed, rolling off her unconscious body as if after sexual climax.

The production style, like the auditorium, encouraged naturalistic acting, and [. . .] speech style tended to the colloquial. The cast was exceptionally strong. Imogen Stubbs's Desdemona was young, beautiful, vulnerable, deeply, physically in love with Othello, and no less loving to her father, so that the sense of her 'divided duty' was touchingly conveyed. The depth of her love was most apparent after her fate was sealed, as she listened entranced to Othello's tale of the handkerchief and for a moment one sensed a return to an earlier stage of their relationship, when she would listen with similar fascination to his traveller's tales.

Othello was played by the black opera singer Willard White [. . .] White is an imposing figure of great natural nobility with a darkly resonant speaking voice of unforced power and authority. Though he never seemed anything less than highly accomplished as an actor, his own speech rhythms were sometimes at odds with the iambic patterns of Shakespeare's verse, resulting in a less than thorough exploration of verbal meaning. For example, in 'Thou dost conspire against thy friend, Iago' (3.3.147) only the second syllable of 'conspire' received a (heavy) accent, so there was no sense of paradox; 'I am bound to thee for ever' was merely a polite statement, and 'Set on thy wife to observe' had none of the sense of self-abasement that Donald Sinden found in it. But Othello's suffering came powerfully to the surface on 'Why did I marry?', his 'farewell', punctuated with the tearing of papers and the drumming of fists on the table, reached an impressive climax, and sheer emotional sincerity won through in the final scenes in which we suffered with him as he made Desdemona suffer. 'Where should Othello go' was a magnificent cry, his final speech both pathetic and noble. The emotional truth of this performance overcame its technical limitations.

And it was matched by Ian McKellen's Iago, a tall, trim figure of military bearing, so professionally disciplined that he was obviously a strong candidate for Cassio's lieutenancy. In Othello's presence he was always under iron control, though his eyes narrowed to slits in intense concentration as he observed anything that might serve his purpose. Only in relaxation, with Roderigo or Cassio, or above all Emilia, did his coarseness of spirit reveal itself. Zoë Wanamaker's subtle portrayal of bemused, long-suffering, but still not quite hopeless incomprehension reminded us that the play is about Emilia's marriage as well as Desdemona's. Iago's contempt for her was barely concealed, yet it was clear why he would have attracted her. McKellen's insolent scorn extended even to the audience in his baleful, challenging gaze. There was a frightening sense of danger in the final scene as he rushed to escape over the bed in which Desdemona lay, and after he had been brought back, captive, he stared fixedly at her body, unresponsive to Lodovico's 'This is thy work', still staring at the dead Desdemona, advancing closer to the foot of the bed to gaze on his handiwork, still staring in impassive, unflinching fascination as the lights went down. It was a chilling conclusion to a fascinating production.

3

Key Passages

Introduction

I have included what I see as the most important passages in the play in this section and annotated them fully. Of course, my choice has not been an easy one. I have selected scenes and passages that I believe have structural and thematic importance. I have therefore included passages from the opening scene in which Iago and Roderigo confront Brabantio with the news that his daughter has married Othello, as their racist comments prefigure much of what is to follow and set the tone of the play. More contentiously perhaps I have included extracts from the third scene ('the trial scene') because it shows how the institutions of Venice function to offset and correct the excesses of its unruly citizens. Obviously I have chosen a number of long passages which deal with the relationship between Othello and Iago, including Iago's first attempt to undermine Othello's confidence in his wife's fidelity (often called 'the temptation scene'); and long extracts from Acts 3 and 4 which show how Iago transforms Othello's suspicions into a plot to murder Desdemona. I have also tried to include a representative selection of passages from the play that concentrate on the three main characters. Desdemona is shown defending her right to marry the man she loves at the start of the play (see McPherson, **pp. 78–84**, and Rosenberg, **pp. 63–6**) and in 'the defamation scene' in Act 4 (see Jardine, **pp. 84–91**). I have also included passages which show Iago at work on Roderigo and Cassio, to give the reader a clear sense that, for all his apparent naïveté, Othello is not the only one who is fooled by the play's villain. This has meant that I have not been able to include any passages which show Bianca and, more importantly, Emilia on stage, so readers are referred to Lisa Jardine's essay above for commentary.

The introductory sections in tinted boxes attempt to give an overall assessment of the function and significance of each passage selected. In compiling the notes I have provided glosses of any unfamiliar words and phrases, as well as pointing out any important themes or clusters of images. Some notes direct readers to contemporary documents and relevant lines in other plays; some to specific critical comments. I have also tried to include a number of cross-references to material reproduced elsewhere in the volume; these appear in bold. I hope my glosses are helpful; they are not intended to be exhaustive or to close off other possible readings. I have not included any textual notes but have followed the Arden 3 text. (For a discussion of the textual problems of *Othello*, see above, **p. 37**, and the relevant items in the bibliography.)

The passages selected are as follows:

1. (**pp. 116–21**) The encounter between Iago and Roderigo and Brabantio in Scene 1, when Desdemona's father is informed of her marriage to Othello.
2. (**pp. 121–33**) 'The trial scene' where Othello and Desdemona defend the reasons for their marriage against Brabantio, and Othello is given his commission in Cyprus.
3. (**pp. 134–7**) The aftermath of 'the brawl scene', when Iago manages to engineer a fight between Montano and Cassio. Iago involves Cassio in his plot before revealing his true motives to the audience in his soliloquy. This is the last point in the play when Othello still enjoys calm and authority.
4. (**pp. 138–47**) The first scene in which Iago undermines Othello's faith in Desdemona as the tragic design accelerates (the most emotionally exhausting scene in the play as Othello is transformed from a secure and happy husband to a jealous and homicidal cuckold).
5. (**pp. 147–55**) A second extract from this scene.
6. (**pp. 155–60**) Iago questions Cassio about Bianca while Othello hides, thinking they are talking about Desdemona.
7. (**pp. 160–3**) Othello denounces and insults Desdemona.
8. (**pp. 164–70**) The final scene in which Othello realises his terrible mistake in murdering Desdemona and Iago is finally exposed.

Abbreviations

I have used the following abbreviations in the notes:

Abbott   E. A. Abbott, *A Shakespeare Grammar* (London: Macmillan, 2nd edn 1870)

Everett   Barbara Everett, '"Spanish" Othello: The Making of Shakespeare's Moor', in Catherine M. S. Alexander and Stanley Wells, eds, *Shakespeare and Race* (Cambridge: Cambridge University Press, 2000), pp. 64–81

Honigmann   *Othello*, ed. E. A. J. Honigmann (London: Nelson, 1997)

Onions   C. T. Onions, *A Shakespeare Glossary*, rev. Robert D. Eagleson (Oxford: Oxford University Press, 1986)

Sanders   *Othello*, ed. Norman Sanders (Cambridge: Cambridge University Press, 1994)

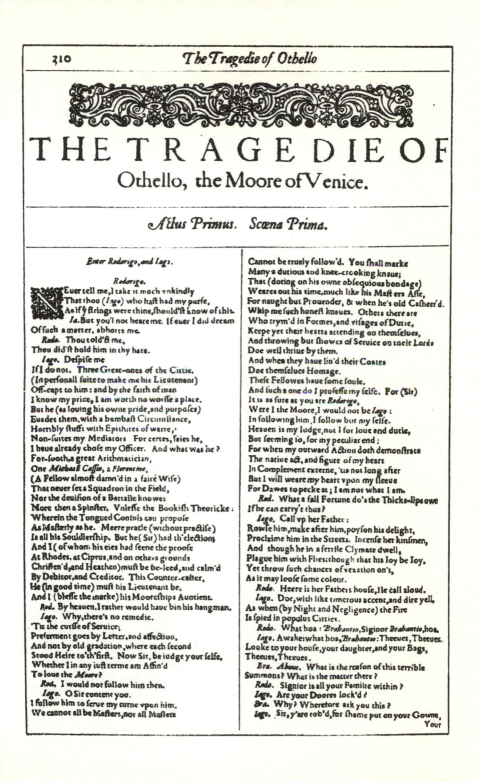

THE TRAGEDIE OF
Othello, the Moore of Venice.

Actus Primus. Scœna Prima.

Enter Rodorigo, and Iago.

Roderigo.

Euer tell me,I take it much vnkindly
That thou (*Iago*) who haft had my purfe,
As if ŷ ftrings were thine,fhould'ft know of this.
  *Ia.*But you'l not heare me. If euer I did dream
Of fuch a matter, abhorre me.
  Rodo. Thou told'ft me,
Thou did'ft hold him in thy hate.
  Iago. Defpife me
If I do not. Three Great-ones of the Cittie,
(In perfonall fuite to make me his Lieutenant)
Off-capt to him : and by the faith of man
I know my price, I am worth no worffe a place.
But he (as louing his owne pride,and purpofes)
Euades them,with a bumbaft Circumftance,
Horribly ftufft with Epithites of warre,·
Non-fuites my Mediators For certes,faies he,
I haue already chofe my Officer. And what was he ?
For-footh,a great Arithmatician,
One *Michael Caffio*, a *Florentine*,
(A Fellow almoft damn'd in a faire Wife)
That neuer fet a Squadron in the Field,
Nor the deuifion of a Battaile knowes
More then a Spinfter. Vnleffe the Bookifh Theoricke :
Wherein the Tongued Confuls can propofe
As Mafterly as he. Meere pratle (without practife)
Is all his Souldierfhip. But he(Sir) had th'election;
And I (of whom his eies had feene the proofe
At Rhodes, at Ciprus,and on others grounds
Chriften'd,and Heathen)muft be be-leed,and calm'd
By Debitor,and Creditor. This Counter-cafter,
He (in good time) muft his Lieutenant be,
And I (bleffe the marke) his Mooreſhips Auntient.
  Rod. By heauen,I rather would haue bin his hangman.
  Iago. Why,there's no remedie.
'Tis the curffe of Seruice;
Preferment goes by Letter,and affection,
And not by old gradation ,where each fecond
Stood Heire to'th'firft. Now Sir, be iudge your felfe,
Whether I in any iuft terme am Affin'd
To loue the *Moore* ?
  Rod. I would not follow him then.
  Iago. O Sir content you.
I follow him to ferue my turne vpon him.
We cannot all be Mafters,nor all Maſters

Cannot be truely follow'd. You fhall marke
Many a dutious and knee-crooking knaue;
That (doting on his owne obfequious bondage)
Weares out his time,much like his Maft ers Affe,
For naught but Prouender, & when he's old Cafheer'd.
Whip me fuch honeft knaues. Others there are
Who trym'd in Formes,and vifages of Dutie,
Keepe yet their hearts attending on themfelues,
And throwing but fhowes of Seruice on their Lords
Doe well thriue by them.
And when they haue lin'd their Coates
Doe themfelues Homage.
Thefe Fellowes haue fome foule,
And fuch a one do I profeffe my felfe. For (Sir)
It is as fure as you are *Roderigo*,
Were I the Moore,I would not be *Iago* :
In following him,I follow but my felfe.
Heauen is my Iudge,not I for loue and dutie,
But feeming fo, for my peculiar end :
For when my outward Action doth demonftrate
The native act, and figure of my heart
In Complement externe, 'tis not long after
But I will weare my heart vpon my fleeue
For Dawes to pecke at ; I am not what I am.
  Rod. What a fall Fortune do's the Thicke-lips owe
If he can carry't thus ?
  Iago. Call vp her Father :
Rowfe him,make after him,poyfon his delight,
Proclaime him in the Streets. Incenfe her kinfmen,
And though he in a fertile Clymate dwell,
Plague him with Flies:though that his Ioy be Ioy,
Yet throw fuch changes of vexation on't,
As it may loofe fome colour.
  Rodo. Heere is her Fathers houfe,Ile call aloud.
  Iago. Doe,with like timerous accent,and dire yell,
As when (by Night and Negligence) the Fire
Is fpied in populus Citties.
  Rodo. What hoa : *Brabantio*,Siginor *Brabantio*,hoa.
  Iago. Awake:what hoa,*Brabantio*:Theeues, Theeues.
Looke to your houfe,your daughter,and your Bags,
Theeues,Theeues.
  Bra. Aboue. What is the reafon of this terrible
Summons? What is the matter there ?
  Rodo. Signior is all your Familie within ?
  Iago. Are your Doores lock'd ?
  Bra. Why? Wherefore ask you this ?
  Iago. Sir, y'are rob'd,for fhame put on your Gowne,
Your

Key Passages

Act 1, Scene 1, lines 81–180

The opening scene of the play shows how volatile Venetian society is and what tensions exist within it. In confronting Brabantio with the secret marriage of his daughter to Othello, Iago and Roderigo introduce not only the familiar Shakespearian theme of the heavy-handed father who wishes to have complete control over his daughter, but also that of racial conflict.

Brabantio appears as a ridiculous figure in his nightgown, like the stock figure of the cuckolded older husband in many comedies. He should be compared to other angry fathers in Shakespeare such as Egeus in *A Midsummer Night's Dream* (c.1595–6). His desire to enclose his daughter contrasts with the reputation of Venice for liberty and of its women for sexual licentiousness (see Coryat and McPherson above, **pp. 25–8, pp. 78–84**). Locking daughters or wives up was usually a recipe for disaster; compare with the treatment and behaviour of Bianca in Thomas Middleton, *Women Beware Women* (1625?). One of the main themes of the play is that of race and essential nature. Brabantio fails to come to terms with the fact that his daughter, his own flesh and blood, has not obeyed him in every way. He sees her as a traitor who erodes his legitimate authority, just as Othello later sees his Turkish side as a traitor to Venice that must be destroyed (see below, **pp. 168–9**). We must consider what is an individual's nature and to whom they owe loyalty.

Iago's words and actions prefigure his role throughout the play. He is later able to undermine Othello's faith in his wife by pointing out that she had earlier deceived her father in choosing him as a husband (see below, **pp. 133, 144**). The language he uses to insult Othello casts him as an old husband performing his marital duties in a depraved and unseemly fashion. Old husbands of young wives were a traditional butt of comedy on stage and in other literary works. Imagery of copulating animals continues throughout the play (see, for example, 4.1.274). Iago does not miss an opportunity to insult Othello in racial terms in the first scene, attempting to establish himself as an honest Venetian scandalised by the mixed marriage and so reproducing what those he wishes to influence expect to hear. In reminding Brabantio that he may soon have a grandchild, Iago is playing on Brabantio's fear of miscegenation, the production of children of mixed race, as well as making the familiar connection between black and evil. The appearance of the first grandchild is, of course, supposed to be a significant and happy event. Iago is trying to emphasise to Brabantio how disastrous his daughter's choice of husband is and how their union will ruin all his hopes (for comment, see McPherson above, **pp. 78–84**).

In the final soliloquy Iago reveals his true nature to the audience and shows that he is the stage Machiavellian villain, deceiving others to further his own ends. Readers might wish to compare his behaviour to characters such as Barabas in Christopher Marlowe's *The Jew of Malta* (c.1589–90).

BRABANTIO [*appears above*] *at a window.*[1]

BRABANTIO
    What is the reason of this terrible summons?
    What is the matter there?
RODERIGO
    Signior,[2] is all your family within?
IAGO
    Are your doors locked?
BRABANTIO   Why? Wherefore ask you this?
IAGO
    Zounds,[3] sir, you're robbed, for shame put on your gown!   85
    Your heart is burst, you have lost half your soul,
    Even now, now, very now, an old black ram[4]
    Is tupping[5] your white ewe! Arise, arise,
    Awake the snorting[6] citizens[7] with the bell
    Or else the devil will make a grandsire of you,   90
    Arise I say!
BRABANTIO   What, have you lost your wits?

---

1   Perhaps indicating that Brabantio appears above the main stage, on an upper stage or gallery.
2   A recognition of Brabantio's importance in Venice, referring to his age and status, and also his membership of the Signiory, the ruling council of Venice which is shown sitting in the following scene.
3   By God's (or Christ's) wounds; a strong oath.
4   Rams were traditionally thought of as lustful animals.
5   Copulating with (only usage by Shakespeare).
6   Snoring, perhaps hinting that they, like Othello, are animals because they sleep so heavily and noisily.
7   A clear reminder to the audience that in Venice people enjoyed the status of citizens with rights, including that of determining who ruled them, unlike their counterparts in England.

RODERIGO
    Most reverend[8] signior, do you know my voice?[9]
BRABANTIO
    Not I, what are you?
RODERIGO   My name is Roderigo.
BRABANTIO
    The worser[10] welcome!
    I have charged thee not to haunt about my doors: 95
    In honest plainness thou hast heard me say
    My daughter is not for thee;[11] and now in madness,
    Being full of supper and distempering[12] draughts,
    Upon malicious bravery[13] dost thou come
    To start my quiet?   100
RODERIGO
    Sir, sir, sir –
BRABANTIO   But thou must needs be sure
    My spirit and my place have in them power
    To make this bitter to thee.[14]
RODERIGO   Patience, good sir!
BRABANTIO
    What tell'st thou me of robbing? This is Venice:
    My house is not a grange.[15]
RODERIGO   Most grave Brabantio,   105
    In simple and pure soul I come to you –
IAGO   Zounds,[16] sir, you are one of those that will not
    serve God, if the devil bid you. Because we come to
    do you service, and you think we are ruffians, you'll
    have your daughter covered with a Barbary horse;[17]   110

---

8 Respected.
9 It is too dark for Brabantio to see Roderigo.
10 An emphatic comparative to give greater emphasis (see Abbott, p. 11).
11 Presumably because Roderigo is too humble in status and too foolish to be able to expect to marry
    a woman such as Desdemona.
12 Intoxicating or disturbing (Onions). Brabantio implies that Roderigo and Iago are drunk.
13 Excessive bravado, hinting at the possibility of violence.
14 Brabantio shows that he has the presence to browbeat a weak character such as Roderigo, even if
    he has just been summoned out of bed to hear bad news. He is referring to his important position
    within the Venetian city-state and is warning Roderigo that he has the power to cause the younger
    man much harm.
15 Isolated farmhouse. In trying to contrast his sophistication as a city-dweller with that of the rural
    farmer, Brabantio plays into Iago's hands. Farms contained animals, and Iago will exploit this
    connection to continue his attack on Othello.
16 Iago's repetition of the oath enables him to appear as an honest man pushed beyond his limits by
    the night's events. Under normal circumstances a low-ranking army office, would not dare to
    use profane language in front of a high-ranking senator; certainly not twice. Either Iago has a
    well-constructed plan, or he reacts quickly to the flow of events.
17 Barbary was the area that the Berbers and Moors of North Africa inhabited, and from where,
    presumably, Othello originated. Barbary was famous for its thoroughbred horses. Iago is employ-
    ing Brabantio's reference to the grange to suggest that Othello's marriage to Desdemona is exactly
    the same as her transgressing one of society's fundamental taboos and having sex with an animal.

you'll have your nephews[18] neigh to you, you'll have
coursers[19] for cousins and jennets[20] for germans![21]

BRABANTIO   What profane wretch art thou?

IAGO   I am one, sir, that comes to tell you your daughter
and the Moor are now making the beast with two backs.[22]   115

BRABANTIO   Thou[23] art a villain!

IAGO   You are a senator![24]

BRABANTIO
This thou shalt answer. I know thee, Roderigo!

RODERIGO
Sir, I will answer anything. But I beseech you,
If't be your pleasure and most wise consent,
As partly I find it is,[25] that your fair[26] daughter   120
At this odd-even[27] and dull watch o'th' night,
Transported with no worse nor better guard
But with a knave of common hire,[28] a gondolier,
To the gross clasps of a lascivious Moor[29] –
If this be known to you, and your allowance,[30]   125
We then have done you bold and saucy[31] wrongs.
But if you know not this, my manners[32] tell me
We have your wrong rebuke. Do not believe
That from the sense of all civility
I thus would play and trifle with your reverence.[33]   130
Your daughter, if you have not given her leave,
I say again, hath made a gross[34] revolt,
Tying her duty, beauty, wit and fortunes
In an extravagant and wheeling[35] stranger

Iago mercilessly plays on Brabantio's fears of miscegenation. There may also be a submerged pun on 'barbarian'.

18 Grandsons and other immediate relatives.
19 Powerful race or military horses.
20 Small Spanish horses. There is probably a reference to the Spanish connection with the Moors of North Africa, too (see Everett).
21 Near relatives (Onions).
22 A graphic and visual image of copulation. Othello's words later (2.3.10) suggest that the marriage is not yet consummated.
23 'Thou' is used to address inferiors.
24 Iago's echoing of Brabantio's line suggests that if he cannot keep his own house in order then he has no business running the city-state, hence Brabantio's fury in the next line.
25 Implying that when Brabantio knows the facts he will change his mind.
26 Stressing her colour in contrast to Othello's black skin.
27 i.e. midnight.
28 Male servant.
29 Again the link between skin colour and excessive sexual desire is made.
30 Has your approval.
31 Insolent (Onions).
32 Understanding (of human behaviour).
33 The respect owed to you.
34 Great, disgusting.
35 Vagrant, unstable. Roderigo tries to contrast Brabantio's sense of the stability of the native Venetians with those whom the city-state adopted, a common manoeuvre in the argument of one threatened by immigrants.

Of here and everywhere. Straight satisfy yourself: 135
If she be in her chamber or your house
Let loose on me the justice of the state
For thus deluding you.

BRABANTIO   Strike on the tinder, ho!
Give me a taper,[36] call up all my people.
This accident is not unlike my dream,   140
Belief of it oppresses me already.[37]
Light, I say, light!   *Exit above.*

IAGO   Farewell, for I must leave you.
It seems not meet,[38] nor wholesome to my place,[39]
To be produced,[40] as, if I stay, I shall,
Against the Moor. For I do know the state,   145
However this may gall him with some check,
Cannot with safety cast[41] him, for he's embarked
With such loud reason[42] to the Cyprus wars,[43]
Which even now stands in act, that for[44] their souls
Another of his fathom[45] they have none   150
To lead their business – in which regard,
Though I do hate him as I do hell-pains,[46]
Yet for necessity of present life
I must show out a flag and sign of love,
Which is indeed but sign. That you shall surely find him,   155
Lead to the Sagittary[47] the raised search,
And there will I be with him. So farewell.[48]   *Exit.*

Enter BRABANTIO *in his night-gown and Servants with torches.*

BRABANTIO
It is too true an evil, gone she is,
And what's to come of my despised time

---

36 Candle.
37 These lines show how cleverly Iago in particular has played on Brabantio's fears. Brabantio has
    already entertained the prospect that his daughter will elope with Othello.
38 Fitting.
39 As Othello's ensign (the lowest rank of commissioned officer: Iago resents – or claims to resent – his
    lowly status).
40 i.e., as a witness.
41 Discharge.
42 Iago admits that Othello has risen through merit to his exalted position.
43 On the longstanding struggle in the Mediterranean for control of Cyprus, see above **p. 10**.
44 i.e., to save.
45 Ability.
46 The torments reserved for the damned in hell. In contrast to Cinthio's novella, we never find out
    why Iago hates Othello so bitterly (see above, **pp. 19–21**).
47 Presumably the name of an inn or house where the newly-weds have taken lodgings.
48 This speech indicates that news travels fast in Venice and that a great deal of information enters the
    public domain. It also prepares us for the second scene of the play where Othello and Desdemona
    defend themselves against their accusers.

Is nought but bitterness. Now Roderigo,   160
Where didst thou see her? – O unhappy[49] girl! –
With the Moor, say'st thou? – Who would be a father? –
How didst thou know 'twas she? – O, she deceives me
Past thought! – What said she to you? – Get more tapers,
Raise all my kindred. Are they married, think you?[50]   165

RODERIGO
Truly I think they are.

BRABANTIO
O heaven, how got she out? O treason of the blood!
– Fathers, from hence trust not your daughters' minds
By what you see them act. – Is there not charms[51]
By which the property[52] of youth and maidhood   170
May be abused? Have you not read, Roderigo,
Of some such thing?[53]

RODERIGO   Yes sir, I have indeed.[54]

BRABANTIO
Call up my brother. – O, would you had had her![55]
Some one way, some another. – Do you know
Where we may apprehend her and the Moor?   175

RODERIGO
I think I can discover him, if you please
To get good guard and go along with me.

BRABANTIO
Pray you lead on. At every house I'll call,
I may command at most:[56] get weapons, ho!
And raise some special officers of night.   180
On, good Roderigo, I'll deserve your pains.[57]   *Exeunt.*

Act 1, Scene 3, lines 1–294

This scene shows the Venetian council at work. It serves as a vivid contrast to
the opening scene, which showed how divisive and destructive the conflicts in

---

49 Miserable, wretched.
50 Brabantio's disordered syntax, reflecting his obvious distress, resembles that of Shylock in *The
    Merchant of Venice* (*c.*1596–7), when his daughter, Jessica, elopes (2.8.15–22).
51 Magical powers.
52 Nature.
53 Brabantio will not accept any blame or responsibility for Desdemona's behaviour.
54 Roderigo is echoing Iago's tactic of telling people what they want to hear.
55 Brabantio has now reversed his stated position at line 97, indicating that even a foolish Venetian of
    dim prospects ranks above a black general. When under pressure such racist sentiments come to the
    surface.
56 Brabantio shows the extent of his power and his confidence in it, leading us to expect that he may
    triumph when he tries to have the marriage annulled in Act 1, Scene 3.
57 Repay you.

Venetian society could be. Here the Duke and council manage to sort out the twin problems of the threat of the Turks to Cyprus and Othello's marriage. Brabantio's views are not held by most members of the Venetian ruling council, and we see an example of successful government at work (for comment see Hadfield above, **pp. 92–3**). The audience may have been aware that the defeat of the Turks was, in essence, a fantasy, given the potent threat of the Ottoman Empire to Europe in the late sixteenth and early seventeenth centuries (see Fynes Moryson above, **pp. 24–5**).

The scene further explores the question of race and identity signalled in the opening scene. In the speech that explains how he won Desdemona's heart, Othello is defining himself as an Elizabethan traveller against the savages of Africa and America. He refers to 'cannibals' and 'anthropophagi' (lines 144–5). Cannibals were man-eaters from the newly discovered Americas; anthropophagi were man-eaters found in the chronicles of ancient historians such as Herodotus and Diodorus Siculus. He then mentions 'men whose heads / Do grow beneath their shoulders'. Strange creatures such as these were found in a number of medieval histories still in circulation such as *Mandeville's Travels*. These details show how desperate he is to fit into European society. Later, Iago transforms him back into the savage that Brabantio always believes him to be (see below, **pp. 151–3, 158–60**; for comment see the essay by Newman, **pp. 74–8**). Perhaps there is a hint of irony in the fabulous stories that Othello tells because many of these were being questioned by more sceptical observers. *Mandeville's Travels* was included in the first edition of Richard Hakluyt's collection of voyages, *The Principal Navigations* (1589), but excluded in the expanded edition of 1598–1600 because of doubts about its authenticity.

Desdemona's reaction to Othello's stories is equally significant. Her attempt to balance her desire to listen to Othello's tales with her chores neatly illustrates the dual nature of the play as a domestic tragedy and a work of exotic promise (see above, **pp. 13–14**). It also indicates how exciting Othello must have seemed to a young woman of independent spirit dominated by an overbearing father. When she states that she saw Othello's 'visage in his mind' she shows that she has not come to terms with Othello's colour. She asserts that his true worth lies in his soul, indicating that she makes the standard equation of black and evil. This a central element of the tragedy, showing that the best motives can help precipitate a disaster in a divided society, and also revealing that the newly-weds do not know each other that well, a limitation that is to help precipitate the tragedy. When the Duke tells Brabantio that his son-in-law is 'more fair than black', he shows that he accepts the same binary oppositions as Desdemona: white/black, fair/dark, good/evil all operate in Venice despite attempts to run a liberal city-state. The Duke is a man of goodwill but he has his limitations too.

Enter DUKE *and* Senators, *set at a table, with lights and Attendants.*

DUKE
    There is no composition[1] in these news
    That gives them credit.[2]
1 SENATOR   Indeed, they are disproportioned.[3]
    My letters say a hundred and seven galleys.
DUKE
    And mine a hundred forty.
2 SENATOR   And mine two hundred.
    But though they jump not on a just account[4] –   5
    As in these cases, where the aim[5] reports,
    'Tis oft with difference – yet do they all confirm
    A Turkish fleet, and bearing up to Cyprus.[6]
DUKE
    Nay, it is possible enough to judgement:[7]
    I do not so secure me in the error   10
    But the main article I do approve
    In fearful sense.[8]
SAILOR (*within*)   What ho, what ho, what ho!

Enter Sailor.

OFFICER
    A messenger from the galleys.
DUKE
    Now? what's the business?
SAILOR
    The Turkish preparation makes for Rhodes,[9]   15
    So was I bid report here to the state
    By Signior Angelo.[10]
DUKE
    How say you by this change?
1 SENATOR   This cannot be,
    By no assay of reason: 'tis a pageant[11]
    To keep us in false gaze. When we consider   20
    Th'importancy of Cyprus to the Turk,

---

1 Consistency.
2 Again, Venice is established as a place where news travels fast.
3 Exaggerated.
4 Agree on the exact number.
5 Guess.
6 The need to separate fact from fiction prefigures Iago's manipulation of Othello with rumour and its consequent uncertainty.
7 Make a decision.
8 The Duke means that the discrepancies in the numbers do not detract from the essential truth of the observations and the consequent dangers they will have to face.
9 Another island in the Mediterranean under Venetian control.
10 Presumably, a captain of a galley (Sanders) or the governor of Cyprus (Honigmann).
11 Show or trick.

And let ourselves again but understand
That as it more concerns the Turk than Rhodes
So may he with more facile question bear it,[12]
For that it stands not in such warlike brace[13]   25
But altogether lacks th'abilities
That Rhodes is dressed in. If we make thought of this
We must not think the Turk is so unskilful
To leave that latest which concerns him first,
Neglecting an attempt of ease and gain   30
To wake and wage a danger profitless.

DUKE

Nay, in all confidence, he's not for Rhodes.

OFFICER

Here is more news.[14]

Enter a Messenger.

MESSENGER

The Ottomites,[15] reverend and gracious,
Steering with due course toward the isle of Rhodes,   35
Have there injointed[16] with an after fleet –

1 SENATOR

Ay, so I thought; how many, as you guess?

MESSENGER

Of thirty sail; and now they do re-stem
Their backward course, bearing with frank appearance
Their purposes toward Cyprus. Signior Montano,   40
Your trusty and most valiant servitor,[17]
With his free duty[18] recommends you thus[19]
And prays you to relieve him.

DUKE

'Tis certain then for Cyprus.
Marcus Luccicos, is not he in town?[20]   45

1 SENATOR

He's now in Florence.

DUKE

Write from us to him; post-post-haste, dispatch.

---

12 i.e. Cyprus.
13 State of defence.
14 The Venetians show good sense in distinguishing between truth and falsehood, in direct contrast to
    Othello later in the play.
15 Turks.
16 Joined.
17 Servant. Montano is governor of Cyprus.
18 Willingness to serve.
19 Reports this to you.
20 Obviously a trusty military leader.

1 SENATOR
Here comes Brabantio and the valiant[21] Moor.

Enter BRABANTIO, OTHELLO, CASSIO, IAGO, RODERIGO *and Officers.*

DUKE
Valiant Othello, we must straight employ you
Against the general enemy Ottoman.   50
[*to Brabantio*] I did not see you: welcome, gentle signior,
We lacked your counsel and your help tonight.[22]
BRABANTIO
So did I yours. Good your grace, pardon me,
Neither my place[23] nor aught[24] I heard of business
Hath raised me from my bed, nor doth the general care   55
Take hold on me, for my particular grief
Is of so flood-gate and o'erbearing nature
That it engluts[25] and swallows other sorrows
And it is still itself.
DUKE   Why? What's the matter?
BRABANTIO
My daughter, O my daughter!
1 SENATOR   Dead?
BRABANTIO   Ay, to me: 60
She is abused, stolen from me and corrupted
By spells and medicines bought of mountebanks,[26]
For nature so preposterously to err
Being not deficient, blind, or lame of sense,
Sans witchcraft could not.[27]   65
DUKE
Whoe'er he be, that in this foul proceeding
Hath thus beguiled your daughter of herself,
And you of her, the bloody book of law[28]
You shall yourself read, in the bitter letter,
After your own sense,[29] yea, though our proper[30] son   70

---

21 A sign that the council values Othello more highly than Brabantio.
22 The Duke's lines show that he can easily accommodate both Brabantio and Othello as valuable members of Venetian society.
23 Social position.
24 Anything.
25 Engulfs. The image is of a flood swamping everything in its wake.
26 Charlatans, often selling fake medicines to the unwary. Brabantio continues his assertion that magic must have been used on Desdemona. His assumptions mirror those of Othello later.
27 Brabantio also continues to assert that Desdemona must be acting against her nature in choosing Othello for a husband.
28 Compare Egeus' demand that Demetrius be tried because he has bewitched his daughter, Hermia, in the first scene of *A Midsummer Night's Dream* (1.1.22–45).
29 i.e. the Duke will interpret the law himself (and agree with Brabantio).
30 i.e. own (and not illegitimate).

    Stood in your action.[31]

BRABANTIO   Humbly I thank your grace.
    Here is the man, this Moor, whom now it seems
    Your special mandate for the state affairs
    Hath hither brought.

ALL   We are very sorry for't.

DUKE [to Othello]
    What in your own part can you say to this?   75

BRABANTIO
    Nothing, but this is so.

OTHELLO
    Most potent, grave, and reverend signiors,
    My very noble and approved good masters:
    That I have ta'en away this old man's daughter
    It is most true; true, I have married her.   80
    The very head and front[32] of my offending
    Hath this extent, no more. Rude[33] am I in my speech
    And little blest with the soft phrase of peace,
    For since these arms of mine had seven years' pith
    Till now some nine moons wasted, they have used   85
    Their dearest action in the tented field,
    And little of this great world can I speak
    More than pertains to feats of broil[34] and battle,
    And therefore little shall I grace my cause
    In speaking for myself. Yet, by your gracious patience,   90
    I will a round unvarnished tale deliver
    Of my whole course of love, what drugs, what charms,
    What conjuration and what mighty magic[35] –
    For such proceeding I am charged withal –
    I won his daughter.

BRABANTIO   A maiden never bold,   95
    Of spirit so still and quiet that her motion
    Blushed at herself;[36] and she, in spite of nature,
    Of years, of country, credit, everything,
    To fall in love with what she feared to look on?[37]
    It is a judgement maimed and most imperfect
    That will confess perfection so could err

---

31 Were the defendant.
32 Whole extent (Sanders).
33 Rough, unskilled (a form of politeness which only serves to draw attention to Othello's polished
    performance).
34 Conflict.
35 An urbane piece of sarcasm.
36 This suggests that Brabantio does not know his daughter very well, that he has not observed her
    awakening maturity and independence, which we observe later in the scene.
37 This predicts Desdemona's line (253).

Against all rules of nature, and must be driven
To find out practices of cunning hell
Why this should be.[38] I therefore vouch again
That with some mixtures powerful o'er the blood   105
Or with some dram[39] conjured to this effect
He wrought upon her.

DUKE   To vouch this is no proof,
Without more certain and more overt test
Than these thin habits and poor likelihoods
Of modern seeming[40] do prefer against him.[41]   110

I SENATOR
But, Othello, speak:
Did you by indirect and forced courses
Subdue and poison this young maid's affections?
Or came it by request and such fair question
As soul to soul affordeth?

OTHELLO   I do beseech you,   115
Send for the lady to the Sagittary,[42]
And let her speak of me before her father.
If you do find me foul in her report
The trust, the office I do hold of you
Not only take away, but let your sentence   120
Even fall upon my life.

DUKE
Fetch Desdemona hither.

OTHELLO
Ancient,[43] conduct them, you best know the place.[44]
And till she come, as truly as to heaven

                              Exeunt [Iago and] two or three.

I do confess the vices of my blood[45]   125
So justly to your grave ears I'll present
How I did thrive in this fair lady's love
And she in mine.

DUKE   Say it, Othello.

OTHELLO
Her father loved me, oft invited me,

---

38 Note not only that Brabantio repeats his assertions, but also the words he uses.
39 Draught of medicine.
40 Commonplace assumptions.
41 The Duke shows that without proof Brabantio has no case. Honigmann suggests that these lines may be an 'appeal against racial prejudice'.
42 See 1.1.156.
43 Ensign, meaning Iago.
44 A further indication of how much was public knowledge in Venice. Othello is shown to be an outsider.
45 Othello means moral failings, but the lines clearly have racial implications, too, and predict the subsequent action of the play.

Still questioned me the story of my life   130
From year to year – the battles, sieges, fortunes
That I have passed.
I ran it through, even from my boyish days
To th' very moment that he bade me tell it,
Wherein I spake of most disastrous[46] chances,   135
Of moving accidents by flood and field,
Of hair-breadth scapes i'th' imminent deadly breach,[47]
Of being taken by the insolent[48] foe
And sold to slavery; of my redemption thence
And portance[49] in my travailous[50] history;   140
Wherein of antres[51] vast and deserts idle,[52]
Rough quarries,[53] rocks and hills whose heads touch heaven
It was my hint[54] to speak – such was my process –
And of the cannibals that each other eat,
The Anthropophagi, and men whose heads   145
Do grow beneath their shoulders. This to hear
Would Desdemona seriously incline,
But still the house affairs would draw her thence,
Which ever as she could with haste dispatch
She'd come again, and with a greedy ear   150
Devour up my discourse; which I, observing,
Took once a pliant[55] hour and found good means
To draw from her a prayer of earnest heart
That I would all my pilgrimage dilate,
Whereof by parcels[56] she had something heard   155
But not intentively.[57] I did consent,
And often did beguile her of her tears
When I did speak of some distressful stroke
That my youth suffered. My story being done
She gave me for my pains a world of sighs,   160
She swore in faith 'twas strange, 'twas passing strange,
'Twas pitiful, 'twas wondrous pitiful;[58]
She wished she had not heard it, yet she wished

46 With the added sense of unlucky.
47 Gap in fortified defences which could be penetrated. Compare Henry V's speech in *Henry V* (1599), 3.1.1–34.
48 Insulting.
49 Behaviour.
50 Tiring, laborious (quarto has 'travels').
51 Caves.
52 Empty, desolate.
53 Precipices, mountainsides (Sanders).
54 Chance.
55 Suitable.
56 In bits and pieces.
57 Attentively.
58 Othello attempts to recapture the sighs of the smitten Desdemona for his interrogators.

That heaven had made her such a man.[59] She thanked me
And bade me, if I had a friend that loved her,   165
I should but teach him how to tell my story
And that would woo her.[60] Upon this hint I spake:
She loved me for the dangers I had passed
And I loved her that she did pity them.[61]
This only is the witchcraft I have used: 170

Enter DESDEMONA, IAGO, *Attendants.*

Here comes the lady, let her witness it.
DUKE
    I think this tale would win my daughter too.[62]
    Good Brabantio, take up this mangled matter at the best:[63]
    Men do their broken weapons rather use
    Than their bare hands.
BRABANTIO   I pray you, hear her speak.   175
    If she confess that she was half the wooer,
    Destruction on my head if my bad blame
    Light on the man. Come hither, gentle mistress:
    Do you perceive, in all this noble company,
    Where most you owe obedience?
DESDEMONA   My noble father,   180
    I do perceive here a divided duty.
    To you I am bound for life and education:
    My life and education both do learn me
    How to respect you; you are the lord of duty,
    I am hitherto your daughter. But here's my husband: 185
    And so much duty as my mother showed
    To you, preferring you before her father,
    So much I challenge that I may profess
    Due to the Moor my lord.
BRABANTIO
    God be with you, I have done.   190
    Please it your grace, on to the state affairs;
    I had rather to adopt a child than get[64] it.
    Come hither, Moor:

---

59 Again showing Desdemona's spirit and her frustration at the limitations of her life. 'Romance
    heroines sometimes wished they were men' (Honigmann).
60 Compare the wooing of Orlando and Rosalind disguised as Ganymede in *As You Like It*, Acts 3–4.
61 The audience is invited to consider this statement in the light of later events. Othello and Desde-
    mona know each other less well than most couples who marry for love.
62 See below, line 198.
63 Make the best of a bad bargain.
64 Produce one. Brabantio clearly expected Desdemona to choose him; and his sense of the natural
    order is, once again, affronted. As in so many reconciliations in Shakespeare, at least one character
    is left outside the circle affirming harmony: compare Malvolio in *Twelfth Night* (1600–1).

I here do give thee that with all my heart
Which, but thou hast already, with all my heart   195
I would keep from thee. For your sake, jewel,
I am glad at soul I have no other child,
For thy escape would teach me tyranny[65]
To hang clogs[66] on them. I have done, my lord.

DUKE

Let me speak like yourself,[67] and lay a sentence   200
Which as a grise[68] or step may help these lovers
Into your favour.
When remedies are past the griefs are ended
By seeing the worst which late on hopes depended.
To mourn a mischief that is past and gone   205
Is the next way to draw new mischief on.
What cannot be preserved when fortune takes,
Patience her injury a mockery makes.[69]
The robbed that smiles steals something from the thief,
He robs himself that spends a bootless[70] grief.   210

BRABANTIO

So let the Turk of Cyprus us beguile,
We lose it not so long as we can smile;[71]
He bears the sentence well that nothing bears
But the free comfort which from thence he hears.
But he bears both the sentence and the sorrow   215
That, to pay grief, must of poor patience borrow.[72]
These sentences to sugar or to gall,[73]
Being strong on both sides, are equivocal.[74]
But words are words:[75] I never yet did hear
That the bruised heart was pierced through the ear.[76]   220

---

65 The play has already shown Brabantio to be a tyrant as a father, a pointed contrast to the successful mechanisms of the Venetian government which sort out problems well. See the Duke's comment above, line 172, where he stands as a surrogate father of Desdemona.
66 Wooden blocks to prevent escape.
67 As a counsellor or adviser.
68 Step.
69 i.e. patience helps you to overcome and defeat injuries.
70 Pointless.
71 Given the impending danger from the Turks, Brabantio's imitation of the Duke's sententious wisdom seems to undercut his blithe confidence in the inevitable good conclusion of bad situations. Smiling in the face of adversity will not deter the Turks.
72 i.e. he who can be convinced by platitudes will be fine, but he who has to suffer without believing in their consolation is less fortunate.
73 Bitterness.
74 Brabantio means that one can take the Duke's platitudes either way (indicating that they are of little significance or help to him). Again, these lines point towards Iago's use of equivocation to undermine Othello.
75 A platitude that is deeply ironic in view of the action of the play.
76 These lines prefigure Othello's suicide (5.2.354).

I humbly beseech you, proceed to th'affairs of state.[77]

DUKE　The Turk with a most mighty preparation makes
　　for Cyprus. Othello, the fortitude of the place is best
　　known to you,[78] and, though we have there a substitute[79]
　　of most allowed sufficiency, yet opinion, a sovereign　　　　225
　　mistress of effects, throws a more safer voice on you.[80]
　　You must therefore be content to slubber[81] the gloss of
　　your new fortunes with this more stubborn and
　　boisterous expedition.

OTHELLO
　　The tyrant custom, most grave senators,　　　　　　　　230
　　Hath made the flinty and steel couch of war
　　My thrice-driven bed of down.[82] I do agnize[83]
　　A natural and prompt alacrity[84]
　　I find in hardness, and do undertake
　　This present war against the Ottomites.　　　　　　　　235
　　Most humbly therefore, bending to your state,
　　I crave fit disposition for my wife,
　　Due reverence of place, and exhibition,
　　With such accommodation and besort[85]
　　As levels with her breeding.　　　　　　　　　　　　240

DUKE
　　Why, at her father's.

BRABANTIO　　　　　　　I'll not have it so.

OTHELLO
　　Nor I.

DESDEMONA　Nor would I there reside
　　To put my father in impatient thoughts
　　By being in his eye. Most gracious duke,
　　To my unfolding lend your prosperous[86] ear　　　　　245
　　And let me find a charter[87] in your voice
　　T'assist my simpleness.[88]

77　An abrupt change that shows how easily the Venetian council can return to the business of state
　　politics.
78　Indicating that Othello must have served in Cyprus earlier.
79　Deputy, probably referring to Montano.
80　Again the importance of news is stressed.
81　Obscure, make dirty.
82　Othello shows himself to be comfortable with military langauge and assumptions. The reference to
　　tyranny shows how military life has no time for the niceties of justice and political representation as
　　practised in Venice. Yet again, the lines prefigure Othello's inability to cope with what he claims to
　　know – the male intimacies of barrack life.
83　Acknowledge.
84　Readiness.
85　Company.
86　Favourable, perhaps hinting at Venice's commercial success and wealth.
87　Permission.
88　Like Othello, Desdemona claims that she has no skill in expressing herself.

DUKE

    What would you, Desdemona?

DESDEMONA

    That I did love the Moor to live with him

    My downright violence[89] and scorn of fortunes   250

    May trumpet to the world.[90] My heart's subdued

    Even to the very quality[91] of my lord:

    I saw Othello's visage in his mind,

    And to his honours and his valiant parts

    Did I my soul and fortunes consecrate,   255

    So that, dear lords, if I be left behind,

    A moth of peace,[92] and he go to the war,

    The rites for which I love him are bereft me,

    And I a heavy interim shall support

    By his dear absence. Let me go with him.   260

OTHELLO

    Let her have your voice.

    Vouch[93] with me, heaven, I therefore beg it not

    To please the palate of my appetite,

    Nor to comply with heat, the young affects

    In me defunct, and proper satisfaction,   265

    But to be free and bounteous to her mind.[94]

    And heaven defend your good souls that you think

    I will your serious and great business scant

    When she is with me. No, when light-winged toys

    Of feathered Cupid seel[95] with wanton dullness   270

    My speculative and officed instrument,[96]

    That my disports[97] corrupt and taint my business,[98]

    Let housewives make a skillet of my helm[99]

---

89 Desire to overturn normal expectations of social behaviour. The reference to violence is, of course, ironic in view of later events.

90 Again, Desdemona asserts her independence and shows how little her father understood of her nature even as he was making assumptions of family loyalty and shared identity (lines 95–107).

91 Nature.

92 Alluding to the moth's attraction to the light. The phrase again shows how Desdemona accepts the dark/light, black/white colour coding of contemporary society.

93 Bear witness.

94 Othello plays down the sexual nature of their union (understandably, given the situation) and emphasises their spiritual compatibility. There is an obvious irony in this, given that the scene has demonstrated how little they really know each other. The lines are appropriate to an ageing soldier, but are also simply good sense in the circumstances.

95 Close (the eyes).

96 Powers of perception, eyes.

97 Pleasures (sexual).

98 These lines also contrast the valour and virtue of war with the soft luxury of pleasure to be found in places of liberty such as Venice. But Othello will find that he is less at home in Cyprus than he imagines he will be.

99 Make a cooking pot out of my helmet. A humorous image to relieve the tension of the scene?

And all indign[100] and base adversities
Make head against my estimation.[101]   275

DUKE

Be it as you shall privately determine,
Either for her stay or going: th'affair cries haste
And speed must answer it.

I SENATOR   You must away tonight.

DESDEMONA

Tonight, my lord?

DUKE   This night.

OTHELLO   With all my heart.

DUKE

At nine i'th' morning here we'll meet again.   280
Othello, leave some officer behind
And he shall our commission bring to you,
And such things else of quality and respect
As doth import you.

OTHELLO   So please your grace, my ancient:
A man he is of honesty and trust.   285
To his conveyance I assign my wife,
With what else needful your good grace shall think
To be sent after me.

DUKE   Let it be so.
Good-night to everyone. And, noble signior,
If virtue no delighted beauty lack   290
Your son-in-law is far more fair than black.[102]

I SENATOR

Adieu, brave Moor, use Desdemona well.

BRABANTIO

Look to her, Moor, if thou hast eyes to see:
She has deceived her father, and may thee.[103]

                              Exeunt [Duke, Brabantio, Senators, Officers].

---

100 Shameful.
101 Rise up to spoil my reputation.
102 The Duke's words recall those of Desdemona (253) (see above, **p. 122**).
103 These lines are part of an on-going series of images concerned with sight and vision. Few plays are
     as concerned with the need for visual proof, or the need to see through to the heart of the matter, as
     Othello, as Iago's attempts to make Brabantio 'see' Othello and Desdemona copulating in the first
     act, or Desdemona's confidence that she can see through to the real essence of Othello (253), make
     clear. The irony, of course, is that Brabantio, like Othello, sees fit to blame women when the real
     villains are men.

Act 2, Scene 3, lines 255–357

This scene shows Iago working on Cassio to further his evil plot. It shows that Cassio is also vulnerable to Iago's designs and that Othello is not his only victim, indicating that it would be a mistake to see the play in terms of a sophisticated white man duping a foolish and trusting black man.

Cassio's sense of the loss of his reputation furthers the play's discussion of identity. His lament is both sincere and exaggerated (fuelled by his drunken state). On the one hand he is clearly right that reputation matters in Venetian society, as the early scenes in the play demonstrated. On the other, his equation of the loss of reputation with the loss of his soul is absurd, and may be designed to show the superficial nature of Venetian/Italian society and its over-reliance on the concept of honour. Cassio thinks that he has become a beast and lost his humanity through his foolish actions. Beasts were not thought to have souls, a fact which distinguished them from humans. Compare John Donne's lines, 'If lecherous goats, if serpents envious/Cannot be damned; alas, why should I be?' ('Divine Meditations', 9, lines 3–4).

When Iago discusses Desdemona with Cassio (317ff.) we should note the potentially sexual nature of the language and imagery that he uses, from Othello surveying Desdemona to Cassio importuning her and using her free and open nature. Iago, as he does later, is playing on assumptions of the liberal nature of Venetian women and their freedom with their favours (see Coryat and McPherson above, **pp. 25–8, 78–84**). He always brings matters down to physical needs and desires; hence the irony of his dismissal of Cassio's comments on reputation and its spiritual importance. Iago's advice always seems sound to those who receive it, while the audience can see its deliberately malign purpose. Iago's ability to use people's good points to destroy them is a key to his success and shows his acute understanding of human nature. The dramatic irony that structures the play and determines the course of the action contributes to the intensity many critics have noted as central to an experience of *Othello*.

IAGO	What, are you hurt lieutenant?[1]	255
CASSIO	Ay, past all surgery.	
IAGO	Marry, God forbid!	
CASSIO	Reputation, reputation, reputation! O, I have	
	lost my reputation, I have lost the immortal part of	
	myself – and what remains is bestial. My reputation,	260
	Iago, my reputation![2]	
IAGO	As I am an honest man I thought you had	

---

1   Cassio's wound is to be contrasted with the physical wound suffered by Montano in the fight ('I am hurt to th'death' (2.3.161)).
2   See also *Richard II*, 1.1.177–8, 'The purest treasure mortal times afford/Is spotless reputation'.

received some bodily wound; there is more of sense[3]
in that than in reputation. Reputation is an idle[4] and
most false imposition, oft got without merit and lost   265
without deserving. You have lost no reputation at all,
unless you repute yourself such a loser.[5] What, man,
there are ways to recover[6] the general again. You are
but now cast in his mood, a punishment more in
policy than in malice,[7] even so as one would beat his   270
offenceless dog to affright an imperious lion.[8] Sue[9] to
him again, and he's yours.

CASSIO   I will rather sue to be despised, than to deceive
so good a commander with so slight,[10] so drunken, and
so indiscreet an officer. Drunk? and speak parrot?[11] and   275
squabble? swagger? swear? and discourse fustian[12] with
one's own shadow? O thou invisible spirit of wine, if
thou hast no name to be known by, let us call thee
devil![13]

IAGO   What was he that you followed with your sword?   280
What had he done to you?

CASSIO   I know not.

IAGO   Is't possible?

CASSIO   I remember a mass of things, but nothing distinctly; a quarrel, but nothing wherefore. O God, that   285
men should put an enemy in their mouths, to steal
away their brains! that we should with joy, pleasance,
revel and applause, transform ourselves into beasts![14]

IAGO   Why, but you are now well enough: how came you
thus recovered?   290

CASSIO   It hath pleased the devil drunkenness to give
place to the devil wrath;[15] one unperfectness shows me
another, to make me frankly despise myself.

IAGO   Come, you are too severe a moraler. As the time,
the place and the condition of this country stands, I   295

3 Feeling.
4 Useless.
5 Iago argues the exact opposite case later when he is undermining Othello's confidence in Desdemona's purity: 3.3.159–64.
6 Win back the trust of.
7 i.e., more for public show than reality.
8 i.e., meaning that Cassio has to be humiliated to show Othello's power in front of the Venetian
   army and the local Cypriots.
9 Petition.
10 Insignificant (Onions).
11 Nonsense.
12 Gibberish (Onions).
13 Again, the theological imagery of Cassio's language is notable.
14 A possible allusion to the Circe story in *The Odyssey*. Circe was a witch who turned men into
   beasts through her obvious charms.
15 Cassio is alluding to the seven deadly sins. His language reminds us of the morality play tradition
   that underlies *Othello*. Compare Iago's lines on jealousy (3.3.167–72).

could heartily wish this had not befallen; but since it
is as it is, mend it for your own good.

CASSIO   I will ask him for my place again, he shall tell
me I am a drunkard: had I as many mouths as Hydra,[16]
such an answer would stop them all. To be now a   300
sensible man, by and by a fool, and presently a beast!
O strange! – Every inordinate cup is unblest, and the
ingredience is a devil.[17]

IAGO   Come, come, good wine is a good familiar creature, if it be well used: exclaim no more against it.[18]   305
And, good lieutenant, I think you think I love you.[19]

CASSIO   I have well approved[20] it, sir. I drunk?

IAGO   You, or any man living, may be drunk at some
time, man. I'll tell you what you shall do. Our
general's wife is now the general. I may say so in this   310
respect, for that he hath devoted and given up himself
to the contemplation, mark and denotement[21] of her
parts and graces. Confess yourself freely to her,
importune her help to put you in your place again.
She is of so free, so kind, so apt, so blest a disposition   315
that she holds it a vice in her goodness not to do
more than she is requested. This broken joint between
you and her husband entreat her to splinter – and my
fortunes against any lay worth naming, this crack of
your love shall grow stronger than it was before.[22]   320

CASSIO   You advise me well.

IAGO   I protest, in the sincerity of love and honest
kindness.

CASSIO   I think it freely, and betimes in the morning I
will beseech the virtuous Desdemona to undertake   325
for me. I am desperate of my fortunes if they check[23]
me here.

IAGO   You are in the right. Good-night, lieutenant, I
must to the watch.   329

---

16 A many-headed monster in Greek mythology, eventually killed by Hercules. When a head was cut
off, another two grew in its place. Often used as a symbol of threatening chaos, disorder and the
danger of mob rule, hence its relevance here.
17 Cassio oscillates between blaming the drink itself and his own nature.
18 Iago often adopts reasonable arguments for his own evil ends when it suits him.
19 A deliberately misleading statement that tells Cassio nothing at all. Compare Iago's words to
Othello later (3.3.119)
20 Experienced. An acknowledgement of Iago's seeming affirmation of close friendship. Presumably,
Cassio is simply taken in.
21 Signs (Onions).
22 There is an irony in Iago's imagery of bones knitting again and being stronger, given that he later
stabs Cassio in the leg (5.1.26).
23 Stop.

CASSIO   Good-night, honest Iago.[24]   *Exit*

IAGO

And what's he then that says I play the villain?
When this advice is free I give and honest,
Probal[25] to thinking and indeed the course
To win the Moor again? For 'tis most easy
Th'inclining[26] Desdemona to subdue   335
In any honest suit. She's framed as fruitful
As the free elements: and then for her
To win the Moor, were't to renounce his baptism,[27]
All seals and symbols of redeemed sin,
His soul is so enfettered to her love   340
That she may make, unmake, do what she list,
Even as her appetite shall play the god
With his weak function.[28] How am I then a villain
To counsel Cassio to this parallel course
Directly to his good? Divinity of hell![29]   345
When devils will the blackest sins put on
They do suggest at first with heavenly shows
As I do now.[30] For whiles this honest[31] fool
Plies Desdemona to repair his fortune,
And she for him pleads strongly to the Moor,   350
I'll pour this pestilence into his ear:[32]
That she repeals[33] him for her body's lust.
And by how much she strives to do him good
She shall undo her credit with the Moor –
So will I turn her virtue into pitch[34]   355
And out of her own goodness make the net
That shall enmesh them all.

---

24 One of the frequent uses of this adjective which is generally joined to Iago's name.
25 i.e. plausible.
26 Willing (with obvious sexual innuendo).
27 A reminder that Iago is well aware that Othello is an outsider who has only recently become a Christian.
28 Natural instincts (again, with obvious sexual innuendo). Iago suggests that Othello's Christianity is only superficial and that his love for Desdemona is more important for his sense of stability and identity, a factor he is about to exploit ruthlessly.
29 The theological language of Cassio is now being developed by Iago for his own ends as he turns himself into a devil.
30 Compare Christopher Marlowe, *Dr Faustus* (*c*.1589), when Faustus asks Mephistopheles to disguise himself as a friar.
31 For 'honest' Iago, real honesty is stupidity. The trick is to appear honest (see the discussion by Empson above, **pp. 59–62**).
32 Compare the description of the death of Hamlet senior, who died when poison was poured into his ear (*Hamlet*, 1.5.63–4).
33 Pleads for his reinstatement.
34 'Type of something foul' (Onions). Also suggests blackness.

Act 3, Scene 3, lines 90–281

Probably the key scene in the play and one that produces an intense effect on an audience. Here Iago destroys Othello's faith in Desdemona and sets in motion a tragedy that cannot be prevented. At the start of this passage Othello has such a clear faith in his wife's love and devotion that he associates his union with her as a means of salvation and a protection against the forces of chaos. By the end of Act 3 his love has turned to hate and he plans to murder her (see below, **pp. 153–5**), making the opening lines an ironically accurate prophecy rather than a statement of undying love. Othello's transformation and his sense of himself should be compared with that of Michael Cassio in the passage above, which now can be read as a prediction of the more significant change of identity that Othello will have to undergo.

A good example of Iago's devious and skilful use of language is his use of the apparently proverbial 'Men should be what they seem,/Or those that be not, would they might seem none' (129–30). The second line here takes away the certainty that the first appears to assert. Shakespeare, here and elsewhere, is aware of the ambiguous and misleading nature of so many proverbs and maxims, which can be reversed, placed against ones which imply the exact opposite, or simply refuted. Any schoolboy who attended a Tudor grammar school, as Shakespeare undoubtedly did, would have learnt the art of rhetoric, which taught pupils how to construct a persuasive argument. Often they were required to argue for and against certain propositions using reason and examples. Shakespeare's plays, like those of many other Renaissance dramatists, are full of argument. As readers and playgoers, we need to attend to the larger structures and meanings as well as to the minutiae of each speech act to determine the sense of a play or a passage within it. The tentative exchange between Othello and Iago here, on one level, shows the problematic nature of apparently secure statements.

Iago also manages to bring to the fore some of Othello's assumptions about his relationship with Desdemona. In his tormented speech that concludes this passage (261–81), Othello compares Desdemona to a hawk who has to be trained. Given the Venetians' perception of Othello and his race, an image Othello has absorbed, he is attempting to assert the control of a husband over his wife and so reverse the usual racial traffic. Seeing marriage relations in terms of hawking is a frequent image in Renaissance literature; compare the extended use of the comparison in *The Taming of the Shrew*. Othello plays with the image of himself as the falconer and Desdemona as the hawk, but undermines the sense of the relationship by indicating that he will not exercise the control over his bird that the falconer must exert. In doing so he renders the comparison ironic, retaining its sense of violent domination without any useful end product, a rather sad comment on their marriage. In seeing himself as a cuckold Othello resembles the stock figure of comedy, the old, foolish husband who is deceived by his clever and frustrated young wife. Shakespeare has transplanted this figure to tragedy. *Othello* is all the more tense and intense a play for recycling motifs, situations and images normally found in comedy, constantly reminding the audience how near all the issues are to being resolved happily (and bringing out the brutal possibilities inherent in much comedy).

OTHELLO

    Excellent wretch![1] perdition[2] catch my soul   90
    But I do love thee! and when I love thee not
    Chaos is come again.[3]

IAGO

    My noble lord –

OTHELLO   What dost thou say, Iago?

IAGO

    Did Michael Cassio, when you wooed my lady,
    Know of your love?

OTHELLO   He did, from first to last,   95
    Why dost thou ask?

IAGO

    But for a satisfaction[4] of my thought,
    No further harm.

OTHELLO   Why of thy thought, Iago?

IAGO

    I did not think he had been acquainted with her.

OTHELLO

    O yes, and went between us very oft.[5]   100

IAGO

    Indeed?

OTHELLO

    Indeed? Ay, indeed. Discern'st thou aught[6] in that?
    Is he not honest?

IAGO

    Honest, my lord?[7]

OTHELLO

    Honest? Ay, honest.   105

1   A term of familiar endearment, but clearly pointing to later developments.
2   Damnation. Again, continuing the theological imagery and significance of the plot.
3   'The allusion is to the classical legend that Love was the first of the gods to spring out of original chaos' (Sanders). The prediction is chillingly accurate.
4   Confirmation.
5   i.e., acted as a go-between and messenger for them. There is a possible innuendo, given the story Iago tells of sleeping in barracks with Cassio (3.3.416–28).
6   Anything (strange).
7   Iago's tactic of repeating key words that Othello uses serves to undermine his certainty in the signs he recognises.

IAGO
  My lord, for aught I know.
OTHELLO
  What dost thou think?
IAGO
  Think, my lord?
OTHELLO
  Think, my lord! By heaven, thou echo'st me
  As if there were some monster in thy thought   110
  Too hideous to be shown.[8] Thou dost mean something,
  I heard thee say even now thou lik'st not that
  When Cassio left my wife: what didst not like?
  And when I told thee he was of my counsel
  In my whole course of wooing, thou criedst 'Indeed?'   115
  And didst contract and purse thy brow together
  As if thou then hadst shut up in thy brain
  Some horrible conceit.[9] If thou dost love me
  Show me thy thought.[10]
IAGO   My lord, you know I love you.[11]
OTHELLO
  I think thou dost.   120
  And for I know thou'rt full of love and honesty
  And weigh'st thy words before thou giv'st them breath,[12]
  Therefore these stops of thine fright me the more.
  For such things in a false disloyal knave
  Are tricks of custom, but in a man that's just   125
  They're close delations, working from the heart,
  That passion cannot rule.
IAGO   For Michael Cassio,
  I dare be sworn, I think, that he is honest.
OTHELLO
  I think so too.
IAGO   Men should be what they seem,
  Or those that be not, would they might seem none.   130
OTHELLO
  Certain, men should be what they seem.
IAGO
  Why then I think Cassio's an honest man.
OTHELLO
  Nay, yet there's more in this:

---

8 See below, lines 167–72.
9 Idea, conception. Instead of children, the product of the union of Othello and Desdemona is Iago's
   hideous plot which leads to their death (and his).
10 Yet another bitter irony.
11 Compare 2.3.306 above.
12 Obviously true, but not in the way that Othello imagines.

I prithee speak to me, as to thy thinkings,
As thou dost ruminate, and give thy worst of thoughts   135
The worst of words.

IAGO   Good my lord, pardon me;
Though I am bound to every act of duty
I am not bound to that all slaves are free to –[13]
Utter my thoughts? Why, say they are vile and false?[14]
As where's that palace whereinto foul things   140
Sometimes intrude not? Who has a breast so pure
But some uncleanly apprehensions
Keep leets[15] and law-days[16] and in session sit
With meditations lawful?

OTHELLO
Thou dost conspire against thy friend, Iago,[17]   145
If thou but think'st him wronged and mak'st his ear
A stranger to thy thoughts.

IAGO   I do beseech you,
Though I perchance am vicious[18] in my guess
– As I confess it is my nature's plague
To spy into abuses, and oft my jealousy   150
Shapes[19] faults that are not – that your wisdom
From one that so imperfectly conceits[20]
Would take no notice, nor build yourself a trouble
Out of his scattering[21] and unsure observance:[22]
It were not for your quiet nor your good   155
Nor for my manhood, honesty and wisdom
To let you know my thoughts.[23]

OTHELLO   Zounds![24] What dost thou mean?

IAGO
Good name in man and woman, dear my lord,
Is the immediate jewel of their souls:

---

13 Iago is suggesting that his love for Othello binds him more closely than slaves, and that he cannot reveal his thoughts, even when commanded by Othello to whom he owes duty.
14 Iago is now using the tactic of disarming Othello by actually telling the truth, which he knows will be taken in a way that harms Othello (another way of using people's virtues against them).
15 Special court sessions, often held twice yearly by the lord of the manor to sort out local legal issues.
16 Court meetings.
17 Note that Othello assumes a male camaraderie here and dispenses with military rank, suggesting that he is more at home with men than with women.
18 Mistaken.
19 'Devises, imagines' (Honigmann).
20 Imagines, conjectures.
21 Random, scattered.
22 Observation.
23 Iago's feigned attempt to conceal the bad news he must tell Othello succeeds in making Othello need to know what he has to say and so initiate the destruction of Desdemona and the tragedy.
24 The first oath uttered by Othello. Compare the language used by Iago and Roderigo to Brabantio in the opening scene.

Who steals my purse[25] steals trash – 'tis something-nothing,   160
'Twas mine, 'tis his, and has been slave to thousands –
But he that filches from me my good name
Robs me of that which not enriches him
And makes me poor indeed.[26]

OTHELLO   By heaven, I'll know thy thoughts!

IAGO
You cannot, if my heart were in your hand,   165
Nor shall not whilst 'tis in my custody.

OTHELLO
Ha!

IAGO   O beware, my lord, of jealousy!
It is the green-eyed monster, which doth mock
The meat it feeds on.[27] That cuckold lives in bliss
Who, certain of his fate, loves not his wronger,[28]   170
But O, what damned minutes tells he o'er
Who dotes yet doubts, suspects yet strongly loves!

OTHELLO
O misery!

IAGO
Poor and content is rich, and rich enough,
But riches fineless[29] is as poor as winter   175
To him that ever fears he shall be poor.[30]
Good God, the souls of all my tribe defend
From jealousy.

OTHELLO
Why – why is this?
Think'st thou I'd make a life of jealousy   180
To follow still the changes of the moon
With fresh suspicions?[31] No: to be once in doubt
Is once to be resolved.[32] Exchange me for a goat[33]

25 i.e. money. Compare Iago's advice to Roderigo when he effectively argues the opposite case (1.3.340–62).
26 Compare the advice to Cassio, 2.3.262–320. The use of the word 'souls' in line 159 suggests that we are meant to realise that Iago is deliberately echoing Cassio's words earlier.
27 Torments the victim. The image suggests self-consumption (compare the similar imagery in *Coriolanus*).
28 A deliberate prediction of the fate of Othello, who will believe himself to be a cuckold, but will be unable to ignore what he mistakenly takes to be the truth.
29 Boundless.
30 The fear of poverty for the rich is worse than the reality for those who have never known riches. The sentiment is designed to act on Othello's worst fears (see his lines at the start of this section, 90–2).
31 The moon is notoriously unstable because its movements vary (unlike those of other heavenly bodies). It is the traditional sign of inconstancy, as well as lunacy (again, a definite hint of what is in store for Othello).
32 Othello indulges in a proverbial statement (or, at least, something that sounds like a proverb). But it does him no good and fails to set his mind at rest, as the audience clearly realises.
33 Goats were notoriously lustful animals (cf. 4.1.263). Othello is also predicting his status as a cuckold (wearing the horns as a sign of his wife's infidelity).

When I shall turn the business of my soul[34]
To such exsufflicate and blown surmises,[35]   185
Matching thy inference. 'Tis not to make me jealous
To say my wife is fair, feeds well,[36] loves company,
Is free of speech, sings, plays and dances well:[37]
Where virtue is, these are more virtuous.
Nor from mine own weak merits will I draw   190
The smallest fear or doubt of her revolt,
For she had eyes and chose me.[38] No, Iago,
I'll see before I doubt, when I doubt, prove,
And on the proof there is no more but this:[39]
Away at once with love or jealousy![40]   195

IAGO

I am glad of this, for now I shall have reason
To show the love and duty that I bear you
With franker spirit: therefore, as I am bound,
Receive it from me. I speak not yet of proof:[41]
Look to your wife, observe her well with Cassio.   200
Wear your eyes thus, not jealous nor secure;
I would not have your free and noble nature
Out of self-bounty be abused:[42] look to't.
I know our country disposition well[43] –
In Venice they do let God see the pranks   205
They dare not show their husbands; their best conscience
Is not to leave't undone, but keep't unknown.[44]

OTHELLO

Dost thou say so?[45]

---

34 Like Cassio, Othello desires to have control over his soul and fears the loss of the will to do so.
35 Improbable rumours and surmises. 'Blown' implies inflated.
36 Is reliable on public social occasions and so is a good wife for a man in Othello's responsible position(?).
37 A list of many of the accomplishments demanded of women of aristocratic and gentry status in the Renaissance.
38 A line that ominously recalls Desdemona and Othello's lack of intimate knowledge of each other before they married, especially Desdemona's 'I saw Othello's visage in his mind' (1.3.253), which suggests that vision is not as straightforward a sense as Othello wishes it to be.
39 Lines that look forward to the handkerchief plot and the need for 'ocular proof' (3.3.363).
40 A dangerous equation which indicates how far Iago has succeeded already in undermining Othello's confidence. Whereas Othello contrasted love to chaos at the start of this exchange (90–2), he now wants to be rid of either and return to his former security as an army officer with friends like Iago.
41 Iago picks up Othello's word in lines 193 and 194, a characteristic trait.
42 Iago states exactly what he is doing, drawing his victim in by showing his knowledge of human nature, and then attacking what he purports to be defending.
43 Iago, despite his Spanish name, assumes a Venetian identity, whether by birth or by culture.
44 A reference to the reputation of Venetian women for promiscuity and liberal attitudes to sexuality (see above, **pp. 25–8, 78–83**). Othello's status as an outsider who needs to be informed and protected by the insider, Iago, is established.
45 The normal relationship between superiors and inferiors in the army is reversed, and Othello has to look up to Iago to help him understand his predicament.

IAGO

> She did deceive her father, marrying you,
> And when she seemed to shake, and fear your looks,   210
> She loved them most.[46]

OTHELLO   And so she did.

IAGO   Why, go to then:

> She that so young could give out such a seeming[47]
> To seel[48] her father's eyes up, close as oak[49] –
> He thought 'twas witchcraft.[50] But I am much to blame,
> I humbly do beseech you of your pardon   215
> For too much loving you.[51]

OTHELLO

> I am bound to thee for ever.[52]

IAGO

> I see this hath a little dashed your spirits.[53]

OTHELLO

> Not a jot, not a jot.

IAGO   I'faith, I fear it has.

> I hope you will consider what is spoke   220
> Comes from my love.[54] But I do see you're moved;
> I am to pray you not to strain[55] my speech
> To grosser[56] issues nor to larger reach
> Than to suspicion.

OTHELLO

> I will not.

IAGO   Should you do so, my lord,   225

> My speech should fall into such vile success
> As my thoughts aimed not at: Cassio's my worthy friend.[57]
> My lord, I see you're moved.

---

46 Iago plays on Othello's fears of being despised in Venice because of his race. It is a sign of Othello's nervousness and his lack of knowledge of his wife that he agrees with Iago's reading of the situation between Desdemona and himself.

47 Pretence.

48 Close. The allusion is to falconry as young hawks had their eyes seeled (hooded) in training to make them obedient.

49 A proverb, meaning as close together as grains in wood.

50 A reference that links Brabantio's assertions and fears to Othello's superstitious faith in the power of the handkerchief (an aspect of the plot especially loathed by Thomas Rymer (see above, pp. 44–7)).

51 Again, Iago's cleverness is in his audacious hypocrisy.

52 Another prediction that says more than Othello knows at this point in the play. It is further demonstrates the reversal of ranks in the relationship between the two men.

53 An obvious understatement that shows how important preserving a calm exterior is for military men.

54 Again Iago covers his villainy with the pretence of love.

55 Over-interpret, over-elaborate.

56 More substantial or more overtly sexual.

57 Iago, as he often does, predicts the exact effects of his words, denies that he intends the effect they will have, and so ensures his success.

OTHELLO   No, not much moved.
I do not think but Desdemona's honest.[58]

IAGO
Long live she so; and long live you to think so.[59]   230

OTHELLO
And yet how nature, erring from itself[60] –

IAGO
Ay, there's the point: as, to be bold with you,
Not to affect many proposed matches
Of her own clime,[61] complexion[62] and degree,
Whereto we see, in all things, nature tends[63] –   235
Foh! one may smell[64] in such a will[65] most rank,[66]
Foul disproportion, thoughts unnatural.[67]
But pardon me, I do not in position
Distinctly speak of her,[68] though I may fear
Her will, recoiling[69] to her better judgement,[70]   240
May fall to match you with her country forms,[71]
And happily[72] repent.

OTHELLO   Farewell, farewell.
If more thou dost perceive, let me know more:
Set on thy wife to observe. Leave me, Iago.

---

58 The word 'honest' links Desdemona to Iago in Othello's imagination, showing how the statement in line 217 has become a truth that will trigger the tragic denouement.

59 Yet more irony given how short a time both have to live in a naturalistic and tightly constructed play which takes place over a few days.

60 A line which shows how much Iago has undermined Othello's confidence and how fragile Othello's universe has become. The chaos he fears if Desdemona is untrue manifests itself in his perception that nature is in crisis.

61 Climate, region. Refers to the theory that people from the same geographical area developed the same appearance and characteristics.

62 i.e. colour.

63 Iago is suggesting that Desdemona has acted against nature in marrying Othello rather than one of her own kind, because people naturally choose a partner from their own rank, class, society and colour. Othello's doubts about her faithfulness have enabled Iago to press his plot even further.

64 Suspect. 'Smell' invariably indicates foul behaviour in Shakespeare; cf. Claudius' description of his guilt: 'my offence is rank, it smells to heaven' (*Hamlet* 3.3.36).

65 Purpose, desire (carnal). 'Will' had a huge variety of meanings in Renaissance English, of which Shakespeare, being called 'Will', makes use. Cf. the meanings generated in Sonnets 135 and 136. Its sexual overtones are invariably important.

66 Literally foul-smelling, rancid, but signifying corrupt, lascivious (Sanders).

67 In these lines Iago has expanded Othello's initial comment to make sure that Othello follows Iago's train of thought. Compare his treatment of Brabantio in the opening scene, where he makes Brabantio's fears more real by conjuring up verbal images before his eyes. Iago later works more aggressively on Othello when he describes his supposed encounter with Cassio in the barracks (3.3.416–42).

68 Speak specifically of her.

69 Returning.

70 Iago implies that Desdemona has married Othello in a fit of lust or passion and will eventually repent of her error and return to her natural kind.

71 I.e. will start to compare you (unfavourably) with her own countrymen.

72 Possibly. The modern meaning is also present, reinforcing Iago's representation of a natural order that Othello's marriage has violated.

IAGO

My lord, I take my leave.

OTHELLO   Why did I marry?   245

This honest[73] creature doubtless

Sees[74] and knows more – much more – than he unfolds.

IAGO

My lord, I would I might entreat your honour

To scan[75] this thing no farther. Leave it to time;

Although 'tis fit that Cassio have his place,   250

For sure he fills it up with great ability,[76]

Yet if you please to hold him off a while

You shall by that perceive him, and his means:

Note if your lady strain his entertainment[77]

With any strong or vehement importunity,   255

Much will be seen in that. In the meantime

Let me be thought too busy[78] in my fears

– As worthy cause I have to fear I am[79] –

And hold her free,[80] I do beseech your honour.

OTHELLO

Fear not my government.[81]   260

IAGO

I once more take my leave.   *Exit.*

OTHELLO

This fellow's of exceeding honesty

And knows all qualities, with a learned spirit,

Of human dealings.[82] If I do prove her haggard,[83]

Though that her jesses[84] were my dear heart-strings,   265

I'd whistle her off and let her down the wind[85]

To prey at fortune.[86] Haply for[87] I am black

---

73 cf. line 229.

74 Again, note the emphasis on sight in a play which is based on the visual difference of its protagonist.

75 Scrutinise (Sanders).

76 Iago says the opposite of what he really means, given that he is partly motivated against Othello by his sense of injustice that Cassio has been promoted over him, as he states in his first speech in the play (1.1.7–32). This motive more clearly developed in Cinthio's narrative (see above, pp. 19–20).

77 Insist on his reinstatement (Honigmann).

78 Interfering.

79 Iago gives the appearance of blunt honesty through minor self-criticism (a frequent tactic).

80 Consider her to be innocent.

81 Self-government. The word reminds the audience of the crucial link between personal and public behaviour.

82 Othello is right that Iago is a keen student of human behaviour.

83 Wild, untamed.

84 The straps tied round a hawk's feet to fasten it the falconer's wrist.

85 i.e. set her free before she is ready.

86 To fend for herself. Hawks released too early would inevitably die, again emphasising the way in which the metaphor undermines Othello's position.

87 Perhaps because.

And have not those soft parts of conversation
That chamberers[88] have, or for I am declined
Into the vale of years[89] – yet that's not much –   270
She's gone, I am abused,[90] and my relief
Must be to loathe her. O curse of marriage
That we can call these delicate creatures ours
And not their appetites![91] I had rather be a toad[92]
And live upon the vapour of a dungeon   275
Than keep a corner[93] in the thing I love
For others' uses. Yet 'tis the plague of great ones,
Prerogatived[94] are they less than the base;
'Tis destiny unshunnable,[95] like death[96] –
Even then this forked plague[97] is fated to us   280
When we do quicken.[98]

Act 3, Scene 3, lines 333–482

This scene shows Othello transformed into the state of chaos that he felt his marriage to Desdemona protected him from. Othello claims that Iago has set him 'on the rack' (339). The rack was the most extreme instrument of torture in Elizabethan England. Victims were tied to a wooden table and a wheel was turned which stretched them until their limbs were dislocated and broken. Virtually no one managed to keep silent when tortured in this way and no one survived unscathed because the damage to the victim was permanent. Othello's choice of imagery is indeed pertinent and expressive of his suffering.

Iago continues to prey on Othello's worst fears. He appeals first to Othello's sense of masculinity, obviously having noted his general's representation of himself as a military man more comfortable with other men. Then he preys on Othello's fear that, as an African in Venetian society, he may not be fully human. The persona he adopts is equally important. In his speech (377–83) Iago pretends to be debating his actions with himself and assumes the guise of the

88 Court gallants, indicating their frequenting of ladies' chambers. Othello again emphasises his military experience among men.
89 Alluding to 'the valley of the shadow of death' (Psalms 23:4).
90 Deceived, disgraced (Sanders).
91 Othello has already accepted Iago's story that Desdemona's nature and reason are at odds.
92 Traditionally a loathsome creature notable for producing poison and so used by witches (cf. Macbeth, 4.1.6–9).
93 Reserve a small place.
94 Privileged.
95 Inescapable.
96 Another sign of how unstable Othello's universe is and how he veers towards thoughts of death when his love proves not to be as secure as he would wish it to be.
97 Forked means horned. Othello means the plague of all husbands that their wives will cuckold them.
98 Are conceived or born. Othello sees life as a cycle of misery.

wounded friend knowing that Othello's anger will turn away from him and to Desdemona (especially after he has begun his speech with a hint that Othello should trust men more than women because they both know that the former are more reliable and honest (see Empson, **pp. 59–62**)). He then suggests that the world has become strange, unfamiliar and frightening: no longer fit for honest and straightforward men like the two of them. These lines also recall the monsters Othello described when wooing Desdemona (1.3.129–70), showing that Othello can deal with such exotic and strange creatures but not ones closer to home.

When Othello plans to wreak a dreadful vengeance on his wife, he is once again in control of his language. He signals this in his reference to the 'Hellespont' (459), an exotic location that also reminds the audience of his earlier 'traveller's speech'. The Hellespont is the Dardanelles Straits, notorious for their strong currents. In classical mythology the Hellespont gets its name from Helle, daughter of Athamas and Nephelle, who fled from her father and stepmother on a golden ram. When Helle fell off its back into the sea the place was named the Hellespont. In the legend of Hero and Leander (retold by Christopher Marlowe in a version published in 1598), Leander meets his death when dragged down by Neptune while swimming across the Hellespont to meet Hero. Othello's image has a variety of associations: his purpose is now as unstoppable as a force of nature; his course of action will be like a furious and violent outburst like the currents of the Hellespont; and the inevitable result will be premature death. His image of 'marble heaven' reinforces this image. Marble implies a stony indifference to the fate of humans below. Othello sees the universe in terms of classical tragedy, notably those of Sophocles (496–406 BCE), who represents the Gods as uninterested and unwilling to alter the fate of suffering humans on earth.

Enter OTHELLO.

IAGO
[. . .]
Look where he[1] comes. Not poppy nor mandragora[2]
Nor all the drowsy[3] syrups of the world
Shall ever medicine thee to that sweet sleep   335
Which thou owedst[4] yesterday.
OTHELLO   Ha! Ha! false to me?[5]

---

1   Othello.
2   The juice of the mandrake plant. Like poppy, it is a sedative.
3   Sleep-inducing.
4   Possessed.
5   Note how the control Othello has over language is now slipping away.

IAGO

    Why, how now, general? No more of that.[6]

OTHELLO

    Avaunt, be gone, thou hast set me on the rack!
    I swear 'tis better to be much abused[7]
    Than but to know't a little.[8]

IAGO   How now, my lord?   340

OTHELLO

    What sense had I of her stolen hours of lust?
    I saw't[9] not, thought it not, it harmed not me,
    I slept the next night well, fed well, was free[10] and merry;
    I found not Cassio's kisses on her lips;[11]
    He that is robbed, not wanting what is stolen,   345
    Let him not know't, and he's not robbed at all.

IAGO

    I am sorry to hear this.

OTHELLO

    I had been happy if the general camp,[12]
    Pioneers[13] and all, had tasted her sweet body,
    So I had nothing known.[14] O now for ever   350
    Farewell the tranquil mind, farewell content![15]
    Farewell the plumed troops[16] and the big[17] wars
    That makes ambition virtue! O farewell,
    Farewell the neighing steed and the shrill trump,[18]
    The spirit-stirring drum, th'ear-piercing fife,   355
    The royal banner, and all quality,
    Pride, pomp and circumstance of glorious war![19]
    And, O you mortal engines[20] whose rude throats
    Th'immortal Jove's dread clamours[21] counterfeit,

---

6 Iago openly – and contemptuously – assumes control.
7 Wronged, deceived (Honigmann).
8 A graphic reworking of the cliché that a little knowledge is a dangerous thing.
9 Again, note the emphasis on the visual imagination.
10 Compare Othello's use of the falconry metaphor earlier in the scene in lines 266–7.
11 Another key concept in the play, the need to have tangible proof.
12 i.e. army.
13 The lowest rank of soldier, required to carry spades, pickaxes and so on for other soldiers. Sometimes soldiers were demoted to the rank of pioneer for misdemeanours.
14 Compare the imagery of military debauchery that surrounds both Helen and Cressida in *Troilus and Cressida*.
15 The chaos that Othello feared has come to haunt him.
16 Giving a sense of military display.
17 Important. Othello states that the military encounters which made his reputation and gave him a sense of worth are now in the past and cannot comfort him.
18 Trumpet.
19 These lines do not show Othello in a wholly favourable light and show how closely his identity and success are tied to violent struggle.
20 i.e. cannons.
21 i.e. thunder.

Farewell: Othello's occupation's gone.[22]   360
IAGO
    Is't possible? my lord?
OTHELLO
    Villain, be sure thou prove my love a whore,
    Be sure of it, give me the ocular proof,[23]   [*Catching hold of him*]
    Or by the worth of man's eternal soul
    Thou hadst been better have been born a dog   365
    Than answer my waked wrath![24]
IAGO   Is't come to this?
OTHELLO
    Make me to see't, or at the least so prove it
    That the probation[25] bear no hinge nor loop
    To hang a doubt on, or woe upon thy life!
IAGO
    My noble lord –   370
OTHELLO
    If thou dost slander her and torture me
    Never pray more, abandon all remorse;[26]
    On horror's head horrors accumulate,
    Do deeds to make heaven weep, all earth amazed,
    For nothing canst thou to damnation add   375
    Greater than that![27]
IAGO   O grace! O heaven forgive me!
    Are you a man? have you a soul, or sense?
    God buy you,[28] take mine office.[29] O wretched fool
    That lov'st to make thine honesty a vice!
    O monstrous world! Take note, take note, O world,   380
    To be direct and honest is not safe.[30]
    I thank you for this profit, and from hence

---

22 Othello is referring specifically to his military career, but this only serves to show how much his identity is tied to the military.

23 The clearest demand for visual evidence. Othello's need to catch his wife out shows how easily he has adopted Iago's way of seeing.

24 Referring to the common belief that the possession of a soul distinguished men from animals. Iago can only escape punishment if he becomes a beast rather than a man. Othello, as he does throughout the play, sees the world in terms of absolutes, heaven and hell.

25 Proof.

26 A possible echo of the words written on the gates of hell in Dante's *Inferno*, a work which Shakespeare could easily have known: 'All hope abandon, ye who enter here' (*Inferno*, canto III, line 9).

27 The suggestion that Iago may as well commit more horrific acts because he has committed such a terrible sin if he has lied about Desdemona recalls Macbeth's sense that there is no point in turning back from his course of action because he is 'in blood/Stepp'd in so far, that, should I wade no more,/Returning were as tedious as go o'er' (3.4.135–7).

28 God be with you, God help you.

29 i.e. Take away my commission, ignore my friendship, 'position of trust' (Honigmann).

30 Iago claims that the world is wrong, not men like himself. Again, this is designed to appeal to Othello's paranoia.

I'll love no friend, sith[31] love breeds such offence.

OTHELLO

Nay, stay, thou shouldst be honest.[32]

IAGO

I should be wise, for honesty's a fool   385
And loses that it works for.

OTHELLO   By the world,[33]
I think my wife be honest, and think she is not,
I think that thou art just, and think thou art not.
I'll have[34] some proof. Her name, that was as fresh
As Dian's visage,[35] is now begrimed and black   390
As mine own face.[36] If there be cords or knives,
Poison, or fire, or suffocating streams,
I'll not endure it.[37] Would I were satisfied![38]

IAGO

I see, sir, you are eaten up with passion.[39]
I do repent me that I put it to you.   395
You would be satisfied?

OTHELLO   Would? nay, and I will![40]

IAGO

And may – but how? how satisfied, my lord?
Would you, the supervisor,[41] grossly gape on?
Behold her topped?[42]

OTHELLO   Death and damnation! O!

IAGO

It were a tedious difficulty, I think,   400
To bring them to that prospect.[43] Damn them then

---

31 As, since.
32 Iago has manipulated Othello into accepting the world-view he has created in the previous speech, that the world is at odds with their desire to be honest and that both are victims of its treachery.
33 A common oath. The ambiguity that Othello expresses shows that Iago has shattered his sense of security and trust in appearances.
34 I must have. Again, the need for (visual) evidence is stressed.
35 Diana, the goddess of chastity.
36 Othello shows that he accepts the denigration of black as a colour signifying moral decay or evil (just as Desdemona does 1.3.253).
37 Othello implies that the best way of dealing with such radical instability and personal misery is to commit suicide. The list of weapons refers to the possible methods that he might use. The lines show how tormented Othello is when his certainty in the things dear to him is challenged.
38 Certain, sure.
39 Iago is suggesting that Othello is not being a proper man in giving way to the excessive nature of his passions.
40 Yet again Othello has taken the debate enabling Iago to ensnare him further by demanding proof (Iago has clearly already planned the handkerchief plot).
41 Spectator, onlooker.
42 cf. 1.1.88. Iago, as he has done throughout the play, conjures up vivid images which will then help him establish what his victim imagines is proof. Compare his words to Brabantio in 1.1.84–157.
43 'view, spectacle' (Honigmann).

If ever mortal eyes do see them bolster[44]
More[45] than their own. What then? how then?
What shall I say? where's satisfaction?
It is impossible you should see this   405
Were they as prime as goats, as hot[46] as monkeys,
As salt[47] as wolves in pride,[48] and fools as gross
As ignorance made drunk. But yet, I say,
If imputation[49] and strong circumstances
Which lead directly to the door of truth   410
Will give you satisfaction, you may have't.

OTHELLO
Give me a living[50] reason she's disloyal.

IAGO
I do not like the office.[51]
But sith I am entered in this cause so far,
Pricked[52] to't by foolish honesty and love,   415
I will go on. I lay with Cassio lately
And being troubled with a raging tooth
I could not sleep. There are a kind of men
So loose of soul that in their sleeps will mutter
Their affairs – one of this kind is Cassio.[53]   420
In sleep I heard him say 'Sweet Desdemona,
Let us be wary, let us hide our loves,'
And then, sir, would he gripe and wring my hand,
Cry 'O sweet creature!' and then kiss me hard
As if he plucked up kisses by the roots   425
That grew upon my lips, lay his leg o'er my thigh,
And sigh, and kiss, and then cry 'Cursed fate
That gave thee to the Moor!'[54]

---

44 Go to bed together; perhaps meaning 'share the same pillow' (Sanders). Given that Othello
    smothers Desdemona after Iago's suggestion (4.1.204–7), this may have an especially sinister
    connotation.
45 Other.
46 Sexually excited.
47 Lustful.
48 Lust. Iago produces images of animals thought to be especially bestial and lustful to poison
    Othello's imagination.
49 Attribution.
50 Valid.
51 Task, duty.
52 Encouraged. The image is that of a horse being urged on by the rider's spurs, implying that Iago is
    helpless in his need to tell the truth, a virtue that always lands him in difficult situations.
53 Iago deliberately represents Cassio as the opposite of himself: a loose-tongued boaster, not a tight-
    lipped and trustworthy friend.
54 This speech may depend for its effect on the fact that all actors were male and so be hinting at the sort of
    relationship between men that was inevitably performed on stage, even if the story narrated a hetero-
    sexual relationship. Such self-consciously theatrical references were far more common in comedies,
    illustrating that the close links between the plot of Othello and some of the comedies was quite
    deliberate and an important aspect of its tragic plot. There is also a sly hint at the sort of relationships
    and closeness encouraged by the herding of men together in army barracks. Iago knows that

OTHELLO   O monstrous! monstrous![55]

IAGO

   Nay, this was but his dream.[56]

OTHELLO

   But this denoted a foregone conclusion.[57]   430

IAGO

   'Tis a shrewd doubt,[58] though it be but a dream,
   And this may help to thicken[59] other proofs
   That do demonstrate thinly.[60]

OTHELLO

   I'll tear her all to pieces![61]

IAGO

   Nay, yet be wise, yet we see nothing done,   435
   She may be honest yet. Tell me but this,
   Have you not sometimes seen a handkerchief
   Spotted with strawberries,[62] in your wife's hand?

OTHELLO

   I gave her such a one, 'twas my first gift.

IAGO

   I know not that, but such a handkerchief,   440
   I am sure it was your wife's, did I today
   See Cassio wipe his beard with.

OTHELLO   If it be that –

IAGO

   If it be that, or any that was hers,
   It speaks against her with the other proofs.[63]

OTHELLO

   O that the slave[64] had forty thousand lives!   445
   One is too poor, too weak for my revenge.
   Now do I see 'tis true. Look here, Iago,
   All my fond love thus do I blow to heaven:
   'Tis gone!

Othello will believe him, showing that his story is plausible, perhaps repeating other known incidents in the army.

55 Othello is, of course, right, but not in the way he thinks.

56 Iago now holds back, letting Othello make the running and absorb the impact of the story himself.

57 i.e. something that had already happened.

58 'suspicion, fear' (Honigmann).

59 Establish.

60 Having lured Othello into a world of suspicion, doubt and innuendo, Iago can now establish 'proof' on his terms, making the pretence of independent verifiability that Othello craves a fiction.

61 Othello is now turning into the violent, irrational savage that many Europeans perceive him to be.

62 Such handkerchiefs were fashionable and highly valued among Elizabethans. The strawberries may symbolise purity, or hint at a hidden evil.

63 Iago moves quickly and easily from telling Othello that he cannot be certain that Desdemona is unfaithful to asserting that there is proof against Desdemona. He is able to do this because he has established Othello's fears so carefully in this scene.

64 i.e. Cassio.

Arise, black vengeance, from the hollow hell,   450
Yield up, O love, thy crown and hearted throne
To tyrannous hate! Swell, bosom, with thy fraught,
For 'tis of aspics'[65] tongues![66]

IAGO   Yet be content!

OTHELLO
O blood, blood, blood![67]   *Othello kneels.*

IAGO
Patience, I say, your mind perhaps may change.[68]   455

OTHELLO
Never, Iago. Like to the Pontic sea[69]
Whose icy current and compulsive course
Ne'er keeps retiring ebb but keeps due on
To the Propontic[70] and the Hellespont:
Even so my bloody thoughts with violent pace   460
Shall ne'er look back, ne'er ebb to humble love
Till that a capable and wide revenge
Swallow them up. Now by yond marble heaven
In the due reverence of a sacred vow
I here engage my words.[71]

IAGO   Do not rise yet.   *Iago kneels.*
Witness, you ever-burning lights above,   466
You elements that clip[72] us round about,
Witness that here Iago doth give up
The execution of his wit, hands, heart,
To wronged Othello's service. Let him command   470
And to obey shall be in me remorse
What bloody business ever.[73]

OTHELLO   I greet thy love
Not with vain thanks but with acceptance bounteous,
And will upon the instant put thee to't.
Within these three days let me hear thee say   475
That Cassio's not alive.

IAGO   My friend[74] is dead,

---

65 Asps. Cleopatra died when she applied an asp to her bosom (*Antony and Cleopatra*, 5.2.279–311).
66 One of the clearest expressions Othello gives of his conception of the universe, divided between heaven and hell.
67 Again, Othello's savagery is emphasised by the repetition of words, showing how his eloquence and rhetorical control are disappearing.
68 Iago's suggestion is designed to make Othello stick more resolutely to the path he has chosen.
69 The Black Sea.
70 The Sea of Marmora, which connects the Black Sea and the Aegean Sea.
71 Othello's vow and the mock-ceremony with Iago serves as a parody of Christian ceremony and shows how Othello has divested himself of the trappings of Christianity in his thirst for revenge.
72 Encompass.
73 i.e. Iago will do anything for Othello because he feels pity for his suffering. Iago pretends that Othello is still the master and gives the general the illusion that he is still in control.
74 Iago casts Cassio as his friend to make his killing seem an even greater sacrifice, and to add greater power to his false pleading for the life of Desdemona.

’Tis done – at your request. But let her live.[75]

OTHELLO

    Damn her, lewd minx:[76] O damn her, damn her![77]
    Come, go with me apart; I will withdraw
    To furnish me with some swift means of death   480
    For the fair devil.[78] Now art thou my lieutenant.[79]

IAGO   I am your own for ever.[80]

Act 4, Scene 1, lines 60–142

In this scene Iago proves his mastery over Othello, forcing him to watch as he questions Cassio about Bianca when Othello thinks that they are talking about Desdemona. Iago assumes control at the start of the passage, showing how his plea to serve Othello easily fooled the general. He taunts Othello with a lack of masculinity, something the general finds hard to bear (see above, **pp. 150–1**). The theme of monsters and monstrosity again assumes importance. Othello has been turned into a beast and a monster, but not in the way that he imagines.

Iago uses a series of degrading images to demean Othello. He refers to Othello's marriage as a 'yoke' (see note to line 66); later (line 89) he refers to him as 'all in spleen' (the organ that was thought to govern passion and melancholy). In the fashionable 'comedies of humours' produced at the time that *Othello* was performed, characters were represented as having an excess of one humour – bile, phlegm, choler and blood – which made them especially vicious, indolent, angry or lecherous. Iago suggests that Othello is rather like a character in a play such as Ben Jonson's *Every Man in His Humour* (1598), again showing how often *Othello* alludes to comedy and deliberately makes use of comic images, motifs and structures.

Cassio's treatment of Bianca and his laughter at the mention of her suffering for him (100) is indicative of how men use women in the play. There is an obvious irony in Iago's slander of Desdemona and the bad reputation of Venetian women that enables Iago's plot to work at all. The women in the play – Desdemona, Emilia and Bianca – are all shown in a sympathetic light (see Jardine above, **pp. 84–91**). The reference to laughter also points out the links between *Othello* and Renaissance comedy. The scene we witness with Othello hiding while he mistakes what he sees and hears resembles scenes in plays by

---

75 Iago knows that after his vow this will persuade Othello to kill her.
76 Lascivious and worthless woman.
77 Othello mixes theological language and notions with a pagan conception of the universe. His understanding of Christian ideas serves only to make his revenge seem even more extreme and ruthless, as he wishes Desdemona to suffer the torments of hell after her death.
78 Again, the use of the coded colour scheme is notable.
79 A moment of bathos; after all this intensity, Iago finally gets his desired promotion.
80 Emphasising to the audience that the fate of the two men is inextricably linked.

Roman authors such as Terence and Plautus, as well as Shakespeare's *The Comedy of Errors* (early 1590s). Again we are reminded how easily the play might have been resolved in a comic manner with a few different twists in the plot.

The last line cited here shows how vicious Othello has become, however. The reference to Cassio's nose being thrown to a dog is undoubtedly obscure and has troubled commentators. The sense of violence is clear enough, and it is likely that 'nose' can stand for 'penis', showing that Othello wishes to dismember the man who has seduced his wife. Othello has now become a bloodthirsty and vengeful savage, his eloquence gone, replaced by curt and vicious threats. It is possible that the key reference is in line 119 when Othello refers to Cassio as a 'Roman'. Romans were renowned for their prominent noses (see below, note 36). If this is the case, then the passage recalls the action of one of Shakespeare's first plays, *Titus Andronicus* (c.1593), in which the triumphant Romans contrive to fall into dissension, allowing the barbarians to wield a destructive influence on life in Rome. One of the cruellest characters is Aaron the Moor. Othello's threat recalls the words and actions of Aaron in the earlier play.

OTHELLO

    Dost thou mock me?

IAGO   I mock you? no, by heaven!   60

    Would you would bear your fortune like a man!

OTHELLO

    A horned man's[1] a monster, and a beast.

IAGO

    There's many a beast then in a populous city,

    And many a civil monster.[2]

OTHELLO

    Did he confess it?

IAGO   Good sir, be a man,[3]   65

    Think every bearded fellow[4] that's but yoked[5]

    May draw with you. There's millions now alive

    That nightly lie in those unproper beds

---

1   A cuckold.

2   Is Iago taunting Othello by admitting his guilt here, and showing Othello that his problem is that he does not really know where to look for the evil that afflicts him? Or is he simply referring to Cassio as an urbane and civilised Florentine who is really a monster?

3   Iago taunts and manipulates Othello as he does Roderigo.

4   i.e. old enough to be an adult and so have responsibilities and troubles.

5   Married. The image is also one of oxen pulling a cart together. Iago means that Othello needs to bear his troubles like a man because everyone has them (so indicating that what he claims is true is commonplace and to be expected in Venice). He also suggests that because Othello is a great man he should deal with them in accordance with his status (by killing his wife). The image of the bearded man pulling with him also has an obscene connotation, of the bearded Cassio sharing his wife.

Which they dare swear peculiar:[6] your case is better.
O, 'tis the spite of hell,[7] the fiend's arch-mock,[8]   70
To lip[9] a wanton[10] in a secure couch[11]
And to suppose[12] her chaste. No, let me know,
And, knowing what I am, I know what she shall be.[13]

OTHELLO
    O, thou art wise, 'tis certain.

IAGO
    Stand you a while apart,   75
    Confine yourself but in a patient list.[14]
    Whilst you were here o'erwhelmed with your grief
    – A passion most unsuiting such a man[15] –
    Cassio came hither. I shifted him away[16]
    And laid good 'scuse upon your ecstasy,[17]   80
    Bade him anon return and here speak with me,
    The which he promised. Do but encave[18] yourself
    And mark the fleers,[19] the gibes and notable scorns
    That dwell in every region of his face;
    For I will make him tell the tale anew   85
    Where, how, how oft, how long ago, and when
    He hath and is again to cope[20] your wife.
    I say, but mark his gesture; marry, patience,
    Or I shall say you're all in all in spleen[21]
    And nothing of a man.

OTHELLO   Dost thou hear, Iago?   90
    I will be found most cunning in my patience
    But – dost thou hear? – most bloody.

IAGO   That's not amiss,
    But yet keep time[22] in all. Will you withdraw?   [*Othello withdraws.*]

---

  6 Their own.
  7 Iago appeals to Othello's sense of the punitive and indifferent universe.
  8 Chief insult.
  9 Kiss.
 10 Unfaithful woman.
 11 Safe bed.
 12 Imagine.
 13 The sense is that Iago knows because he understands human nature and so knows what women
     such as Desdemona are like. The implication is that he has made everything up and that people
     conform to his fictions.
 14 i.e. control yourself and be patient.
 15 Iago again implies that Othello can deal with the problem if he reasserts his masculine control and
     gets on with the job of murdering his wife rather than indulging in womanly grief at his unfortunate
     situation.
 16 Got him out of the way.
 17 Trance, fit.
 18 Hide.
 19 Sneers.
 20 Meet, copulate with.
 21 Turned completely into spleen (see my comment on **p. 155**).
 22 Retain control.

Now will I question Cassio of Bianca,
A housewife[23] that by selling her desires   95
Buys herself bread and clothes: it is a creature[24]
That dotes on Cassio – as 'tis the strumpet's plague
To beguile many and be beguiled by one.[25]
He, when he hears of her, cannot refrain
From the excess of laughter. Here he comes.   100

Enter CASSIO.

As he shall smile, Othello shall go mad.
And his unbookish[26] jealousy must construe
Poor Cassio's smiles, gestures and light[27] behaviour
Quite in the wrong. How do you now, lieutenant?
CASSIO
The worser, that you give me the addition[28]   105
Whose want even kills me.[29]
IAGO
Ply[30] Desdemona well, and you are sure on't.[31]
[*Speaking lower*] Now if this suit lay in Bianca's power
How quickly should you speed!
CASSIO   Alas, poor caitiff![32]
OTHELLO
Look how he laughs already!   110
IAGO
I never knew a woman love man so.
CASSIO
Alas, poor rogue,[33] I think i'faith she loves me.
OTHELLO
Now he denies it faintly,[34] and laughs it out.[35]

---

23 Possibly a loaded description. Housewife could be pronounced as 'hussy', a prostitute, showing
    how respectability and the underworld were often closely linked through puns and allusions (com-
    pare the use of 'nunnery' meaning brothel in *Hamlet*, 3.1.151). It is also a sign of Iago's sneering
    contempt for women.
24 Note how Iago dehumanises the unfortunate Bianca.
25 Proverbial. Iago's words could be applied to many in the play and recall Brabantio's words to
    Othello (1.3.293–4).
26 Unlettered, unlearned. Iago is showing his contempt for Othello's origins as an African (an irony,
    of course, given Othello's studied and careful use of rhetoric throughout the play and the learned
    allusions contained in his speech explaining how he won Desdemona's heart (1.3.129–70)).
27 Frivolous (with the implication of flirtatious sexuality).
28 Title.
29 A reminder to the audience that Iago is now Othello's lieutenant.
30 Manipulate, work on.
31 'sure to get what you want' (Honigmann).
32 Wretch.
33 Probably a term of endearment, albeit rather patronising.
34 Without conviction, falsely.
35 Laughs it off.

IAGO
    Do you hear, Cassio?
OTHELLO   Now he importunes him
    To tell it o'er; go to, well said, well said.   115
IAGO
    She gives it out that you shall marry her;
    Do you intend it?
CASSIO
    Ha, ha, ha!
OTHELLO
    Do ye triumph, Roman,[36] do you triumph?
CASSIO   I marry! What, a customer![37] prithee bear some   120
    charity to my wit,[38] do not think it so unwholesome.[39]
    Ha, ha, ha!
OTHELLO   So, so, so, so: they laugh that win.[40]
IAGO   Faith, the cry goes that you shall marry her.
CASSIO   Prithee say true!   125
IAGO   I am a very villain else.[41]
OTHELLO   Have you stored me?[42] Well.
CASSIO   This is the monkey's[43] own giving out. She is
    persuaded I will marry her, out of her own love and
    flattery, not out of my promise.[44]   130
OTHELLO   Iago beckons me: now he begins the story.
CASSIO   She was here even now, she haunts me in every
    place. I was the other day talking on the sea-bank[45]
    with certain Venetians, and thither comes the bauble[46]
    and, by this hand, falls me thus about my neck –   135
OTHELLO   Crying 'O dear Cassio!' as it were: his gesture
    imports it.
CASSIO   So hangs and lolls[47] and weeps upon me, so
    shakes and pulls me! Ha, ha, ha!

36 Othello imagines Cassio as a triumphant Roman returning with his trophies of war. The reference
    may be to *Julius Caesar* (1599). Caesar returned in triumph over his rivals in the bloody civil war only
    to be murdered by the republican faction led by Brutus. Given that Othello later refers to Cassio's
    nose (141), the suggestion may be that Cassio has a Roman nose. Romans were supposed to have
    prominent noses. Of course, the lines may be highlighting the nose of the actor who played Cassio.
37 Cassio's perception of Bianca is quite clear.
38 Give me some credit for common sense.
39 Defective.
40 Indicating that Cassio's laughter will soon cease and the laughter of the revenger will replace it.
41 Iago, yet again, actually tells the truth knowing that it cannot be read by the characters on stage,
    only by the audience.
42 Honigmann suggests this is a reference to providing 'for the continuance of a stock or breed', i.e.
    Cassio is siring the children Othello should be. Sanders suggests the reading 'scored', and interprets
    this to mean either (*a*) branded or wounded, or (*b*) cuckolded.
43 Another playful term of affection for a foolish child.
44 Cassio revels in his power over someone less powerful than himself being deceived while Iago uses
    him as a dupe in his plot, a good example of the power games taking place in the play.
45 Coast or seashore.
46 'Worthless plaything' (Sanders).
47 Dangles.

OTHELLO   Now he tells how she plucked him to my   140
chamber. O, I see that nose of yours, but not that
dog I shall throw it to.

Act 4, Scene 2, lines 30–92

This scene shows how clearly Othello has accepted Iago's world view and cannot be changed from his course of action – as he stated (see above, **p. 154**) – whatever Desdemona protests. Desdemona's opening words refer the audience back to the trial scene (1.3) and the explanation of their falling in love. The lack of knowledge they have of each other is now exposed: a gap has become a chasm. In addition we are invited to consider how the noble Othello has been transformed from an eloquent warrior who could explain what he meant to someone whose anger prevents him from speaking in a straightforward way. The ambiguity of Iago's speech has changed Othello's language. Othello now imagines that everything is deceptive and is really the opposite of what it appears to be. In a sense the logic that he adopts resembles the racist assumption exhibited throughout the play that black is an evil colour and black people can only be good when they have white souls. Furthermore, Othello now has to choose between the honesty of his wife and the honesty of Iago (see line 66). He chooses Iago, which contrasts to Desdemona's choice of Othello over her father and shows just how deluded he has become.

Othello's use of theological language (e.g. 'damn', line 35) casts him as the righteous avenger who can perform God's work for him. Compare the role of Hieronimo in Thomas Kyd's *The Spanish Tragedy* (c.1589), when he decides that he must avenge the murder of his son after the mechanisms of state fail to track down Horatio's killers. It is clear that Hieronimo is wrong to take the course of action that he does because the audience would have been acutely conscious of the biblical injunction, 'avenge not yourselves, but *rather* give place unto wrath: for it is written, Vengeance *is* mine; I will repay, saith the Lord' (Romans 12:19). Othello shows that his understanding of Christianity is limited.

The powerful and disturbing image of Desdemona being no more honest than summer flies is a complex and bitter commentary on the state of their marriage as Othello sees it (lines 67–70). Othello refers to flies growing in slaughter-houses as babies do in the womb ('quicken'). The implicit suggestion is that the hopes the couple might have had of the normal course of marriage – i.e. having children – have turned to a disgusting and repellent legacy. Flies were thought to receive life and grow from the wind. Othello implies that Desdemona values the sexual act no more highly (and risks an unwanted pregnancy from her adulterous lover).

When Othello then refers to Desdemona as a book upon which the word 'whore' has been written (lines 72–3), he repeats what Iago has done. Othello has read the book that Iago has written, not what Desdemona actually is. The men have conspired to write 'whore' on the woman. Compare Vittoria Corombona's defence of her character and her refusal to accept that the men can label her a 'whore' in John Webster's, *The White Devil* (1612), 3.2. The scene shows that Othello cannot be deflected from the course of action he has become determined to pursue and, at the start of the play's terrible last scene, he duly murders Desdemona, finally transforming her into the silent, obedient wife that convention demanded.

DESDEMONA
  Upon my knees, what doth your speech import?[1]
  I understand a fury in your words
  But not the words.
OTHELLO
  Why, what art thou?
DESDEMONA
  Your wife, my lord: your true and loyal wife.   35
OTHELLO
  Come, swear it, damn thyself,
  Lest, being like one of heaven, the devils themselves
  Should fear to seize thee:[2] therefore be double-damned,[3]
  Swear thou art honest!
DESDEMONA   Heaven doth truly know it.
OTHELLO
  Heaven truly knows that thou art false as hell.   40
DESDEMONA
  To whom, my lord? with whom? how am I false?
OTHELLO
  Ah, Desdemon, away, away, away!
DESDEMONA
  Alas the heavy day, why do you weep?
  Am I the motive of these tears, my lord?
  If haply[4] you my father do suspect   45
  An instrument of this your calling back,[5]
  Lay not your blame on me: if you have lost him[6]

---

1 In a coded insult Othello has just told Desdemona to 'Leave procreants alone' (28). She kneels before him just as Iago and Othello knelt in the ceremony of revenge that condemned Desdemona to death.
2 The words recall the ending of Christopher Marlowe's *Dr Faustus* (*c*.1589) when Faustus is seized by devils and taken off to Hell.
3 For perjury and adultery.
4 Perhaps.
5 Othello has been recalled to Venice.
6 As a friend.

Why, I have lost him too.[7]

OTHELLO   Had it pleased heaven[8]
To try me with affliction, had they rained
All kinds of sores and shames on my bare head,[9]   50
Steeped me in poverty to the very lips,
Given to captivity me and my utmost hopes,[10]
I should have found in some place of my soul
A drop of patience; but, alas, to make me
The fixed figure for the time of scorn   55
To point his slow and moving finger at![11]
Yet could I bear that too, well, very well:
But there where I have garnered up[12] my heart,
Where either I must live or bear no life,
The fountain from the which my current runs   60
Or else dries up – to be discarded thence![13]
Or keep it as a cistern[14] for foul toads
To knot and gender in![15] Turn thy complexion[16] there,
Patience, thou young and rose-lipped cherubin,
Ay, here look, grim as hell![17]   65

DESDEMONA
I hope my noble lord esteems me honest.

OTHELLO
O, ay, as summer flies are in the shambles,[18]
That quicken even with blowing. O thou weed
Who art so lovely fair and smell'st so sweet[19]
That the sense aches at thee,[20] would thou hadst ne'er been born!   70

DESDEMONA
Alas, what ignorant sin have I committed?

---

7 Desdemona reiterates her loyalty to her husband and repeats the choice she made in the first act (1.3.180–9).
8 Othello's lines refer to the afflictions of Job, a good man who was tested by God to see if his faith was pure. Given that Othello has planned to murder his wife the lines are deeply ironic.
9 Job suffered boils and other afflictions which Satan and God rained down upon him (Job, 2–7, 20–3).
10 Recalls Othello's narrow escape from being sold into slavery (1.3.136–8).
11 Othello imagines himself as a fixed figure (a statue?) mocked by all around him. He has become a caricature and a moral example to all. Othello shows that he especially dreads public humiliation.
12 Stored (the affections of my heart).
13 Compare the grand image of the currents leading to the Hellespont (3.3.456–63).
14 Reservoir of water.
15 Compare the image of the toad earlier (3.3.274–7). The image continues the references to ugly and lustful animals copulating made throughout the play.
16 Face.
17 The sense seems to be that if Patience were to look at the scene before her the shock would start to change her from a rosy-lipped cherub to a grim and pale creature.
18 Slaughterhouse or meat market. Another foul animal image.
19 Desdemona is an unwanted flower, a weed, but she is, unlike weeds, beautiful, so she cannot be destroyed easily as they can be.
20 A line which expresses the sexuality that Othello tries to control throughout the play (see, for example, 1.3.262–9).

OTHELLO
>Was this fair paper, this most goodly book
>Made to write 'whore' upon? What committed![21]
>Committed? O thou public commoner![22]
>I should make very forges[23] of my cheeks   75
>That would to cinders burn up modesty
>Did I but speak thy deeds.[24] What committed!
>Heaven stops the nose at it, and the moon[25] winks,
>The bawdy wind that kisses all it meets
>Is hushed within the hollow mine[26] of earth   80
>And will not hear't. What committed!
>Impudent[27] strumpet!

DESDEMONA   By heaven, you do me wrong.

OTHELLO
>Are not you a strumpet?

DESDEMONA
>No, as I am a Christian.
>If to preserve this vessel[28] for my lord   85
>From any hated foul unlawful touch
>Be not to be a strumpet, I am none.

OTHELLO
>What, not a whore?

DESDEMONA   No, as I shall be saved.[29]

OTHELLO
>Is't possible?

DESDEMONA
>O heaven, forgive us!

OTHELLO   I cry you mercy then,[30]
>I took you for that cunning whore of Venice[31]   90
>That married with Othello.

---

21 Othello twists Desdemona's innocent words so that it appears as if she is confessing to committing adultery, a further sign of his decline from straightforward honesty.
22 Common whore. Othello makes Desdemona seem to be like Bianca, who is indeed a common whore. But, as the play demonstrates, Bianca is an abused and sympathetic character who suffers at the hands of men who label her and fail to see her as a human being.
23 An open hearth for heating iron.
24 The image is of the cheeks as bellows blowing out fire to burn up Desdemona's pretence of modesty. Othello means that if he had enough time and energy to speak the truth they might be consumed by the heat of the act.
25 The symbol of chastity.
26 Cave.
27 Shameless (stronger in Elizabethan English than now).
28 Body.
29 Desdemona pits her theological language against that of Othello. While he appears like an Old Testament avenger, she is more obviously New Testament in her meek demeanour and desire for forgiveness.
30 Sarcastic.
31 Othello now employs the stereotypes that Iago presented him with.

Act 5, Scene 2, lines 257–369

The final lines of the play containing Iago's capture, the explanation of events to the assembled characters on stage and Othello's suicide. The theological imagery that has been building up in the previous scenes reaches a climax as Othello has to admit the atrocity he has committed in murdering his innocent wife. Othello thinks that he is too evil to be allowed the sight of the dead Desdemona. He shows a typical male perception of women, alternately worshipping her as an angel and damning her as a whore. In his opening speech he begs for the damnation he had earlier wished for his wife (see above, p. 155) and predicts his damnation on the Day of Judgement when he meets Desdemona again (line 271). It was commonly believed that the bodies would rise from the graves on the last day and be sent to heaven or hell. The subject is represented in numerous pictures and literary texts. See, for example, John Donne, 'Divine Meditation', 7, 'At the round earth's imagined corners', in which he imagines all the dead bodies being reunited with their souls. Othello longs for death (line 287). He means that he would rather have oblivion than suffer the torments that he has to endure. Again the comparison with John Donne may be appropriate. In 'Divine Meditation', 9, Donne, fearing that he may be sent to hell on the Day of Judgement, asks God to forget his sins and pretend that, like a goat or a serpent, he has no responsibility for the fate of his soul.

Iago is seen as a devil, an impression confirmed by his refusal to explain his actions (lines 300–1). Othello suggests that Iago must have cloven feet as he is the devil (line 183) and later (line 299) that he has damned him to hell, the logical culmination of their bonding in 3.3. Iago's refusal to explain recalls the similar refusal of Hieronimo when he is finally captured in The Spanish Tragedy. It is also possible that Iago, whose name is Spanish, may well resemble a captured Jesuit priest. His characteristic mode of speech throughout the play was to pretend to be honest whilst actually speaking in ambiguous words. Jesuits were routinely accused of equivocation. Lodovico's response ('What, not to pray', line 302) further emphasises the possible religious connotations of the ending of Othello, casting Iago outside the norm of religious behaviour. This was exactly how Catholics were represented in the last decade of Elizabeth's reign, as threats to the state and its religion. Gratiano's reference to 'torments' (torture) in the same line further suggests the link between Iago's fate and that of captured Jesuit priests, as they were invariably tortured to make them confess.

The scene shows the Venetian officials acting sensibly to sort out a crisis, as they did at the start of the play. Note how swiftly Lodovico, sent over from Venice in Act 4, sums up what has to be done (lines 328–35).

Othello's final speech has been much analysed (see, for example, Leavis above, pp. 62–3). Several points can be made. It is worth noting that Othello starts with a plea for others to get his story right and accept his sense of himself as the truth. Othello is trying to establish the story that will be told about him through his final words. Note also that he is speaking about himself;

Desdemona features very little in this final speech. Othello's last lines establish an opposition between the good, loyal Venetian and the evil Turk. Othello kills himself because he feels that part of him has acted as an enemy to the state and he is now summoning his better side to assert control. The audience is reminded of the fact that the Turks never actually appear in the play and that the dangers faced by the Venetians are of their own making. After the Turkish fleet has been scattered by the storm Othello asks whether his troops have 'turned Turks? And to ourselves do that/Which heaven hath forbid the Ottomites?' (2.3.166–7).

[*Enter* GRATIANO.]

GRATIANO
    What is the matter?
OTHELLO   Behold, I have a weapon,
    A better never did itself sustain
    Upon a soldier's thigh.[1] I have seen the day
    That with this little arm and this good sword   260
    I have made my way through more impediments
    Than twenty times your stop: but, O vain boast,
    Who can control his fate?[2] 'Tis not so now.
    Be not afraid, though you do see me weaponed:
    Here is my journey's end, here is my butt[3]   265
    And very sea-mark[4] of my utmost sail.
    Do you go back dismayed? 'tis a lost fear:
    Man but a rush against Othello's breast
    And he retires.[5] Where should Othello go?[6]
    Now: how dost thou[7] look now? O ill-starred[8] wench,   270
    Pale as thy smock. When we shall meet at compt[9]
    This look of thine will hurl my soul from heaven
    And fiends will snatch at it.[10] Cold, cold, my girl,

---

1 A deliberate phallic image given that Othello has just strangled his wife for her alleged adultery.
2 Othello retreats into the military world where he feels comfortable and has to stop himself so that he can face the reality of what he has done.
3 Target (as in archery), goal.
4 Beacon to guide sailors into harbour.
5 Othello is contrasting his present position with the usual resolution he took up in battle.
6 Some editions suggest that Othello moves over to the bed on which Desdemona lies dead.
7 Desdemona.
8 Ill-fated. Othello acknowledges that Desdemona was caught up in forces far too strong for her to deal with.
9 The Day of Judgement.
10 Again, the lines recall the fate of Dr Faustus staged recently (see above, 4.2.36). Whereas Othello saw Desdemona as one of the damned, he now realises that he is more likely to end up in hell.

Even like thy chastity.[11] O cursed, cursed slave![12]
Whip me, ye devils,   275
From the possession of this heavenly sight!
Blow me about in winds, roast me in sulphur,
Wash me in steep-down gulfs of liquid fire![13]
O Desdemon! dead, Desdemon. Dead! O, O![14]

Enter LODOVICO, MONTANO, *Officers with* IAGO, *prisoner, and* CASSIO *in a chair.*

LODOVICO
Where is this rash and most unfortunate man?   280
OTHELLO
That's he that was Othello? here I am.[15]
LODOVICO
Where is that viper? bring the villain forth.
OTHELLO
I look down towards his feet, but that's a fable.
If that thou be'st a devil, I cannot kill thee.

[*Wounds Iago.*]

LODOVICO
Wrench his sword from him.
IAGO   I bleed, sir, but not killed.[16]   285
OTHELLO
I am not sorry neither, I'd have thee live:
For in my sense 'tis happiness to die.
LODOVICO
O thou Othello, that wert once so good,
Fallen in[17] the practice of a cursed slave,
What shall be said to thee?
OTHELLO   Why, anything;   290
An honourable murderer, if you will,
For nought I did in hate, but all in honour.[18]

---

11 Othello links death and chastity. Men realising the effects of their – or others' – sins over the dead body of a woman is a standard trope in Western literature.
12 Othello has now become the slave he nearly became in Africa when he escaped capture by hostile natives (1.3.137–9).
13 All punishments which the damned suffered in visions of hell such as that in Dante's *Inferno* (early fourteenth century). See also Revelation 19:20 and Claudio's vision of hell in *Measure for Measure* (1604–5), 3.1.121–5.
14 Compare Lear's anguish at the death of Cordelia in *King Lear* (1605–6), 5.3.309.
15 Othello's experience in the play has made him wish to deny his identity in the hope of salvaging what he was before he became entangled by Iago's plot.
16 Iago suggests that he may in fact be a devil because he bleeds rather than dies.
17 Through.
18 There was a great deal of criticism of the cult of masculine military honour in the last decade of Elizabeth's reign. It is likely that Othello's lines and sense of his actions at this point show him to be deluded in his sense of honour – which involved smothering his wife without checking the evidence very carefully – and acting in part to save his reputation.

LODOVICO
    This wretch hath part confessed his villainy.
    Did you and he consent in Cassio's death?
OTHELLO
    Ay.   295
CASSIO
    Dear general, I never gave you cause.[19]
OTHELLO
    I do believe it, and I ask your pardon.[20]
    Will you, I pray, demand that demi-devil[21]
    Why he hath thus ensnared my soul and body?
IAGO
    Demand me nothing. What you know, you know.   300
    From this time forth I never will speak word.
LODOVICO
    What, not to pray?
GRATIANO   Torments will ope your lips.
OTHELLO
    Well, thou dost best.
LODOVICO
    Sir, you shall understand what hath befallen,
    Which, as I think, you know not. Here is a letter[22]   305
    Found in the pocket of the slain Roderigo,
    And here another: the one of them imports
    The death of Cassio, to be undertook
    By Roderigo.
OTHELLO
    O villain!
CASSIO   Most heathenish[23] and most gross![24]   310
LODOVICO
    Now here's another discontented[25] paper
    Found in his pocket too, and this, it seems,
    Roderigo meant t'have sent this damned villain
    But that, belike,[26] Iago in the nick[27]
    Came in, and satisfied him.[28]   315

---

19 Compare with Desdemona's protestations of innocence (4.2).
20 Compare Othello's response with his reaction to Desdemona's protestations in that scene.
21 Presumably because he bleeds but does not actually die (284–5).
22 A convenient and frequently used plot device which helps to clear up loose ends in the action.
23 Again establishing the boundaries between proper religion and what lies beyond the civilised state. This is a key theme in the play, given Venice's precarious position on the borders of Europe and Othello's status as a naturalised African general.
24 Flagrant, monstrous.
25 'letter expressing resentment' (Sanders).
26 Probably.
27 In the nick of time.
28 i.e. gave a satisfactory answer.

OTHELLO

O thou pernicious caitiff![29]
How came you, Cassio, by that handkerchief
That was my wife's?

CASSIO   I found it in my chamber,
And he himself confessed but even now
That there he dropped it for a special purpose   320
Which wrought to his desire.[30]

OTHELLO   O fool, fool, fool![31]

CASSIO

There is besides in Roderigo's letter
How he upbraids Iago, that he made him
Brave[32] me upon the watch, whereon it came
That I was cast;[33] and even but now he spake,   325
After long seeming dead, Iago hurt him,
Iago set him on.

LODOVICO   [to Othello]

You must forsake this room and go with us.
Your power and your command is taken off
And Cassio rules in Cyprus. For this slave,   330
If there be any cunning cruelty
That can torment him much and hold him long,[34]
It shall be his. You[35] shall close[36] prisoner rest[37]
Till that the nature of your fault be known
To the Venetian state. Come, bring him away.   335

OTHELLO

Soft you,[38] a word or two before you go.
I have done the state some service, and they know't:[39]
No more of that. I pray you, in your letters,
When you shall these unlucky deeds relate,
Speak of me as I am. Nothing extenuate,[40]   340
Nor set down aught in malice. Then must you speak
Of one that loved not wisely, but too well;[41]

---

29 Villain, scoundrel.
30 'which had the effect he wanted' (Honigmann).
31 Othello is at last seeing the extent of his errors, indicating that he still has a way to go from his perception of himself as an 'honourable murderer' (291).
32 Defy.
33 Dismissed.
34 'Keep him alive a long time before he dies' (Honigmann). The state plans to take a cruel revenge on Iago, as was the case with traitors in England, who were severely tortured and mutilated before being publicly executed.
35 Othello.
36 Confined, guarded.
37 Remain.
38 Wait or stay.
39 Othello asserts a sense of self through his relationship to the Venetian state.
40 Diminish, lessen.
41 The audience is clearly invited to ask whether this is true.

Of one not easily jealous, but, being wrought,
Perplexed in the extreme;[42] of one whose hand,
Like the base[43] Indian,[44] threw a pearl[45] away   345
Richer than all his tribe;[46] of one whose subdued[47] eyes,
Albeit unused to the melting mood,
Drops tears as fast[48] as the Arabian trees
Their medicinable[49] gum.[50] Set you down this,
And say besides that in Aleppo[51] once,   350
Where a malignant[52] and a turbanned[53] Turk
Beat a Venetian and traduced[54] the state,
I took by th' throat the circumcised dog[55]
And smote him – thus!   *He stabs himself.*

LODOVICO
O bloody period![56]

GRATIANO   All that's spoke is marred.   355

OTHELLO
I kissed thee ere I killed thee: no way but this,
Killing myself, to die upon a kiss.[57]

                                [Kisses Desdemona, and] dies.

CASSIO
This did I fear, but thought he had no weapon,
For he was great of heart.

---

42 Ditto.
43 Lowly, probably in the scheme of creation.
44 Indians were renowned for their tremendous wealth, but were seen as an ignorant people who did
   not know the value of what they had. It is possible that the folio text's 'Judean' is correct,
   making this an allusion to either Judas's betrayal of Christ or King Herod's rejection of his wife,
   Mariamne. If we accept 'Indian' this helps to emphasise our sense of Othello as a man who is
   establishing a binary opposition between civilised Venice and the world of savages beyond its
   boundaries.
45 The only reference to Desdemona in the speech, indicating Othello's focus on himself after her
   murder.
46 Either of India or of Israel.
47 'Overcome by emotion' (Sanders).
48 Viscous, thick. The sense is that the tears roll down his cheeks slowly and he cannot wipe them
   away as one can normal tears.
49 Medicinal.
50 The reference is undoubtedly to the gum of myrrh trees, which was widely used for perfumes,
   medicine and incense. One of the three kings offers the baby Jesus myrrh (Matt. 2:12). Othello
   employs the striking image to show how extensive is his grief for his wife's death; and, given that
   one of the functions of myrrh was to preserve dead bodies, the appropriate nature of the sentiment
   is clear.
51 An important early modern trading port in Turkey. Sanders notes that 'it was a capital crime for a
   Christian to strike a Turk' there.
52 'Rebellious against God' (Onions).
53 A sign of an adherence to the Islamic faith. Othello was often represented as a 'turbanned Turk' on
   stage, even though these lines suggest otherwise.
54 Defamed, slandered.
55 i.e., the Turk. Muslims were circumcised.
56 Conclusion.
57 Do the lines recall Judas's kissing Jesus before he betrayed him (Luke 22:47)?

LODOVICO   [to Iago]   O Spartan dog,[58]
   More fell[59] than anguish, hunger, or the sea,   360
   Look on the tragic loading of this bed:[60]
   This is thy work. The object[61] poisons sight,
   Let it be hid. Gratiano, keep the house
   And seize upon the fortunes[62] of the Moor
   For they succeed to you. To you, lord governor,[63]   365
   Remains censure[64] of this hellish villain,
   The time, the place, the torture:[65] O, enforce it![66]
   Myself will straight aboard, and to the state
   This heavy act with heavy heart relate.   *Exeunt.*

FINIS.

---

58 Spartan dogs were notoriously savage. The line links Iago not only to the 'circumcised dog' just referred to (line 353), but also to Othello's threat to throw Cassio's nose to a dog (4.1.142). 'Envy, Iago's disease, was sometimes represented as a snarling dog' (Honigmann).
59 Fierce, cruel.
60 This indicates that Othello has died beside Desdemona on the bed.
61 Spectacle.
62 Possessions.
63 i.e. Cassio.
64 Judgement, trial.
65 A reminder that the process that will take place in Venice is similar to that in England, which also licensed torture for serious crimes (albeit not on as large a scale as in some other European states).
66 Perhaps a suggestion that Cassio is not always as eager to establish law and order as he might be.

4

Further Reading

Further Reading

This list makes no attempt to be comprehensive, but is designed to guide readers through the great mass of material on *Othello*. I have tended to avoid citing work I have already reproduced in this book, assuming that readers will realise that I recommend it to them, unless it would distort the sense of the field to omit it. A useful starting point for any bibliographical search is Stanley Wells, ed., *Shakespeare: A Bibliographical Guide* (Oxford: Oxford University Press, 1997). The list of works on Shakespeare produced annually in *Shakespeare Quarterly* should also be consulted. Readers should always consult both *Shakespeare Quarterly* and *Shakespeare Survey* to see what new essays have been written.

Editions and Text

Probably the best current edition is E. A. J. Honigmann's for Arden 3 (London: Nelson, 1997), which contains an extensive introduction with a full discussion of contexts, textual variants, stage history and other important matters. Honigmann argues that the play should be dated back to 1601–2 rather than 1603–4, as is more often assumed, a case made at greater length in his *The Texts of 'Othello' and Shakespearean Revision* (1996). Also useful are Norman Sanders's edition for the New Cambridge Shakespeare (Cambridge: Cambridge University Press, 1984) and Julie Hankey's for the 'Plays in Performance' series (Bristol: Bristol Classical Press, 1987), which has an excellent overview of the stage history of the play. Readers interested in textual matters and controversies should also consult Scott McMillin, 'The *Othello* Quarto and the "Foul-Paper" Hypothesis', *Shakespeare Quarterly*, 51 (Spring 2000), 67–85.

Collections of Essays

There are a large number of collections of essays on *Othello*. Virginia Mason Vaughan and Kent Cartwright's *Othello: New Perspectives* (London: Associated University Presses, 1991) is up to date and contains new essays; Harold Bloom's

William Shakespeare's Othello (Modern Critical Interpretations) (New York: Chelsea House, 1987) collects important essays by Stanley Cavell, Stephen Greenblatt, Patricia Parker, Susan Snyder and others. John Wain's *Othello: A Casebook* (London: Macmillan, 1971) is still useful and contains essays by Helen Gardner, W. H. Auden, Nevill Coghill, and some of the pieces reproduced in this book; Peter Davison's *Othello* (The Critics Debate) (Basingstoke: Macmillan, 1988) is not a collection as such but a useful overview and summary of key debating points and arguments. Catherine M. S. Alexander and Stanley Wells, eds, *Shakespeare and Race* (Cambridge: Cambridge University Press, 2000) contains some key essays on *Othello* and its influence on conceptions of race, the most significant of which is Celia R. Daileader's 'Casting Black Actors: Beyond Othellophilia'. The essays by Barbara Everett and G. K. Hunter are also useful. A more general collection on Shakespearian tragedy that contains an essay on *Othello* by André Green is John Drakakis, ed., *Shakespearian Tragedy* (Longman Critical Readers) (Harlow: Longman, 1992).

Background Reading

Interested readers should first turn to Geoffrey Bullough, ed., *Narrative and Dramatic Sources of Shakespeare*, 8 vols (London: Routledge, 1957–75), vol. 7. Virginia Mason Vaughan's *Othello: A Contextual History* (Cambridge University Press, 1994) is an invaluable guide to the contexts of the play when first performed and its subsequent history. John Gillies, *Shakespeare and the Geography of Difference* (Cambridge: Cambridge University Press, 1994) deals with the conception of the world. Andrew Hadfield, ed., *Amazons, Savages and Machiavels: Travel & Colonial Writing in English, 1550–1630: An Anthology* (Oxford: Oxford University Press, 2001) is a collection of contemporary representations of the nations and peoples available to Tudor and Stuart readers. Questions of race are analysed in Kim F. Hall, *Things of Darkness: Economies of Race and Gender in Early Modern England* (Ithaca, NY: Cornell University Press, 1995), and Jack D'Amico, *The Moor in English Renaissance Drama* (Tampa, Fla: University of South Florida Press, 1991). More straightforward histories are Samuel Chew, *The Crescent and the Rose: Islam and England during the Renaissance* (New York: Octagon, 1974, rpt of 1937); Nabil Matar, *Islam in Britain, 1558–1685* (Cambridge: Cambridge University Press, 1998); and Eldred Jones, *Othello's Countrymen: The African in English Renaissance Drama* (London: Oxford University Press, 1965). The Venetian context and representations of Italy more generally are contained in Michele Marrapodi et al., eds, *Shakespeare's Italy: Functions of Italian Locations in Renaissance Drama* (Manchester: Manchester University Press, 1993). A general guide to historical contexts aimed at students of literature is Julia Briggs, *This Stage-Play World: Texts and Contexts, 1580–1625* (2nd edn, Oxford: Oxford University Press, 1997). The history of Shakespeare criticism collected in Brian Vickers's *Shakespeare: The Critical Heritage*, 6 vols (London: Routledge, 1974–81) should be consulted by anyone keen to follow the reception history of *Othello*.

Critical Interpretations

Patricia Parker's 'Fantasies of "Race" and "Gender": Africa, *Othello*, and Bringing to Light', in Margo Hendricks and Patricia Parker, eds, *Women, "Race", & Writing in the Early Modern Period* (London: Routledge, 1994), pp. 84–100, reads *Othello* in the light of contemporary discourses of monstrosity. Michael Neill's 'Opening the Moor: Death and Discovery in *Othello*', in his *Issues of Death: Mortality and Identity in English Renaissance Tragedy* (Oxford: Oxford University Press, 1997), pp. 141–67, reads the play in terms of theories of anatomy and display. Stephen Greenblatt's 'The Improvisation of Power', in his *Renaissance Self-Fashioning from More to Shakespeare* (Chicago, Ill.: Chicago University Press, 1980), is an influential essay on the forms of identity represented in the play. See also Alan Sinfield's argument in *Faultlines: Cultural Materialism and the Politics of Dissident Reading* (Oxford: Oxford University Press, 1992), ch. 3. A key work is Ania Loomba, *Gender, Race, Renaissance Drama* (Manchester: Manchester University Press, 1989), which has a chapter largely devoted to *Othello*. Arthur L. Little Jr. also has some interesting comments on *Othello* and racial and sexual identities in *Shakespeare Jungle Fever: National-Imperial Re-Visions of Race, Rape, and Sacrifice* (Stanford, Calif.: Stanford University Press, 2000), and there are also useful essays on the same subject in Dympna Callaghan, ed., *A Feminist Companion to Shakespeare* (Oxford: Blackwell, 2000), by Joyce Green MacDonald and Denise Albanese, and by Geraldo U. de Sousa in his *Shakespeare's Cross-Cultural Encounters* (Basingstoke: Macmillan, 1999). Commentary on the representation of sexuality in *Othello* is to be found in Michael Hattaway, 'Male Sexuality and Misogyny', in Catherine M. S. Alexander and Stanley Wells, eds, *Shakespeare and Sexuality* (Cambridge: Cambridge University Press, 2001), pp. 92–115, as well as the works on race and sexuality cited above. More generally see Lisa Jardine, *Still Harping on Daughters: Women and Drama in the Age of Shakespeare* (Hemel Hempstead: Harvester, 1983).

Stage History

See Hankey and Vaughan above. Marvin Rosenberg's *The Masks of Othello: The Search for the Identity of Othello, Iago and Desdemona by Three Centuries of Actors and Critics* (Newark, Del.: University of Delaware Press, 1993, rpt of 1961) is still a thoughtful guide to stage productions. Errol Hill, *Shakespeare in Sable: A History of Black Shakespearean Actors* (Amherst, Mass.: University of Massachusetts Press, 1984) is essential reading for anyone interested in the stage history of *Othello*. Useful comment is also contained in Martin L. Wine, *Othello: Text and Performance* (Basingstoke: Macmillan, 1984), which is good on some recent performances. Russell Jackson, ed., *The Cambridge Companion to Shakespeare on Film* (Cambridge: Cambridge University Press, 2000) is a definitive guide to *Othello* on screen. More specialized comment is available in Micheál MacLiammóir, *Put Money in Thy Purse: The Making of Othello* (London: Methuen, 1952, rpt Virgin Publishing, 1994), a memoir of the making of Orson

Welles's film by the actor who played Iago. There are essays on films of *Othello* by Judith Buchanan in Mark Thornton Burnett and Ramona Wray, eds, *Shakespeare, Film, Fin de Siècle* (Basingstoke: Macmillan, 2000); by Lynda E. Boose in Lynda E. Boose and Richard Burt, eds, *Shakespeare: The Movie: Popularizing the Plays on Film, TV, and Video* (London: Routledge, 1997); and Jack J. Jorgens, *Shakespeare on Film* (New York: University Press of America, 1991).

Index

NOTE: Page numbers in bold indicate an extract by an author or from a particular work; page numbers followed by an *n* indicate information is found only in a footnote.